The Learning Brain

by Eric Jensen
©1994

Illustrated by Gary Johnson

Library of Congress Cataloging-in-Publication Data

1. Popular-- General Interest
2. Business--Training & Development
3. Reference--Learning skills
4. Psychology--Learning & Brain
5. Science--The Brain

©1995 Eric Jensen
The Learning Brain by Eric Jensen
Protected by International Copyright Laws
ISBN # 0-9637832-2-X

Printed in the United States of America
Published by Turning Point Publishing
San Diego, CA USA

Additional copies may be ordered for $20 each or 6 for $99. For 25 or more copies, write, call or fax for volume pricing. Check, purchase order, Visa and Mastercard accepted. Add $4.95 shipping and handling for each book in USA. For five or more books, add 10% instead. Overseas orders processed with wire transfers, VISA or Mastercard only. For a FREE catalog of Brain-Based products, write to the address below. See free offer in back. Thank you. Send your order to the address below:

Turning Point
P.O. Box 2551
Del Mar, CA 92014, USA
Toll free (800) 325-4769
(619) 755-6670 or fax (619) 792-2858

Acknowledgments

To the crusaders, scientists, writers and theorists who made this book possible including Bill Blakemore, James Botkin, Tony Buzan, Dr. Renate Nummela Caine, Geoffrey Caine, Barbara Clark, Dr. Marian Diamond, Dee Dickinson, Gordon Dryden, Marilyn Ferguson, Dr. Howard Gardner, Leslie Hart, Dr. Jane Healy, Hooper, Dr. Jean Houston, Peter Jennings, Dr. Georgi Lozanov, Dr. Paul Maclean, Dr. Paul Messier, Dr. Lyn Nadel, Dr. Robert Ornstein, Sheila Ostrander, Dr. Candace Pert, Dr. Richard Restak, Colin Rose, Lynn Schroeder and Dr. Robert Sternberg.

The "in-the-trenches" practitioners, supporters and pioneers of a more brain-based learning approach I'd like to acknowledge include: Rob Abernathy, Frank Alessi, Richard Bandler, Garrett Barry, Nancy Bently, Chris Brewer, Stephanie Burns, Annette Cam, Bruce Campbell, Don Campbell, Linda MacRae Campbell, Phillip and Libyan Cassonne, Joan Caulfield, Dr. Frank Clement, Dr. Charles Connolly, Bob Cunningham, Bobbie DePorter, Dr. Lynn Dhority, Glen Doman, James Doran, Nancy Ellis, Launa Ellison, Michael Gelb, John Grassi, Michael Grinder, Ronald Hering, Wayne Jennings, Penny Kelly, Susan Kovalik, Peter and Syril Kline, Charlotte Lettecha, Don Lofland, Nancy Maresh, Laurence Martel, Ron Maxfield, Doug McPhee, David Meier, Greg Meyer, Dr. Ann Nevin, Robert Owen, Lyelle Palmer, Gary Phillips, Barbara Praschnig, Allyn Pritchard, Mark Reardon, Anthony Robbins, Bob Samples, Charles Schmid, Don Schuster, Karen Sliwka, James Smith, Tony Stockwell, Edgar Thomas, Marshall Thurber, Larry Van Etten, Jeannette Vos, John Wade, Michael Wall and Win Wenger.

Finally, I'd like to thank Andrea Simpson for strategic support, Gary Johnson for the illustrations and my wife Diane for more love, support and inspiration than can be measured.

Introduction

*Humans are biologically designed to survive and the
single greatest competitive advantage is the ability to learn*

Learning can, of course, take place in the classroom, but most of it doesn't. Today's learner is not just a student or teacher, it's a displaced factory worker, a "down-sized" middle manager or a cutting edge executive. Learning has suddenly become everybody's business. In fact, learning *how to learn* may now be your most critical survival skill.

Have you ever given much thought about how we learn? The ability to learn, both individually, in groups, in organizations and as a country is now more critical than ever. And how can we all become purposeful and skilled at learning unless we truly understand *how* we learn? The solution, it seems, is right between our ears. It is an approach based on learning the way the brain learns best.

Our amazing brain can learn many ways. For example, we can learn through virtual reality, by talking to a friend, using a computer, reading a book, listening to a lecture, a CD-ROM or going on a field trip. Each has their advantages. And the way in which it is learned will likely dictate our depth of understanding, recall and likelihood of applying the knowledge in our lives. By learning about how our brain learns best, you can take advantage of its marvelous capacity.

This book is the one that researchers and neuroscientists won't write. Why? It's full of speculations and implications. And most scientists are hesitant to speculate for fear of either being wrong or being "unprofessional." Yet, there are astonishing discoveries made weekly in the fields of biology, physics, cognitive science, psychopharmacology, neurology and genetics that provide many, many clues on how we learn. The *old* school of knowledge says, "Let's wait until these become common knowledge." Today's cutting-edge learners say, "I want to know right away what's hot and what's not. Let *me* make the decision about whether to use it or not."

This is a "user-friendly" book. For more in-depth information, you may want to follow-up by: 1) browsing the extensive bibliographical resources in the appendix or, 2) getting some consulting services listed in the back of the book or, 3) you may be interested in purchasing an exciting new 30 min. video, called "The Learning Brain" It's available from the order form in the back of the book.

Table of Contents

CHAPTER FOUR: *Strategies & Styles*

CHAPTER FIVE: *Memory & Recall*

CHAPTER SIX: *Different Learners*

CHAPTER SEVEN: *Intelligence & Learning*

CHAPTER EIGHT: *Nutrition & the Brain*

CHAPTER NINE: *States of Attention*

CHAPTER TEN: *Toxins & Hazards*

CHAPTER ELEVEN: *Music in Learning*

CHAPTER TWELVE: *Stress & Threats*

CHAPTER THIRTEEN: *Prenatal & Preschool*

CHAPTER FOURTEEN: *Motivation & Rewards*

CHAPTER FIFTEEN: *Sex & Gender*

CHAPTER SIXTEEN: *Environments*

APPENDIX:

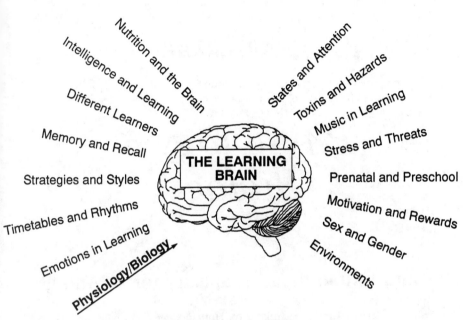

Nutrition and the Brain

Intelligence and Learning

Different Learners

Memory and Recall

Strategies and Styles

Timetables and Rhythms

Emotions in Learning

States and Attention

Toxins and Hazards

Music in Learning

Stress and Threats

Prenatal and Preschool

Motivation and Rewards

Sex and Gender

Environments

THE LEARNING BRAIN

Physiology/Biology

Chapter One

1

CHAPTER ONE

Physiology &
Biology

Brain's Extraordinary Capacity for Learning

Research Summary: Estimates by Huttenlocher, Edelman and Ornstein verify that the brain has almost countless cells. It is the most complex organ known to humans. For the sake of comparison, here are the number of brain cells in a few different organisms:

   * a fruit fly has 100,000.
   * a mouse has 5 million.
   * a monkey has 10 billion.
   * humans have about 100 billion cells, yet when all linked together the number of connections our brain can make is variously estimated by the above researchers to be from 10^{14th} power (a hundred trillion), to 10^{800th} power, to as much as ten followed by millions of zeroes (more than the estimated number of atoms in the known universe, which is estimated to be between $10^{80th-100th}$ power).

   Some researchers say that our brain begins to lose cells starting at birth; others say cell deterioration begins about age twelve. It's not as significant as to how much we lose; we are born with so much, we can afford the loss of a few million cells. Research by Jernigan has revealed that there is evidence of slightly increasing brain volume in subjects aged 25-39 years old. The most striking finding by researchers was the change in the gray matter-to-white matter ratio, especially in the cortical mantle. That area becomes increasingly thinner on MRI scans from age eight through adulthood. As one ages, there are significant increases in the neocerebellar vermal area, too. So we know that the brain's plasticity continues as one ages.

Professor Peter Kouzmich Anokhin of Moscow University, after an investigation into the nature of brain's capacity, said, We can show that each of the ten billion neurons in the human brain has a possibility of connections of one with twenty-eight noughts (zeros) after it! If a single neuron has this quality of potential, we can hardly imagine what the whole brain can do...."

Examples: Leonardo Da Vinci, whose drawings, ideas and predictions were still valid 400 years later; Cardinal Mezzofani, who spoke 60 languages; Yogi Shaa, who could repeat 1,000 phrases after just one hearing; Hideaki Tomoyori of Japan, who has memorized the first 10,000 decimal places of the mathematical ratio "pi"; and Dan Mikels, who once memorized the names and numbers of the Los Angeles Telephone directory.

Implications: We have been vastly underestimating the capacity of the learner. Our expectations have been too low for both the average and the best of learners.

Action steps: Maintain high expectations regardless of the evidence. Teach in many different learning styles so that the potential of every learner is accessed. Then use alternative forms of assessment to provide avenues for those who learn differently. Provide a climate where every learner is respected. Avoid heterogeneous ability grouping. Utilize multi-status, multi-age and multi-ability teamwork.

Best Bet Resources: *The Amazing Brain,* by Ornstein and Sobel, *The Brain* by Restak and *The Three Pound Universe*, by Teresi and Hooper.

Left-Right Brain Theory Recently Updated

Research Summary: The original work of Nobel Prize Laureate Dr. Roger Sperry, who discovered the functioning differences between left and right brain hemispheres, remains valid. The controversy since then has been created by overly zealous enthusiasts who insist on creating a left-right, them vs. us, bad-good, super-logic vs. intuition war. Books have appeared which draw up the battle lines over the "old left-brain way" and the "updated right-brain approach."

However, Levy has confirmed that both sides of the brain are involved in nearly every human activity. It's all a matter of timing and degree of involvement. What we can safely say about each hemisphere is that the left side processes "parts" (sequentially) and the right side processes "wholes" (gestalt). It is best to leave the hemisphericity puzzle as simple and unbiased as possible. Use the two sides more as a metaphor for understanding how we process instead of pigeon-holing all behaviors into either left or right brain as a blueprint for a reductionist model.

To say that one side of the brain is logical or one side is creative is wrong because people can become very creative by following and using logical options, patterns, variations and sequences. The work of DeBono on lateral thinking reminds us that one can use "systems" to be creative. Using the left side of the brain can produce "creative" results. In other words, each side of the brain relies on the other and each is part of a larger "whole."

Example: Listening to another speak may seem like a left hemisphere activity, since it is the side that processes words, definitions and language. But the right hemisphere processes the inflection, tonality, tempo and volume- which are actually more critical to the *meaning* of the conversation. Drawing, composing and painting may seem like a right hemisphere activity, yet artists follow their own logic and rules about shapes, colors and sounds.

Implications: Both parts and wholes are important to learning. Neither should be emphasized at the cost of the other. Some of those who are promoting "right-brain thinking" might do more good by promoting "whole-brain thinking."

Action Steps: Provide learners with global overviews. Provide them with a sequence of steps that will be followed. Alternate between the "big picture" and the details. Validate that we are "whole-brain learners."

Best Bet Resource: *Left Brain-Right Brain Differences* by James Iaccino.

Brain Prefers Complex, Multi-Path Learning

Research Summary: In *Human Brain and Human Learning,* Hart says that the brain simultaneously operates on many levels, processing all at once a world of color, movement, emotion, shape, intensity, sound, taste, weight, and more. It assembles patterns, composes meaning and sorts daily life experiences from an extraordinary number of clues.

Caine and Caine remind us that the brain is always processing on many paths, many modalities, different levels of consciousness, and so on. It's designed to process many inputs at once--in fact, it actually prefers it so much, a slower, more linear pace reduces understanding.

The work of Botella and Eriksen also verifies the parallel processing methods used by the brain in RSVP (rapid, serial, visual presentation) tasks. We all learn in random, personalized, complex real-life patterns that defy description except in the most reductionist terms. In fact, the brain seems to thrive immensely by pursuing multipath, multimodal experiences.

Some scientists say that there is very little learning that the brain does best in an orderly, sequential fashion. In fact, Nobel Prize winning scientist and co-discoverer of DNA's double-helix formation, Francis Crick, says that the functions of the brain "are usually *massively parallel* (author's emphasis). For example, about a million axons go from each eye to the brain, all working simultaneously."

Example: We learn about a city from the full multi-path, sensory experience of it, rather than from sequential information in a book. We learned our neighborhood as a child from scattered, random input, not from a manual or guidebook. Learning is best when it provides many options and inputs.

Implications: Hart puts it bluntly: "[A]ny group instruction that has been tightly, logically planned will have been wrongly planned for most of the group, and will inevitably inhibit, prevent or distort learning."

Action Steps: We learn the most from rich, multi-modal influences such as field trips, simulations, excursions, discussions, real-life projects and personal life activities for your learners. Provide richer environments for learning.

Best Bet Resource: *Human Brain and Human Learning,* by Leslie Hart. Or, for a FREE bulletin, "Amazing New Brain Research Applied to Teaching" see page 351.

Left Hemisphere Processes Faster than Right

Research Summary: Research headed by Dr. Paula Tallal, co-director of the Center for Molecular and Behavioral Neuroscience at Rutgers University, shows that MRI and EEG scans proved the left hemisphere processes information faster than the right. Vos dispute her claims, saying the right is faster. Tallal is finding that this faster speed may be critical for separating language into its distinct word sounds. She has been working with learning impaired children, three to ten percent of which have a processing disorder that makes their brain go in "slow motion", as she calls it. She has found that when they can't process sounds quickly enough, their language learning is stalled.

Example: When the words are electronically slowed down, the learning disorder of Tallal's students disappears and the children understand perfectly. There's nothing else wrong with many children other than an auditory slow motion processing glitch.

Implications: This kind of learner is not slow or stupid. Rather, the learner has a specific disorder that can be dealt with effectively by using appropriate technology. Many learners who are labeled as "slow" may actually have a "slow" left hemisphere but avoid labeling them. They can learn many things in many other ways.

Action Steps: If you have students with auditory processing disorders, find a nearby specialist who understands how to deal with it. Refer learners to the best help you can find. They may be able to learn effectively with help.

Extremities Stimulation Improves Brain

Research summary: If the brain activates the hands and feet, does the reverse hold true? The work of Dr. Jean Houston proved that stimulation of the body can stimulate the brain. Later, Kandel and Hawkins reported on the effects of digital manipulation on the brain. Using an owl monkey, researchers set up a study. The brain areas that related to the digits were measured and recorded. The monkey worked manipulatives for an hour a day for three months. By having the monkey use certain digits, they were able to measure the contrasting effects with those digits NOT used for manipulation. After 90 days, the area of the brain representing the stimulated fingers in the brain had increased (in size and connections) substantially.

Example: Concert pianists are often highly articulate and are able to stay sharp well into old age. The constant playing and manipulation of the fingers seems to stimulate the mind as much as the hands. Elderly who play cards, chess, shuffleboard, golf or who swim all have a greater chance of staying sharp than those who only do gross motor activities such as walking.

Implication: Not only does our mind exercise our body; our body can stimulate the brain.

Action steps: Physical stimulation can be an appropriate part of the learning context. Have your students move, manipulate and exercise their hands each day. Use clapping, dancing, puzzles, manipulatives. Invent new ways to shake hands or work on a keyboard.

Best Bet Resource: *The Possible Human,* by Jean Houston. For a FREE bulletin, "Learning Activities for Grades 7-12", see page 353.

Enormous Variance Found in Human Brains

Research Summary: As with our fingerprints, no two brains are alike. In research by Edelman, the huge variability of retinotectal maps is emphasized. He says that not only are the maps not fixed, but in some brain areas, "there are major fluctuations in the borders of maps over time." Moreover, each individual map is unique. The variability of maps in adults depends on signal input. "In the visual system there may be over 30 interconnected brain centers, each with its own map." The electrical and chemical dynamics of the brain resemble the sound, light and patterns of a jungle more than an electric company. The dynamics all result from chemistry.

Example: Brain size and weight among humans can vary as much as 50%. While Einstein had an average sized brain, the writer Balzac's brain was almost 40% larger. Our brain's internal wiring is quite different, too. Two people are both at the scene of an accident. Each reports on it in such a different way, it's hard to believe that they are describing the same thing.

Implications: In order to account for such differences, different approaches may be necessary to allow all learning to become appropriate.

Action Steps: Often, it may be best to use varying formats to find out what students have learned. Some may need to learn or express their learning with sound, mind maps, song, role play, journals, models, movement, pictures; others may want to combine their learning into special projects.

Best Bet Resource: *Maps of the Mind*, by Charles Hampden-Turner.

HIPPOCAMPAL NEURONS

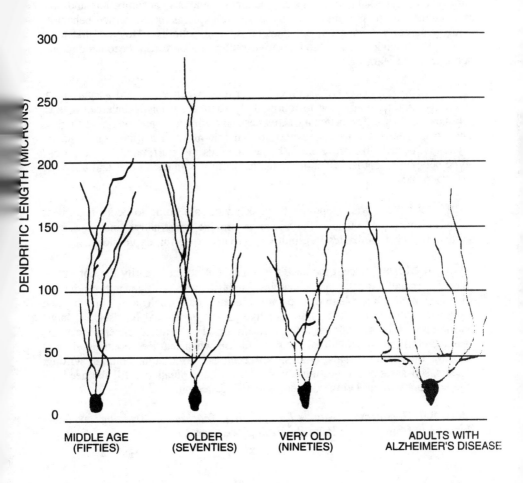

DENDRITIC LENGTH (MICRONS)

300

250

200

150

100

50

0

MIDDLE AGE
(FIFTIES)

OLDER
(SEVENTIES)

VERY OLD
(NINETIES)

ADULTS WITH
ALZHEIMER'S DISEASE

Ritualistic Behaviors May Have Genetic Basis

Research Summary: Dr. Paul MacLean was responsible for a significant shift in our thinking about human behavior. He was the director of the Laboratory of the Brain and Behavior at the U.S. National Institute for Mental Health. He asserts that we actually have three brains in one: the R-Complex (reptilian; our brain stem and cerebellum) the mid-brain (limbic area, amygdala, hypothalamus, pineal, thalamus, nucleus accumbens) and the neomammalian (cerebrum & neo-cortex). He explains many learned behaviors simply as carry-overs from our ancient survival patterns. He says that these ritualistic behaviors may need positive outlets or they can become counter-productive to learning.

Example: You observe reptilian-brain rituals when expressed as playful or taunting games, compulsion to follow daily routines, tropistic behaviors (fads, cliques), preening for better attractiveness, informal debates over meaningless subjects, competition for approval, informal role-plays, a learning environment which is "nested" like an animal's home, the "It's my stuff," and "I'm top dog" type behaviors, learners flocking in teams, flirting with each other and adhering to group fads.

Implications: Some reptilian brain behaviors are going to occur regardless of what you do. You have the power to provide constructive and productive outlets for what are basically primitive, yet very powerful, expressions.

Action Steps: Accept the need for rituals, but not necessarily the content of them, especially if they are negative. Establish new positive and productive rituals which direct learners toward mutual goals such as: arrival and beginning rituals (music fanfare, positive greetings, special handshakes, hugs, etc.), special organizational rituals (team or class names, cheers, gestures, games, etc.), situational rituals (e.g., applause when learners contribute), and closing or ending rituals (songs, affirmations, discussion, journal writing, cheers, self-assessment, gestures, etc.). All of these rituals can fill the needs of the learners without being counterproductive to learning.

Best Bet Resources: *Rituals for Learning, Teaching & Training* available by catalog from Turning Point Publishing, see page 351.

Chimpanzees Smarter than Your Right Brain

Research Summary: Gazzaniga says that while the right hemisphere "remains superior for some activities, such as the recognition of upright faces, some attention skills, and perhaps some emotional processes, it is poor at problem-solving and numerous other mental activities. In fact, it would appear to be *inferior to the mental capacities of a chimp.*"

Gazzaninga says that new brain discoveries suggest that the brain is more modular in its construction than earlier thought. He adds that our "modular systems are fully capable of producing behaviors, mood changes and cognitive activity. This activity is monitored and synthesized by the special system in the left hemisphere, the interpreter. The right hemisphere does not have such a system...."   New studies have shown the error of the bi-lateral symmetry assumption. The functions necessary for human thought are predominantly left hemisphere.

Example: Activities that are designed only for the right brain, like visualizing, drawing or role playing, often leave some learners frustrated unless they are followed up by discussion or some other left-hemisphere activity.

Implications: Avoid subscribing to the attitude that the right brain is the sole secret to our learning. Use a variety of strategies, tools and techniques that use both sides of the brain. By itself, the right brain is not very life-changing.

Action Steps: Avoid the "right-brain bandwagon". But equally, avoid the over dominant "left-brain mold". Make sure that you always activate, integrate and coordinate activities for both sides of the brain. Set up activities for the right brain "aha" of "discovery" and then follow up with the left brain processing.

Made-to-Order: Your New "Designer Brain"

Research Summary: "For the first time in human history, we will be in a position to design our own brain," says noted brain expert, author and neuropsychiatrist, Dr. Richard Restak. The nature of learning is, as we suspected, primarily electrochemical. By changing the chemistry of the brain, you change the behavior of the brain. And this applies to your personality, memory and all learning.

Using the innovative Morris water maze, McNamara & Skelton discovered the specific neurochemical basis for learning and memory. Their work, and that of others, verified the specific roles that brain chemistry plays in every function of the brain. It turns out that we are basically running on a chemical "witch's brew" at all times.

Serotonin levels affect alertness. We know that spatial learning is dependent on glutamatergic and cholinergic processes. Norepinephrine affects alertness, depression and anxiety. The neurotransmitter glutamate triggers neuronal changes that constitute memory. Too much dopamine in the limbic system and you have paranoia and distortion. The peptides in adrenal and sex hormones are necessary for spatial learning. Excessive GABAergic activity prevents memory function. Opiodergic activity reduces motivation.

So, could chemical intervention improve the brain and learning? It turns out that it already does. We already use chemicals that affect our mind including caffeine, sugar, proteins, carbohydrates and so-called "designer drugs." But that's just the tip of the iceberg, so to speak. There are fascinating new drugs being tested now or on the market already that put you in a better frame of mind for learning, increase positive attitudes, reduce mood swings and increase memory. Some are already available now and others, in an enormous new variety, are on the way.

Example: The company Omnitrition already markets "smart products," including powdered concentrates sold in packets called "Focus" and "Go For It". These contain specific combinations of amino acids which some say boost attention, concentration and memory. Great Earth in Santa Monica, California markets pills called "Body Smart: Neuro Support Nutritional Supplement". While there is some political and legal debate as to what these products can claim, even FDA harassment will only drive them to an underground market.

In a dramatic move, another company, Cortex Pharmaceuticals, Inc. of Irvine, California, plans to market a whole range of brain-improvement drugs, including BDP, the so-called "super-memory pill" that reduces the neuronal stimulation required to form memories. Researcher Gary Lynch says that these stimulants may make the action of learning and memorizing virtually effortless.

Implications: Instead of studying for three hours to prepare for a test, a student may well be able to do it in minutes. New drugs are already developed to do just that. Pre-test anxiety may be eliminated by "cousin drugs" of Prozac, Zoloft and Paxil.   Deprenyl, Melatonin, Nimodipine, Vassopressin   and Piracetam have millions of converts worldwide.

Action Steps: Make sure that your learners are in a positive, receptive state of mind before you begin teaching content. Provide opening activities that help to lower stress, increase curiosity and offer challenge. If possible, make sure they have had good nutrition before learning.

Best Bet Resource: *Receptors,* by Richard Restak. Omnitrition supplement packets available through Victor Weisser (619) 579-8571 or (214) 245-8282. Other neuronal stimulants available through fitness and health food stores. You may also want to purchase the book *Smart Drugs I, Mind Food & Smart Pills* and *Smart Drugs II* available by catalog from Turning Point Publishing, see page 351.

Fastest Response Noted to Symbolic Learning

Research Summary: Hooper and Teresi say that our reptilian brain (the fastest part of our brain) is "wired up" to respond to archetypes, to "partial representations", and our response to these is nearly instantaneous.

Dr. Paul Maclean, father of the triune brain research, says, "Our brains take the part for the whole, seeing snakes, mothers and a thousand other symbols in Rorschach inkblots.... Look at our artifacts, the cave paintings." The brain has a tendency to make more out of the symbols than what's there. In other words, what the brain isn't given, it makes up.

Example: A brick is thrown at your head and the reptilian brain does not ask the question, "I wonder how much the brick weighs?" It also does not access emotions such as, "Oh! I'm so disappointed in that person's behavior!" The reptilian brain, being most concerned with instinctive survival, simply tells your body, "Duck----fast!"

Our culture is full of symbols: the heart, the eye, mountains, the sun, a mother, icons in computer programs, the ocean, a can of Campbell's soup, jeans, the golden arches, a soccer ball, the stop light, international picture signs, and more. Each of these symbols has come to represent larger meanings, ranging from hunger, success, happiness, and love, to freedom, independence, power, sex, and satisfaction.

Implications: The influences on learners are more far-reaching and powerful than we first thought. Advertising may have a more powerful effect than previously known. The posters and peripherals in a learning environment may be more important also. The overall ability to reach learners may be greater than we first thought.

Action Steps: Increase the use of learning symbols and images in the learning environment. Utilize student input to create new messages about learning. Could they draw, design or build "learning icons", such as a human brain, to represent curiosity? Inspirational posters of mountain climbers, teamwork and great discoveries may help. Make them on poster paper and post them up high. Let them become a part of the peripheral learning environment.

Spoken Words Actually Alter Physical Brain

Research Summary: Kotulak has reported that words can be just as powerful as prescription drugs in behavior modification. The work of UCLA psychiatrist Dr. Lewis Baxter has proven that carefully chosen words can activate the same areas of the brain as a highly-prescribed drug. The therapeutic value of language indicates that words can, indeed, heal.

In this particular case, Baxter and his colleagues studied the brains of obsessive-compulsive patients using PET (positron emission photography), which measures cell activity in various parts of the brain and creates a color photo of it. They found that the caudate nucleus was overactive in these patients and acted like a behavior "fixative" since it allowed for the repetition of unwanted behaviors. The prescribed drug, Prozac, raises the level of the brain's own sedative, serotonin, so that the behavior ceases. During the test cases of behavior therapy, the patients experienced identical changes in the caudate nucleus, calming down the patients as the drug did.

Example: One of your learners is feeling depressed or upset. Your carefully-chosen words raise his spirits and help generate motivation. The student thanks you.

Implications: Your effect may be much greater than you previously thought. Your potential for effecting change may also be far greater. The importance of choosing words carefully is underscored.

Action Steps: Practice giving your learners encouragement and affirmation. Do this less as an exception, but more as long-term support and verbal definition of the learner's potential genius.

Brain's Just Like Muscles; Use it or Lose It

Research Summary: French researcher and neuroepidemiologist Jean-Francois Dartigues says that nonintellectuals are more likely to face senility later in life. Apparently, if you don't want to lose your marbles, you'd better use them throughout your life. Dartigues did a study of 3,700 people over the age of 65 in which he correlated their intellectual functioning with their former occupations. Then he adjusted for variables such as age, sex and even environmental and toxic risks. He found that the subjects who performed best on the tests were not those with the greatest formal education, but those who had the most intellectually demanding careers. In other words, what counts is how you use your brain, not how much you may know.

On the other hand, Dr. Jonas Salk, Nobel Prize laureate and inventor of the polio vaccine, disagrees. He says that the ability of the brain to think and solve problems may be similar to the functioning of our immune system. In other words, once your body has learned how to fight off an invader, you develop an immunity for life. Salk's opinion was that thinking skills may be dormant for years and still be potent when needed.

Example: In Dartigues's study, after retiring, former farm workers were over six times more likely to become mentally impaired than those who were in more intellectual occupations, such as teachers, trainers, executives, managers and other white collar professionals. But for farm managers, the rate is only 2.9 times that of intellectual occupations.

Implications: Being busy is not enough--many are busy who use very little of their brain. It's not what you have that counts, it's what you do with it that counts. To keep your mind sharp, do the things that challenge it and force it to stay active.

Action Steps: Do challenging reading every day; avoid the temptation of "mindless" TV shows. Do crossword puzzles, problem-solving, memorizing, language learning, travel planning, designing, budgeting, financial planning, workshops, career planning and the playing of music.

Best Bet Resources: *Boost Your BrainPower* by Michaud and Wild, *Pumping Ions,* by Tom Wujec; *How to Be Twice as Smart*, by Scott Witt; and *Creative Growth Games*, by Eugene Raudsepp.

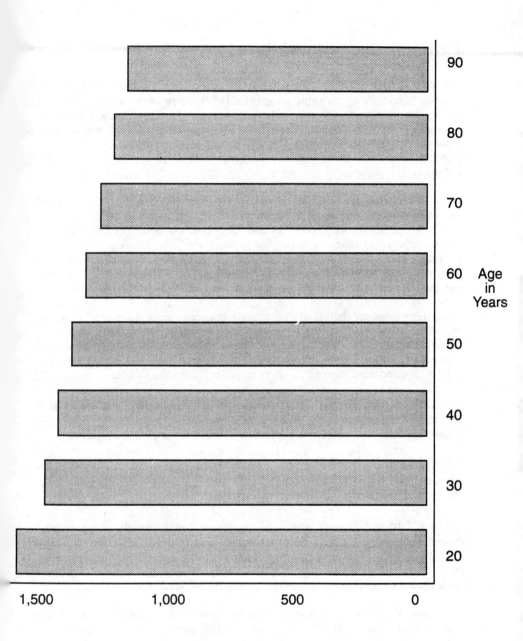

BRAIN WEIGHT (GRAMS)

Effects of Aging on the Human Brain

Research Summary: Khachaturian, Associate Director of the Neuroscience and Neuropsychology of Aging program at the National Institute of Aging, says that in the absence of disease, the brain retains its ability to function well into old age. Overall, the detrimental effects are measurable but with encouraging options, says Selkoe. He adds that while there is some minor shrinkage and slowing of reaction time, some of the great thinkers of all time were active elderly.

The measurable specifics include these facts: The weight of the brain decreases from an average of 1500 grams to 1300 grams by age 60, and to 1100 grams by age 95. In the cerebral cortex, large neurons shrink, as they do in the hippocampus. In other areas of the brain, there is a shrinkage or loss of neurons. But researchers at the University of Rochester Medical Center have observed a net growth of dendrites in some regions. Glial cells increase after age 60, but researchers are uncertain yet of the biological purpose behind it.

A pioneer on the effects of activity and environment on the brain, Dr. William Greenough from the University of Illinois has researched the elderly. He says that if you want to continue to "grow" a better brain well past adulthood into later maturity, "varied experience drives synaptogenesis". In other words, keep active and remember that variety is, indeed, the spice of life.

Example: One 85-year old woman just completed the 1993 New York Marathon. She started long distance running when she turned 70. She has gained confidence, stamina, health and mental agility through her running.

Implications: Being older doesn't mean being senile or mentally handicapped. It means it's even more important than ever to actively challenge the brain with novelty and difficult but achievable tasks.

Action Steps: Provide continued challenges for the minds of the elderly. Never underestimate them. More and more, elderly prove what they can do - and it's a lot. You may also want to research the effects of anti-aging medication and neuronal supplements. They range from Ginklo Biloba to prescription drugs that boost alertness, menory and thinking.

Best Bet Resources: You may want to contact the Cognitive Enhancement Research Institute at 415-321-2374 for a subscription to their newsletter and other products.

Reptilian Brain Affects Posture, "Hot Buttons"

Research Summary: The research of MacLean and Hart has verified that the brain stem is responsible for behaviors which are automatic and occur without planning or thinking. These automatic behaviors are concerned with the immediate protection of your body, your physical property, intellectual property and emotional property. And the behaviors are the same, regardless of whether you're 6 or 60. So what does this reaction-mechanism have to do with our learning? It's simple. There is no distinction between the mind and body.

According to Gelb, threats affect our physiology and posture affects motivation, learning and attitudes. The reptilian portion of our brain is designed to respond quickly to threats. But threats can be so subtle that only the non-conscious mind reacts. He says the work of Alexander has shown him a person's posture reflects a lifetime of threats and learning fears which are constantly re-activated and stimulated in a stressful learning environment. A slumped-over learner breathes poorly, often constricting circulation. A learner in a bad posture can create new tensions and cause the body to compensate laterally with another equally poor posture. With any threat, the body stiffens up and the "fright" posture is re-triggered. Learning potential again decreases.

Example: A student in a classroom or seminar makes an inappropriate comment or behaves improperly. You react immediately by snapping back with a disciplining reaction or a clever verbal comeback: your brain stem is protecting your turf. A hot button is pushed once again. The learner reacts intellectually, emotionally and physically. A defensive posture is taken. That "threat-response" posture continues to be embedded.

Implications: You rarely ever get angry for the reason you think you do. Each time you react, it's the re-triggering of an earlier, stored reaction. The trigger may be nearly insignificant. Nevertheless, your brain says, "React! This is horrible!" Over time, your body becomes a storehouse of defensive postures.

Action Steps: If physically threatened by a learner, let your brain stem act for you instantly. It is designed to save your life. If the threat is, in fact, insignificant, pause for a moment, take a slow, deep breath and relax. After you've allowed yourself a moment to get "past" the reptilian behavior tendency, then you can act more appropriately.

Best Bet Resources: *Sitting on the Job* by Donkin

Optimism is a Left-Brain Learned Behavior

Research Summary: When learners are hooked up to an EEG, which measures brain wave activity, scientists can tell how the brain responds to stimuli. But a PET scan gives us specific locations for brain activity, telling us which part of the brain is used while thinking or feeling. Maguire reports that in research by Yale Researchers Ahern and Schwartz in 1987, it was found that the right side of the brain was the most activated when the learner was feeling depressed, negative, or stressed. But when the learner was feeling optimistic about life and the future, most activity was found on the left hemisphere.

Can the feeling of optimism result from a biological change? Researcher Bandura at Stanford University worked with a group of subjects on strategies for reducing fear and stress. As the subjects improved in their skills, less amounts of catecholamines were released. Those are the body's own chemicals that are released during stress. In short, there is a different biochemistry to feeling capable and confident.

Example: When you feel depressed or negative, you often need to come to a new conclusion about the source of the depression. You think your way out of it, or simply let time pass and quit thinking about the negatives. When you "count your blessings", you often feel contented.

Implications: If people were taught how to process negative moods or events which could impact their learning, they might be much more effective learners.

Action Steps: Make sure that the skills needed for thinking things through and learning optimism are part of the learning. Learning optimism comes from conflict-resolution skills, goal-setting skills, a sense of belonging and acceptance, visioning activities, developing a sense of value and purpose in life, and physical vitality.

Best Bet Resources: *Learned Optimism,* by Martin Seligman and *Strategies of Optimism,* by Vera Peiffer. Or, for a FREE bulletin, "How To Motivate Yourself to Go to Work", see page 353.

Brain Thrives on Pattern-Making & Detection

Research Summary: The work of Hart has highlighted one of the key characteristics of the neocortex: the ability to detect and make patterns of meaning. This process involves deciphering cues, recognizing relationships and indexing information. The clues that the brain assembles are best recognized in a Gestalt format, not in a digital, "adding up" process. Hart reminds us that "...pattern recognition depends heavily on what experience one *brings to* a situation" (emphasis added). These patterns must continually be revised, altered or updated as new experiences add information, insights and corrections. In fact, Hart says that learning is the extraction of meaningful patterns from confusion. In other words, figuring things out *in your way*.

In a study of readers, Bower and Morrow found that comprehension increased when readers created a mental model or pattern of the material while reading. The readers would make patterns, connections, relating the actions of the characters to their goals. The readers also focused attention on the character's movements, visualized locations for several seconds and related them to the model or pattern they were building in their minds. This activation resulted in the reader's improved recall speed and comprehension.

Edelman says that "...learning in any species results from the operation of neural linkages between global mappings and the value centers." Learning is achieved when behavior leads to synaptic changes in global mappings that satisfy set points. Three essentials of higher brain functions are categorization, memory and learning. The last depends on the first two; the second depends on the first. Perceptual categorization is essential for memory. The value centers are located in the hypothalamus and midbrain.

Example: When you arrive in a new city, you not only want to know how to get where you're going, but also where you are in relationship to where everything else is located. In other words, the spatial, contextual relationships are the patterns which help you understand and get around in a city.

Implications: What learners are left with is two basic chunk sizes of information: the unit of knowledge or experience, and the pattern. Facts may provide the answer on a test, but the pattern equals real meaning.

Action Steps: Before beginning a new topic, ask your students to tell you orally or make it graphic in a mind map. Post up a mind map of the patterns of your topic before you begin. That gives the brain "addresses" at which to store key information and make relationships. During a course, continually have students make maps of the material. At the end of the course, ask them to make larger, mural-sized maps of their learning.

Evidence of Non-Conscious Mind Revealed

Research Summary: Two researchers, Pfurtscheller and Berghold, verified that as early as two seconds prior to an actual activity or movement, your brain has already decided what body parts to activate and which side of the brain to use. This means you are already acting on something before you are truly aware that you are even thinking about it.

Dr. Emile Donchin, at the Champaign-Urbana campus of the University of Illinois, has documented something even more profound. He says that more than 99% of all learning is non-conscious. This means you are constantly picking up learning from visual cues, sounds, experiences, aromas and other environmental cues that far exceed any content from a lesson plan or course outline. Most of what's learned in any class or course is <u>not</u> in any lesson plan. In other words, the brain is such an amazing learning machine that it is learning most of the time, even when you think it's not.

Example: You drive from one city to another. You arrive safely and check into a motel or stay with a friend. Someone asks you about something. You say you can't quite recall it. But then they mention the company's name and suddenly a light goes on. "Yes", you say, "I did hear of that company. Weren't they on a billboard somewhere on the road? Oh, yes, now I remember. They are the ones who...." You actually learned that information hours ago. But at the time, you were not conscious of it.

Another example: your students are working on a project in cooperative teams. In their view, they are learning the content. But they are also learning about each other and acquiring collaborative skills. In fact, that may be the majority of the learning. That's an example of non-conscious learning.

Implications: Your learning climate and environment is very important. So are your dress standard and your nonverbal messages. Those are all "learned" by your students even though you may not be "teaching" any of them. How to treat your students, what you say, how you say it, the temperature, the room set-up is all influencing the learner and being processed either consciously or non consciously.

Action Steps: Create a learning environment rich with positive suggestions. Use more congruent body language. Set higher standards for yourself and your environment. Involve your learners in meeting those standards.

Brain Enrichment's Dramatic Impact on Elderly

Research Summary: University of Illinois researcher and neural plasticity pioneer William Greenough selected young and middle-aged rats, and put some in isolation, some with companions and others in enriched environments (stocked with toys). The rats who were with companions showed some improvement over those in isolation. The ones in enriched environments, however, did the best. Greenough says, "[M]ore synapses mean more behavioral repertoires, a wider array of responses, more choices." In short, enriching the environment grew better brains.

But the most interesting of his results came with the older, mature rats. He had expected the younger rats to grow better brains, but he was astonished by the older rats' improvement. He said, "...[e]nrichment had a very dramatic effect on their brains, just as dramatic as in very young rats." While we used to think the brain's architecture was formed early in life, we now know of the incredible structural plasticity of the brain. Even in the elderly? The elderly especially benefit from stimulation.

Example: Dr. Emery of the University of Southern California worked with 48 subjects who were divided into two groups, each meeting three times a week. One of the two groups exercised, the other did not. Among the exercisers, problem-solving and intelligence increased. In the other group, mental skills stayed the same.

Many elderly try to limit their experiences and other forms of sensory input with the thought of "taking it easy". Rest homes often advertise how comforting and relaxing (boring and predictable) their facilities are. But Greenough's study points to significant benefits from just the opposite kind of environment. "People have compared old people in nursing homes to the population still waiting to get in," he says. "And there's a whopping difference in IQ...Nursing homes are badly designed; they starve the brain of experience."

Implications: We may need to re-think how we treat the aged. We all may be accidentally creating dementia, bored brains and even early deaths in rest homes by strictly limiting the experiences, novelty and stimulation to the elderly.

Action Steps: If your parents are in a rest home, choose carefully. Do volunteer work for rest homes by bringing in stimulating activities. Offer classes. Teach a foreign language. Help them create music. Bring in a comedian. Do field trips, travel and excursions. Bring in children. Have a party. Engage elderly in large, meaningful projects.

Can Subliminals Really Affect Our Learning?

Research Summary: After an exhaustive review of research on subliminals, E. Taylor says that subliminals can and do affect the brain. This does not mean that all subliminal messages are effective. It means that the largest body of research says that when done in the appropriate medium, packaged in a brain-compatible way, the right message, "packaged" right, which fits the subject's belief systems, can consistently affect behavior.

A subliminal is defined as a stimulus perceived below the threshold of awareness. In other words, the auditory or visual trigger must be able to be perceived, but you're not aware of it at the moment it's happening. For example, a whisper a block away is well below our threshold of perceptiveness unless you have electronic listening gear. So it's not subliminal because no neural activity was triggered. A poster in a classroom that is out of normal awareness (off to the side, in the back of the room) is not a subliminal, either.

After much research, Wolman says that "[s]ubliminal stimulus does leave an influence upon the content of subsequent cognition.... Subliminal stimuli has affected and can affect secondary process thinking... and that despite failures of replication there are numerous instances where subliminal stimuli 'can measurably influence a variety of subject's behaviors.'"

What are the criteria for whether a subliminal will influence you or not? There are many. They are easy to determine in a controlled environment, but difficult in a random, uncontrolled situation. Dixon has documented over 748 references on subliminals and says that five factors determine whether they will be effective: 1) signal strength, 2) direction of attention, 3) external noise level, 4) internal noise level, and 5) meaning. In other words, subliminals can work, under ideal conditions.

Urban verifies that subliminal visual stimulation is much more easily verified than auditory. So, do those "mega-message" auditory subliminals work? Those are the audio tapes using speech-compressed affirmation subliminal stimuli of up to one million messages per hour. Taylor says they do not work. More is not better. He says, "[S]peech delivered subliminally at high rates of speed... produces more headaches than any other... effect."

The same applies to companies which use "multilayering, multifrequencing, echo and shadow effects." While the brain is capable of processing information at a high rate of speed, unless it is presented in context, with appropriate emotions, in the learning style of the subject, it simply won't attend to a flood of messages; the brain's reticular activating system will filter them out as "noise".

Lewicki says that the non conscious acquisition of information is not only much faster than the conscious, but also it is "structurally more sophisticated." It allows us to multi-path process easier, so that we can better: 1) perform cognitive functioning, 2) interpret stimuli, and 3) trigger emotional reactions.

There are dozens of research articles which document where subliminals have failed to influence a subject's behavior. For some, it may be a matter of learning styles. In others, it may be problems with expectancy, perceptual bias, technical packaging and the emotional content of the message.

Examples: The most famous example was the 1950's New Jersey theater owner who claimed he had flashed a "Drink Coca-Cola" subliminal on the screen during the airing of the movie "Picnic". He claimed that sales increased 58% over a six-week period. Others have disputed his claims.

Taylor reports that one sound engineer, who has asked to remain unnamed, said he mixed subliminal messages into popular music at the request of many "prominent groups and artists". He stopped when "the messages became observable in the music fan's behavior".

Visual subliminals fall into three categories: 1) Altered light levels, 2) High speed flash projection, and 3) Variable insertion. Altered light levels mean that a lower wattage message may be shown on a screen continuously during the time a brighter message is being consciously perceived. The high speed flash projection is similar to tachistoscope and movie theater projection where a message is flashed at 1/100th to 1/3000th of a second continuously. The variable insertion is like adding a flashcard to a deck of cards and flipping it like an old-time movie screen. The most common auditory subliminals are the recordings of voices embedded below the level of awareness and masked by ocean waves or music.

Implications: A common public misconception is that since subliminals are illegal, we are protected from them. A United States FCC code does prohibit the use of subliminals, but here's the reality of the matter: 1) There are no penalties for violating the law. As a result, many advertisers take liberty and do use them often. 2) There are many other kinds of advertising being used that are far more persuasive and intrusive than subliminals.

Action Steps: Subliminals can and do work when used correctly. Use them in a teaching or training context **only when** 1) all learners are over 18 years of age 2) 100% of the learners give approval to the methodology and 3) they have explicit knowledge of and approval of the exact content of the material.

Best Bet Resource: *Subliminal Learning,* by Taylor.

Does Television Affect Learners' Brains?

Research Summary: Of all the areas of brain research, this has proved to be one of the most difficult and controversial to verify. One researcher, Lande, says that "many instances of children and adults imitating video violence have been documented . . . [but] considerable doubt still exists about [its role] . . . in stimulating human aggression." He suggests that a small population group is likely to be more vulnerable to the effects of violent programming.

Centerwall says that the scale of the problem is enormous and recommends controlled studies. Tonge says that "violent and aggressive themes tend to make children more aggressive and disobedient." And, he adds, positive role-modeling does positively affect children's behavior. Gadow says that his studies showed that following viewing of violent themes, children tend to be more antisocial. But, he adds, children watching nonaggressive television programming were equally, and sometimes even more, aggressive later on. In other words, maybe it's not the violence, but the activity itself that is causing these behaviors.

We do know from Armstrong that studying in front of the television hurts student performance. One who has done a great deal of research on the effects of television on the brain is Dr. Jane Healy. In interviews with researchers, scientists, parents, teachers, television consultants, executives and professors, she has determined the following:

* Research strongly indicates that TV has the ability to negatively affect the brain and to impair learning.
* The hypnotic effect may be "neurologically addictive" by changing some of the brain's electrical impulses.
* TV may impair listening, active reading, problem-solving, attention-sustaining, motivation and writing skills.
* TV artificially manipulates the brain into paying attention by "violating its natural defense mechanisms with frequent visual and auditory changes."
* Constant exposure to violence may create higher levels of stress, and that may create a constant downshifting or minimizing of the brain so that it utilizes more of the lower brain reptilian and survival related responses and less of the higher order thinking skills.
* TV may underdevelop many areas of the brain: the left-hemisphere language system, and volitional control centers and their specific cortical connections.
* The largest cost may be "opportunity" cost: all of the brain-developing activities that are NOT being done while TV is being watched.

Can television be an effective babysitter for infants? No, says Janellen Huttenlocher, psychologist at the University of Chicago. "Mothers talk in very short sentences [to their infants]. They describe the here and now. They point out things they are talking about and rarely mention objects that aren't around." Television does exactly the opposite. Its fast changing images, startling noises and lack of interactiveness create a "neural narcotic" for the brain. But does this create more scattered and more dominantly right-brain learners? Right now, the evidence leans that way, but further research needs to be done.

Example: A student sits in class with that "spaced out" look. He doesn't want to participate much and thinks school is boring. School cannot compete with the speed and variety of television.

Implications: Some students may have too rich of a "TV diet". We may be affecting a whole generation of learners adversely by allowing so much television to be watched without limits.

Action Steps: Place limits on TV and video use. Talk to children about TV content, how it manipulates, its point of view. Keep the growing years very active; involve children in thinking, planning, having conversations and doing projects. Demonstrate that you mean what you say; be a role model. You may want to spend much more time reading than watching TV.

Best Bet Resources: *Endangered Minds: Why Our Children Can't Think* by Jane Healy, available by catalog from Turning Point Publishing, see page 351.
If you're a parent, there's an electronic "TV rationing" device you can use that automatically gives your children a weekly "television allowance." It's available from Home Labs, Smyrna, GA. at (800) 466-3522.

Elderly Learners Have Surprising Stamina

Research Summary: We're familiar with the phrase "circadian rhythms" in describing human activity. Those are the daily activity cycles of the body, such as breathing, hormone release, etc. One might think that when compared to a younger group of males and females, the elderly would require more rest and prefer less difficult tasks.

The research of Lieberman et al. revealed that the elderly had surprising daytime activity levels and less sleepiness, especially in the morning, than the youthful volunteers. The elderly had a peak physical activity level at 13:26 (1:26 past noon), while the younger group peaked at 15:13, almost two hours later.

Dr. Cameron Camp says that what we think are "memory defects" in the elderly are often not defects. Instead, they are simply practical decisions about priorities. The elderly have generated so many experiences that less and less of what they are exposed to is novel. And novelty triggers the body's neurochemicals to say, "Save this now!"

Example: Those who have continued to stimulate their minds have remained active well into their "golden years". Good examples are Mother Teresa, Katherine Hepburn, Picasso, Buckminster Fuller, Churchill, George Burns, Leonard Bernstein, and Bob Hope. Continue creating novelty and you'll stimulate the brain and memory

Implications: We may have many elderly who are poor learners because we have treated them that way. When we treat the aged as if they are unable to learn, they don't get the stimulation needed to stay sharp. It's a self-fulfilling prophecy.

Action Steps: Stimulate the brain! It loves challenge and novelty. If you work with the elderly, adjust what you do to include their most likely timetables. If you don't, avoid stereotypic and discriminatory labels.

Personality May Be Genetically Determined

Research Summary: Gazzaniga says that MRI (magnetic resonance imaging) measurements show greater genetic control in the left hemisphere than the right. That means that your inherited characteristics are more likely to be sustained if they are left hemisphere traits. This may explain twins' behavior. In studies of twins, the left hemisphere shows less variation than the right, meaning that the changes are likely to be more right-brain ones.

Maguire has reviewed the research by Dr. Bouchard Jr., the director of the Minnesota Center for Twin and Adoption Research at the University of Minnesota, and says that although our lives are NOT preprogrammed from birth, much is genetically-influenced. The center has extensively profiled twins to determine how much is inherited and how much is environmentally "grown." Included in the findings are the following:

* Leadership is 60% inherited.
* Aggression, social closeness, orderliness are moderately inherited.
* Shyness is dominantly inherited.
* Strong fears are highly subject to inheritance.

Bouchard says that the way genetic influences work can often be subtle, and that genes are only one factor in determining a person's brain power or personality. But his research on twins has proved many of the traits do have a genetic link.

Example: One of many true incidents: Two identical twins (James Lewis and James Springer) were separated at birth. They never knew about each other and were reunited after forty years, at which time they discovered that: 1) both had married women named Linda, 2) both had divorced, 3) each remarried women named Betty, 4) both had undergone police training, 5) both enjoyed the same hobbies (golf and woodworking), 6) each owned blue Chevies, 7) both had dogs named Toy, and 8) both vacationed at the same beach near St. Petersburg, Florida.

Implications: We are all free-choice humans choosing from a genetic menu. In other words, we can all choose any kind of life we want. But the choices available to us may have a fixed number of possibilities.

Action Steps: Understanding one family member or a parent of a family member may provide illumination for the understanding of another in that family.

Summary of Action Steps

1. Make sure that your learners are in a positive, receptive state of mind before you begin teaching content. Provide opening activities that help to lower stress, increase curiosity, and challenge.

2. Maintain high expectations; teach in many different learning styles so that the potential of every learner is accessed. Use alternative forms of assessment. Provide a climate where every learner is respected and give them consistent encouragement and affirmation. Avoid heterogeneous ability grouping. Utilize multi-status, multi-age and multi-ability teamwork.

3. Establish new, positive and productive rituals which direct learners toward mutual goals, such as arrival & beginning rituals (music fanfare, positive greetings, special handshakes, hugs, etc.), special organizational rituals (team or class names, cheers, gestures, games), situational rituals (applause), and closing or ending rituals (songs, affirmations, discussion, journal writing, cheers, self-assessment, gestures).

4. Increase the amount of field trips, simulations, excursions, discussions, real-life projects and personal life activities for your learners.

5. Provide learners with global overviews. Provide them with a sequence of steps that will be followed. Alternate between the "big picture" and the details. Validate that we are "whole-brain learners."

6. Increase the use of learning symbols and images in the learning environment.

7. Create a rich, positive-feeling learning environment. Use more congruent body language. Set high standards for yourself and your environment. Involve your learners in meeting those standards.

8. Do challenging reading every day; avoid the temptation of "mindless" TV shows. Do crossword puzzles, problem-solving, memorizing, language learning, travel planning, designing, budgeting, financial planning, workshops, career planning and the playing of music.

9. Place limits on TV and video use. Talk to children about TV content, how it manipulates, its point of view. Keep the growing up time very active, involve children in thinking, planning, conversations and projects. Demonstrate that you mean what you say by being a role model, reading more often than watching TV.

10. Subliminals can and do work when used correctly. Use them in a teaching or training context **only when** 1) all learners are over 18 years of age 2) 100% of the learners give approval to the methodology and 3) they have explicit knowledge of and approval of the exact content of the material.

11. Understanding one family member may provide illumination for the understanding of another in that family.

12. Never underestimate the elderly. More and more, elderly prove what they can do, and it's a lot. Educate others about the importance of stimulation.. If your parents are in a rest home, take action: do volunteer work by bringing in stimulating activities and engaging the elderly in meaningful projects.

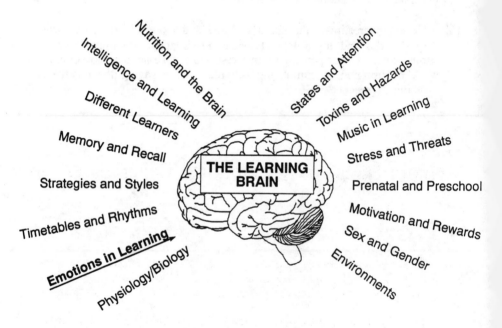

The Learning Brain

- Nutrition and the Brain
- Intelligence and Learning
- Different Learners
- Memory and Recall
- Strategies and Styles
- Timetables and Rhythms
- **Emotions in Learning**
- Physiology/Biology
- States and Attention
- Toxins and Hazards
- Music in Learning
- Stress and Threats
- Prenatal and Preschool
- Motivation and Rewards
- Sex and Gender
- Environments

Chapter Two

CHAPTER TWO

Emotions in Learning

Memory Boosted by Emotional Experiences

Research Summary: MacLean reminds us that our emotions, hormones, and feelings all affect our learning. The role of the mid-brain in learning has been endlessly verified in studies on the memory of mammals. Studies by McGaugh and Introini-Collision with their teams of researchers verify the role of limbic area (mid-brain) hormones and the amygdala in long-term memory. The work of O'Keefe and Nadel was instrumental in establishing the role of the hippocampus (located in the mid-brain area) in emotions, indexing and learning.

Hooper and Teresi document the work of "emotions pioneer" Dr. James McGaugh, psychobiologist at UC Irvine. McGaugh says that when emotions are engaged, the brain is activated. For example, when rats are injected with adrenaline, they remember longer and better. He says, "Arousal causes all these chemical cocktails--norepinephine, adrenaline, enkephalin, vasopressin, ACTH-- to sprits out. We think these chemicals are memory fixatives. They may work directly at the brain, but I think they exert most of their effects indirectly, through the peripheral nervous system....they signal the brain, 'This is important, keep this!'" McGaugh's research on emotions and hormones has consistently led him to conclude that they "can and do enhance retention...."

Example: What you probably remember most from your childhood was your lowest "lows" and your highest "highs." The same for teachers: you probably remember the worst and the best or the most outrageous. This applies across all areas of your life: the best and worst vacations, meals, dates, jobs, weather and so on.

Implications: The philosophy used to be: "Keep things under control. Don't let the students get out of hand. Suppress emotions!" The new philosophy, based on the way the brain learns and remembers best, may well be: "Engage the emotions; make the learning personally compelling, deeply felt and real."

Action Steps: Make a purposeful strategy to engage positive emotions within the learner. Without it, the learner may not code the material learned as important. Long, continuous lectures and predictable lessons are the least likely to be remembered. Utilize the following: enthusiasm, drama, role-plays, quiz shows, music, debates, larger projects, guest speakers, creative controversy, adventures, impactful rituals and celebrations.

Laughter May Help Boost Learning States

Research Summary: Dr. William Fry at Stanford University has discovered that the body reacts biochemically to laughing. Fry inserted catheters into the veins of medical students who were watching and listening to a comedian. He and his associate Lee Berk of the Loma Linda Medical School wanted to measure the changes in blood chemistry. They found an increase in white blood cell activity and changes in the chemical balance of the blood which may boost the body's production of the neurotransmitters needed for alertness and memory.

How could this happen? For one thing, a good laugh can lower stress-- and a low stress brain and body makes for a better learner. In the classic book *Anatomy of an Illness,* Dr. Norman Cousins revealed his laughter therapy which, he stated, was instrumental in his battle with cancer. So, does laughing change the chemistry of the brain? That used to be a joke, but many scientists now think so.

Example: Your students are feeling stressed, and one of them tells a joke. The whole room erupts with laughter and they now seem ready to learn something new.

Implication: Maybe humor and jokes do have more of a place in learning environments, provided, of course, that their use is tasteful and respectful of the time available.

Action steps: Be tolerant of learner contributed humor. At times, having a two minute joke session may be an appropriate way to deal with stress.

Cognitive-Emotive Recognition Link Verified

Research Summary: Researchers Campbell & Grossberg discuss how the structure and function of hippocampal and inferotemporal processing may be linked. Learning areas such as categorization, attention, memory, novelty recognition and memory search all work together at different stages of development.

But while researchers have known that the infero-temporal cortex can recognize both specialized and abstract information, Campbell proposed a link between this ability to recognize and lesions in hippocampal formation. This proposed link may verify the relationship between how we feel and how we learn. Dr. Candace Pert, chief of brain biochemistry at National Institute of Mental Health, says "The emotions are not just in the brain, they're in the body...this may explain why some people talk about gut feelings."

Example: You see a student come into class and immediately have a good feeling about him or her. Or, you are feeling good about yourself one afternoon and you see a student. You now have a positive association with that student. Thoughts and emotions are tied.

Implications: The emotional state of your learners is at least as important as the intellectual-cognitive content of your presentation.

Action Steps: Make sure you put your learners in a good emotional state before you present the material. Allow your learners time to de-stress first, then make the learning enjoyable with amusing activities so that the emotions are positively engaged.

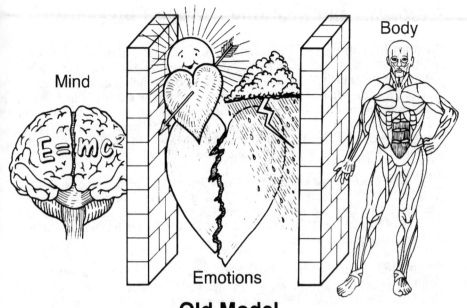

Mind

Body

Emotions

Old Model

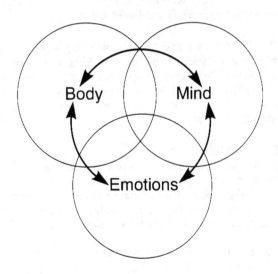

Body

Mind

Emotions

Actual

Emotions and Learning Closely Linked

Research Summary: Researchers have found critical links between emotions and the cognitive patterning needed for learning. Ornstein, Sobel, Lakoff and Rosenfield have documented how emotions influence learning in two ways: First, the "flavor" or "color" of our experiences are likely to make us either want more of it (it was pleasurable) or less of it (it was boring or painful). Second, positive emotions allow the brain to make better perceptual maps (O'Keefe and Nadel). That means that when we are feeling positive, we are able to sort out our experiences better and recall with more clarity.

How much do our emotions rule us? Just talk to anyone who is engaged in sales. Most salespersons will tell you the "buying decision" is usually emotional. In fact, top endorphin (emotion hormone) researcher at National Institute of Mental Health, Dr. Candace Pert, says, "The brain is just a little box with emotions packed into it."

Example: A learner arrives distraught over a domestic dispute, a lost article, or a lost game by a favorite team. The learner is irritable, moody and learns very little. He remembers the class as a waste of time and has a bad day. The opposite: a learner has just had a recent success or positive relationship encounter. The day is rosier, the birds are singing and he's happy. As a result, he learns better and has positive memories of the class.

Implications: As teachers and trainers, we may want to pay much more attention to the emotional state of the learner. First, unless the learner is in a relaxed state of positive expectancy, very little of a constructive nature can happen. Second, as instructional leaders, we have the power to influence the emotional state with activities that release stress or increase bonding or give the emotions a chance to be expressed.

Action Steps: Two-fold:
1) Make sure that the learner has a positive, safe way to "express out" any negative emotions. Suggestions include:
   * a mind-calming visualization or relaxation exercise
   * doing something physical: a walk, cross-crawl, stretching, games
   * dialogue time: with partners, a small group, or sharing with whole group
   * internal time: journal-writing, self-assessment, goal-setting
   * metaphorical rituals: put a "dumping box" near the door so learners can toss in any negative feelings, either on paper or symbolically.

2) Make sure that the learning has positive emotions associated with it.
   Ideas include:
   * use of role-play, theater, drama, mime and simulations
   * use of music, playing instruments, singing, chanting, cheers, shouts
   * use of debate, controversial issues, personal stories, improvisation
   * physical movement: dance, games, exercises, stretching, play
   * excursions, guest speakers, trips, novel or challenging activities

Best Bet Resource: Booklet: *How to Engage Emotions* or *99 Energizing Activities,* available by catalog from Turning Point Publishing, see page 351.

Your "Self-Convincers" Ruled by Emotions

Research Summary: While all of us can be presented with evidence that something is true, it is not verified in our own world until we *feel* that it is true. In spite of all we have learned from reason, science, logic or common sense, we do not feel that anything is true until our mid-brain, the limbic portion, which deals with emotions, says that it is. Dr. Paul Maclean, brain pioneer, says that the most disturbing thing about the way the brain is wired is."[t]hat the limbic system, this primitive brain that can neither read nor write, provides us with the feeling of what is real, true and important." The limbic system insists that ultimately the learner must feel that something is true before it is believed.

Example: Listen for expressions that let you know that others are processing the veracity of an experience. Someone says that "It just doesn't feel right." Another says, "I'll believe it when I see it." A third says, "Wait 'til he hears about this." These phrases indicate an attempt to feel convinced about something. Only then will there be actual belief.

Implications: In a learning context, the engagement of emotions at the end of an activity can help the brain to "know what it knows," to give the needed stamp of approval. Increased learner self-confidence follows, along with intrinsic motivation for future learning. Many rituals that celebrate the learning can do more than just make the learning fun, they can also seal the information and experiences in the brain as real and worth remembering.

Action Steps: Include simple opportunities for learners to engage emotionally after a learning experience. It could be learner enthusiasm, "high fives," acknowledging their partner, drama, role-plays, quiz shows, debates, impactful rituals and simple celebrations. It could even be as simple as an enthusiastic learner conversation about the topic. The key is simple, but critical: engagement of emotions leads to learners "knowing that they know it". And that leads to self-confidence and motivation to learn more.

Best Bet Resource: For more details on self-convincer states, there's an booklet titled, *How to Boost Learning by 30%*, available by catalog from Turning Point Publishing, see page 351.

Learner Emotions Key to Motivation

Research Summary: Utilizing the whole brain approach, acknowledging both left and right hemisphere learning, says Levy, "respects the inseparability of cognition and emotion." She adds that by purposefully engaging your learners in meaningful emotional processes, you'll tap into more of the student's brain.

A top researcher on emotions, N. H. Fridja says that understanding learner emotions is one of the keys to motivation. Although the presence of emotions doesn't give you the content of the problem, it certainly tells you that there is an issue to be addressed. Emotions influence:

* selective attention
* event interpretation
* motivation
* prediction

* recall
* decision-making
* problem-solving
* learning

When strong emotions are engaged, they so flavor the human experience that the learner is unable to bring anything else to conscious attention. Unlike a typical cognitive thought, once emotions are fully engaged, they cannot be hidden or made non-consciously without a great degree of effort. In other words, while some learners may be able to temporarily ignore a powerful emotion for a few minutes, it does need to have a form of expression. Suppression only defers the learner's engagement to a few moments later. Emotions require contexts for expression or they will disable a learner within minutes.

Example: How often are learners distracted from learning by previous argument in the halls, at home or in school playgrounds? Or, you know that you should do an errand, or make a phone call or pay a bill. You have all the reasons to do it. But you still put it off. For how long? Until you _feel_ like doing it.

Implications: By learning to manage our own emotions, we can stay better motivated to be at our best. By empowering our learners to be able to manage their own emotions, they, too, can become self-motivated.

Action Steps: Actively pursue emotion-engaging strategies such as drama, suspense and celebration. Utilize emotions as an ally and powerful strategy for learning. The evidence is strong that it will pay off. Be cautious, however. Make sure to be aware of any students with emotional disturbances.

Summary of Action Steps

1. Put your learners in a good emotional state before presenting material. Allow them time to de-stress first, then make the learning enjoyable with amusing activities so that the emotions are positively engaged.

2. Make a purposeful strategy to engage positive emotions within the learner so that the material learned will be coded as important. Long lectures and predictable lessons are less likely to be remembered than those employing enthusiasm, drama, role-plays, quiz shows, music, debates, larger projects, guest speakers, creative controversy, adventures, impactful rituals and celebrations.

3. Make sure that learners have a positive, safe way to "express out" any negative emotions. Suggestions include relaxation exercises, physical activity, dialoging, journal-writing, and metaphorical rituals, such as a "dumping box" for learners to toss in any negative feelings.

4. Be tolerant of learner contributed humor. At times, having a two minute joke session may be an appropriate way to deal with stress .

5. Include simple opportunities for learners to engage emotionally after a learning experience. It could be learner enthusiasm, "high fives," acknowledging their partner, drama, role-plays, quiz shows, debates, impactful rituals and simple celebrations. The key is simple, but critical: engagement of emotions leads to learners "knowing that they know it." And that leads to self-confidence and motivation to learn more.

6. Actively pursue emotion-engaging strategies such as drama, suspense and celebration. Utilize emotions as an ally and powerful strategy for learning. The evidence is strong that it will pay off. Be cautious, however. Make sure to be aware of any students with emotional disturbances.

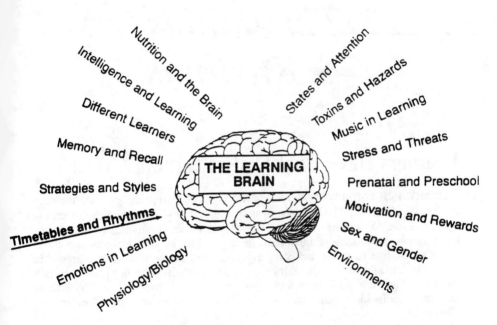

Nutrition and the Brain

Intelligence and Learning

Different Learners

Memory and Recall

Strategies and Styles

Timetables and Rhythms

Emotions in Learning

Physiology/Biology

States and Attention

Toxins and Hazards

Music in Learning

Stress and Threats

Prenatal and Preschool

Motivation and Rewards

Sex and Gender

Environments

THE LEARNING BRAIN

Chapter Three

CHAPTER THREE

Timetables & Rhythms

Learners Have Dual Daily Learning Cycles

Research Summary: Our brains are constantly running on two learning cycles, says Thayer. The first is a "low to high energy" cycle and the second is a "relaxation to tension" cycle. These two cycles dramatically affect our learning and perception of ourselves, he says. Thayer says learners can focus better in the late morning and early evening. Yet they are more pessimistic in middle to late afternoon. Our thinking can get unrealistically negative at certain low times and quite positive during high cycles. These patterns, or "rhythms of learning," coincide with the ultradian cycles described by Brewer and Campbell.

Can these patterns be modified, and are they consistent? Yes, to both. Learners were taught to modify the rhythms by varying their sleep, exercise, diet and exposure to sunlight. In addition, differences in personalities can result in pattern variations. Introverts reported higher tension during the first two-thirds of the day; extroverts, during the last two-thirds.

Example: An elderly woman's daily pattern was entirely reset by exposing her to four extra hours of bright light each day for one week. Researcher Czeisler says that her temperature and cortisol rhythms were actually reset as a result of this therapy.

Implications: Our learners may have much more influence over the quality of their learning than previously thought. By understanding patterns and fluctuations, one can better learn to take preventive action.

Action Steps: Help your learners to become aware of their own best times for learning. Use the influence you have to encourage your learners to manage or stabilize any of their awkward rhythms. They can do that through nutrition, rest and activity.

Time of Day Affects Learning Dramatically

Research Summary: University of Sussex researcher Dr. Oakhill conducted experiments to discover whether the time of day affects memory. She found that we incorporate two different types of memory into our learning: literal and inferential. In the morning we seem to favor literal memory and in the afternoon our brain is better at integrating knowledge with what we already know.

Brewer and Campbell say that from 9-11 a.m., the brain is 15% more efficient for short term memory. Semantic cerebral process is generally more efficient in the afternoon. Campbell says that 9 a.m.-12 noon is the best time for rote learning, spelling, problem-solving, test review, report writing, math, theory, science. Noon to 2 p.m. is best for movement-oriented tasks, paperwork, manipulatives, computer work, music, singing & art. The time from 2-5 p.m. is best for studying literature and history, and for doing sports, music, theater and manual dexterity tasks. Because some of us are "morning people" and others are "night people", there is a 2-4 hour variance among learners for optimal timing.

A Duke University study conducted by Cynthia May took 42 learners and showed that how well you recall depends as much on your age as on the time of day. May reports that young adults do best on memory recall in the afternoon or evenings. Older people proved to perform significantly better in the morning and worse when they were tested in the afternoon.

Given all of the variations in people types, research tells us that no matter when you present a particular topic, it is likely to be out of synch, or the wrong time, for about one-third of your learners, according to Freely, Price, and Virotsko. In fact, Carruthers and Young demonstrated that when adolescents were allowed to learn subjects at their preferred time of day, the motivation, behavior and mathematics scores improved.

Example: If a standardized test is always given at a certain time, some will consistently underperform. If test material is read early in the day, learners are better able to recall exact details; names, places, dates, facts. However, more meaningful information is grasped better in the afternoon.

Implications: It seems that literal memory may decline across the day, forcing learners to pay closer attention and relate more of the information to personal experience.

Action Steps: Present new information earlier in the day. Use the afternoon to integrate what's already known. The morning is best for sourcing information; the afternoon, for synthesizing and applying it. Do reading, listening, watching activities in the morning; role-playing, projects, drama, simulations in the afternoon.

Best Bet Resource: *Rhythms of Learning*, by Chris Brewer and Don Campbell, available by catalog from Turning Point Publishing, see page 351. The Duke University study was reported in *Psychological Science*, available from 40 W. 20 St. New York 10011.

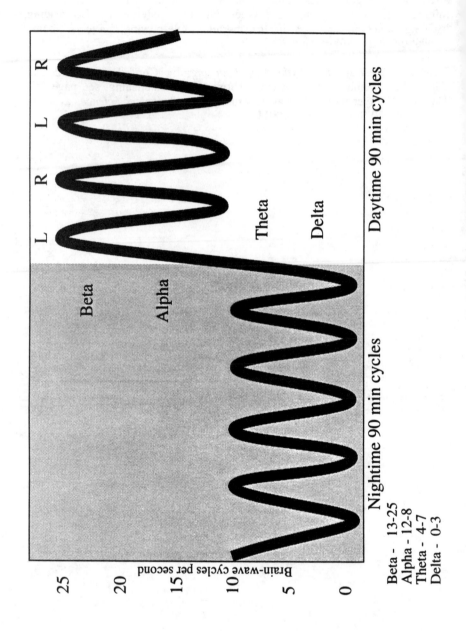

Beta - 13-25
Alpha - 12-8
Theta - 4-7
Delta - 0-3

Relax-Energize Learning Cycles Best

Research Summary: Lozanov says the activation and suppression of cerebral/limbic structures is key to the success of a teacher. He says the relaxing effects of a positively suggestive learning climate are key to "...reducing the vigilance intensity to an optimum by activating the serotonin-energetic systems or suppressing the catecholaminegetic systems." Translated, that means the brain stays alert and relaxed for learning but not anxious and hyper-stressed.

Lozanov adds that the whole brain is a system that needs to be simultaneously satisfied. By purposely activating both the more structured, sequential educational content and the more emotionally satisfying experiences (left and right hemisphere, cerebral and limbic), the system "accelerated... in all levels...." In fact, Lozanov believes that by satisfying the "optimum functional needs of the central nervous system.... [teaching and training can become] a factor in the accelerated development of the personality." In other words, the richer the learning experience, the more individual and personal benefits there are to the learner aside from the intended content.

Example: A simulation/role-play followed by a discussion would fit the activity-rest cycle in learning.

Implications: Any teaching process which is 90-100% lecture or 90-100% any methodology could be more effective if designed better. Many students who are not succeeding now may be impaired by the methodology used.

Action Steps: Make sure that your learning is sequenced to appeal to the abstract/cerebral and emotional/limbic parts of the brain. Alternating formats of activity and rest, instruction and discussion or exploration and de-briefing make the most sense.

Brain Modal Switchover Every 90 Minutes

Research Summary: Each side of our brain has dominance in certain skill areas; with the left being more efficient at verbal skills and the right at spatial. But two Canadian researchers, Klein and Armitage, discovered that there is an alternating period of efficiency for each side. In other words, when verbal is high, spatial is lower.

How dramatic is the switchover in brain dominance? In testing, the researchers found verbal scores improved from 165 to 215 and spatial performance scores improved from 108 to 125. And this alternating efficiency oscillates on 90-100 minute cycles. *In other words, learners switch from right brain to left brain dominance throughout the day.* The day, for our brain, is defined by 16 cycles lasting 90 minutes each.

This discovery fits in well with the earlier discovery that all humans have ultradian rhythms known as the "B-R-A-C" cycle, the "basic rest-activity cycle". These cycles are the alternating periods of REM (rapid-eye-movement) which corresponds with our dream time and our non-REM light rest periods. This nighttime cycle is continued throughout the daytime also.

Orlock says that these 90 minute cycles also coincide with hormone release into the bloodstream, regulating hunger and attention span. She cites experiments in isolation where the subjects consistently "headed for the refrigerator or the coffeepot about every ninety minutes." Sensitivity to pain, appetite and learning varies because the brain is changing continually. She also quotes a study on the hemispheric dominance switches that occurred on learning, thinking, reasoning and spatial skills tests. Once again, the switchover occurred every 90 minutes.

Another researcher, Maryland gerontologist Morton Leeds, suggests that this 90 minute cycle may be the perfect time for suggestion and affirmation. Why? The changeover may be a time when the body is switching gears and entering a neutral time highly receptive for change and healing.

Example: Many teachers, trainers, learners and others might say that the mid-morning and mid-afternoon coffee & snack breaks seem like a natural thing to do.

Implications: As an instructional leader, you may want to know about these cycles, yet not be dominated by them. Caffeine, for example, actually disrupts the body's own natural cycles (Ehret). Your body increases its own levels of norepinephrine throughout the day to increase alertness. Therefore, it may be best to drink decaffeinated coffee or tea.

Action Steps: Learners who are at the peak of the right or left hemisphere dominance may need cross lateral activation to "unstick" them. Dr. Paul and Gail Dennison say that physical activity that moves one side of the body across over to the other side can stimulate both sides of the brain and energize thinking.

Best Bet Resources: *Brain Gym*, Teacher's Edition, by Paul & Gail Dennison. Contact: available by catalog from Turning Point Publishing, see page 351. For research on the 90 minute affirmation cycles, contact Dr. Leeds at: 6219 Lone Oak Dr., Bethesda, MD, 20817.

Sleep Time Builds Complex Memories

Research Summary: Research at the University de Lille in France indicates that sleep time may affect the previous day's learning. By cutting nighttime sleep by as little as two hours, your ability to recall may be impaired the next day. The rule holds truer for complicated and complex material than it does for familiar or simple material. Some scientists speculate that sleep gives your brain time to do some "housekeeping" and rearrange circuits, clean out extraneous mental debris and process emotional events.

Hopfield suggests that the real reason for this may be a concept called "unlearning". Using complex mathematical and computer modeling, he discovered that neural networks can become much more efficient when certain memories are "unlearned". In fact, in his research, the role of REM sleep was critical for the brain to process the days events. By eliminating unnecessary pathways or information, the brain becomes much more efficient.

Example: The fact that you have trouble remembering dreams may indicate how effective dreams are in "cleaning" your cerebral "house".

Implications: Many of your learners may either need more sleep or better quality sleep.

Action Steps: Let your students know of the importance of physical rest and dreams.

Powerful Rhythms Affect Brain's Learning

Research Summary: Human learning and physical performance is dramatically affected by our biological rhythms.   Orlock says that we have temporal cycles of the mind and body that correspond to lunar and solar cycles. We have a 24-hour solar cycle and a 25-hour lunar cycle that affect us in countless ways, including cell division, pulse rate, blood pressure, mood swings, concentration and learning ability.   In addition, these cycles influence memory, accident rate, immunology, physical growth, reaction time and pain tolerance.

Our brain's electrical rhythms (cycles) range from 1-25 per second.   Our hearts beat about once a second. We breathe about 15 times a minute and blink from 5-15 times a minute.   Our skeletal muscles have 4-6 minute cycles of strength.   Overall physical strength and our body's temperature peak in the afternoon.

Hormones are released into our bloodstream every 2-4 hours and can dramatically alter learning.   Women are better learners the two weeks after their period is over.   Sleep and alert cycles are predictable.   The middle peak hour of one's nightly sleep would be the same time and peak of daytime drowsiness, 12 hours later.

Haus says that we also have 7-day (circaseptan) rhythms.   Organ transplant patients have the highest rejection episodes 7, 14, 21 and 28 days after surgery.   Even rats and unicellular organisms have these same seven-day rhythms.   That's because our brain and body periodically change the immune levels and white blood cell counts.

Even our breathing has cycles. On the average, we breathe through one nostril for three hours. The tissue then becomes slightly engorged, then we tend to switch to the other side. This has profound influences on the brain of the learner since it affects which hemisphere of the brain we use. These cycles are the same, day or night. We are simply more alert during the daytime cycles. And the learner may want to know how best to take advantage of them.

Researcher Englund found these rhythms to exist, also. His tests included psychomotor tasks, intellectual tasks, affective states tasks and physiological function tasks.   His research tells us that overall intellectual performance (thinking, problem-solving, debating) is greatest in later afternoon and early evening.   Although comprehension increases as the day progresses, reading speed decreases.

Scientists have found that our levels of minerals, vitamins, glucose and hormones can vary as much as 500% in a given day.   That profoundly affects the brain's efficiency and effectiveness. In general, short-term memory is best in morning, least effective in the afternoon. Long-term memory is best in the afternoon.

Halberg and Cornelissen say that each person has a different time profile, a "chronome", which is a map of our internal rhythms. This personal knowledge, they say, is critical; it is not only what you do, but when that counts. For example, the potency or toxicity of your household medications and prescription drugs vary dramatically, depending on when you take them. For maximum effect, take them two hours before the peak of your daily circadian (blood-pressure) rhythms. You'll need the lowest dose and you'll get the best effect from them.

Example: Very few teachers or trainers want to work with an audience during the "low" times of the afternoon, from 2-4 p.m. Our normal daily cycle is more likely to be 25, not 24 hours!). This can cause problems for our brain as a learner because it means that every day, you "rotate" your efficiency an hour later in the day. But the rest of the world doesn't change for you, so you may be "out of synch". At the Hermann Center for Chronobiology and Chronotherapy in Houston, Texas, the staff helps patients track their biorhythms to aid treatments. One man had a 26-hour daily cycle and was driving him and others around him crazy. With dramatic solar therapy, he was re-synchronized to a normal life.

Implications: We may be underestimating the ability of students if we test them at the wrong times of the day. Options for assessment at varied times could increase learner performance.

Action Steps: Vary your presentation hours to suit the ideal timetable for the brain. Provide diversity of activities to suit different learners. Englund even recommends that testing of students be offered at various times of the day to account for these differences.

Best Bet Resources: Dr. Michael Smolensky at the Hermann Center for Chronobiology and Chronotherapy in Houston, Texas; Dr. Franz Halberg, Director of the Chronobiology Laboratories of the University of Minnesota; *Inner Time*, by Carole Orlock; Ergonomics Program, Naval Health Research Center, Box 85112, San Diego, CA 92138.

Brain Needs "Deep Profound Rest"

Research Summary: Horne has discovered that the brain can become more easily fatigued when conditions for learning are weak. To get the brain's best performance, it needs deep physiological rest, the kind in which you are "dead to the world". Many moderate to high stress learners never get this kind of rest for their brain. Additionally, learners who live under a constant threat of some kind also never get this all-important brain rest. Without it, learning is impaired.

How much is enough? We all know that different learners need different amounts of this deep sleep. While some adults insist on 8-10 hours per night, others seem to function perfectly for years on 4-6 hours a night. The brain has its own particular cycles of functioning and requires deep, non-threatening rest so that it can utilize the REM stages properly for dreams and down-time processing.

Example: Learners who are short on sleep may perform well on short quizzes requiring rote memorization. But learners who are deprived of sleep score lower on extended performance testing and those requiring creativity and higher-level problem-solving.

Implications: Learners may need down-time for optimal brain performance. The Latin tradition of an afternoon "siesta" from 12-2 p.m. may have some biologically sound basis to it.

Action Steps: Encourage your learners to get adequate rest at night.

Brain Prefers "Pulse" Learning Pattern

Research Summary: Hobson reports that the ability to maintain learning attentiveness is affected by normal fluctuations in brain chemistry. These fluctuations occur in cycles of approximately 90 minutes across the entire 24 hour day. At night we all experience periods of "deep sleep", REM time, and light sleep. During the daytime, these cycles continue at a level of greater awareness. Even animals have these periods of basic rest and activity (Jacobs).

The brain learns best in the pattern of a pulse. Learning is best when focused, diffused, focused, diffused. How long is best for a focused activity like a lecture? Take the age of the learner, and add two minutes. The maximum, even for adults, is about 20-25 minutes, say researchers. French researcher Pieron found that the brain learned best when the learning was interrupted by breaks of 2-5 minutes for diffusion or processing.

Campbell says that the break should consist of a diffusion activity, such as a total break from the content or an alternate form of learning the content. Consider a peer teaching session, mind-mapping or project work. He also found that deep breathing and physical relaxation were especially useful in sustaining the learning.

As reported elsewhere in research by Shea, Della Valle, Hodges and Kroon, physical environment flexibility and learning style appropriateness dramatically impact the length of time students can stay sharp and focused.

Example: You go to a lecture. After a half hour or more, the audience is restless, inattentive and frustrated. The learning rate goes down and the presenter wonders why.

Implications: Many times what looks or sounds like learner apathy or fatigue is simply the down side of a predictable attention cycle. You can interfere with that cycle.

Action Steps: If you are working with young learners, you may want to limit your lectures and activities to 5-10 minutes at a time. For adolescents, limit lectures to 10-15 minutes and with adults, 15-25 minutes. After that focused time, have a diffusion activity. It could be something physical, something fun, a stand-up sharing with partner time or learner-generated ideas, teamwork, applications or personal development.

Summary of Action Steps

1. Encourage your learners to get plenty of rest, activity and nutrition. Help them to become aware of their own best times for learning.

2. Present new information earlier in the day. Use the afternoon to integrate what's already known. The morning is best for sourcing information; the afternoon, for synthesizing and applying it. Do reading, listening, watching activities in the morning; role-playing, projects, drama, simulations in the afternoon.

3. "Unstick" learners who are at the peak of right or left hemisphere dominance with physical activity that moves one side of the body across over to the other side, which can stimulate both sides of the brain and energize thinking.

4. Vary your presentation and testing hours to suit the ideal timetable for the brain.

5. If you are working with young learners, limit your lectures and activities to 5-10 minutes at a time. For adolescents, limit lectures to 10-15 minutes and with adults, 15-25 minutes. After that focused time, then have a diffusion activity. It could be something physical, something fun, or learner-generated ideas, teamwork, applications or personal development.

6. Make sure that your learning is sequenced to appeal to the abstract/cerebral and emotional/limbic parts of the brain. Alternating formats of activity and rest, instruction and discussion or exploration and de-briefing make the most sense.

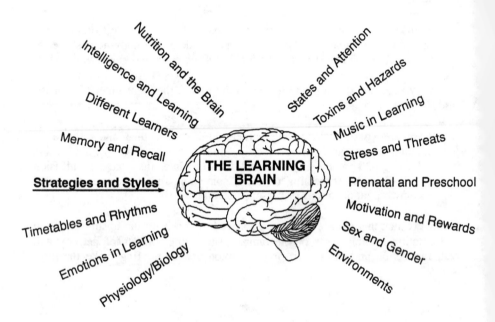

Nutrition and the Brain

Intelligence and Learning

Different Learners

Memory and Recall

Strategies and Styles →

Timetables and Rhythms

Emotions in Learning

Physiology/Biology

States and Attention

Toxins and Hazards

Music in Learning

Stress and Threats

Prenatal and Preschool

Motivation and Rewards

Sex and Gender

Environments

THE LEARNING BRAIN

Chapter Four

CHAPTER FOUR

Strategies & Styles

Learner Beliefs Affect Acquisition

Research Summary: There are three keys to learner goal acquisition, says Ford. They are learner beliefs, goals and emotions. The "personal agency beliefs" are critical for learners reaching goals which are "of the greatest developmental significance--those involving challenging but attainable goals."

There are two types of "PABs" (personal agency beliefs). They are capability beliefs ("I think I could graduate from the university") and context beliefs ("Now that I'm carrying a full load at school, getting good grades is harder than I thought"). Both of these PABs are activated once the goal is set, and not before.

An instructional leader may have no idea that these PABs exist within any particular learner. They would have no effect on a learner's progress in other areas. In fact, unless there is a particular goal in place, no one else around them would know that they hold those beliefs.

In a long-term study of 250 students, ages 12-15, researchers Meece, Wigfield and Eccles found that the single best advance predictor of success in mathematics was *their expectancy* of future math success. In other words, their PABs. Once these students were in the classes, the best predictor of their likelihood of continuing in math classes was *its importance* to them. This fits in with many teachers' experiences of students who first say, "I can't learn this stuff," and then, when they do learn it, say, "What's the point?"

It's very important that the learner believe that he or she is capable simply because of the placebo effect. In an article in the Journal of the American Mediacal Association, Turner says the belief of a supposed cure, action or strategy can have from a 35-70% success rate *and more!*

When the learner does not have the PABs to succeed in a particular context, there is a solution. Co-establish, with significant student input, "controllable short-term goals", says Barden and Ford. By doing this, the long-term outcomes may be in doubt, but with successes, the PABs of the underconfident learner may be enhanced in increments.

Do beliefs affect the teacher or trainer? Yes, powerfully. The research by Rosenthal was one of many compelling arguments for why the instructional leader must always have high expectations. Rosenthal proved that students will turn out, not coincidentally, just about how you expect them to turn out.

Example: You are able to engage some learners with simple, short goals ("Here's what we can get done today"). Other learners want larger, more challenging goals (Let's design a better health care system and get it in the local news").

Implications: Many learners want to succeed. They are capable of succeeding; they simply lack the beliefs to do so.

Action Steps: Ask learners to set their own goals for today's class. Make sure the goals are positive, specific and obtainable by the end of class. For example, a goal could be as simple as wanting to learn two new interesting things. You then need to provide the resources and learning climate to help your learners reach their goals. Then hold them accountable. Check back later to assess results and celebrate, if appropriate.

Best Bet Resources: To understand more about adult learner beliefs, get *Creating Your Future*, by Tad James. For learners under 15, get *Classroom Magic*, by Linda Harper.

Can Standing Up Boost Thinking?

Research Summary: Dr. Max Vercruyssen of the University of Southern California discovered your body's posture affects learning. His research showed that, on the average, standing increased heartbeats by 10 extra times per minute. That sends more blood to the brain, which activates the central nervous system to increase neural firing. Researchers found, that on the average, there's a 5-15% greater flow of blood and oxygen to the brain when standing. Psychologically, he says, standing up also creates more attentional arousal and the brain learns more.

Example: While sitting, you are more likely to get bored and lose focus. But while standing and listening to another, if it's just for a few moments, your focus is stronger.

Implication: We are wasting some learning time by having students sit too much.

Action Steps: When the group energy seems to lag, ask your learners to stand up. Then you can either continue to talk for 1-3 minutes while they stand, or give them a diffusion activity, an energizer, or ask them to start a relevant discussion with a partner.

Best Bet Resources: For a FREE bulletin, "21 Tips on Opening Your Class or Presentation", see page 353.

Learning Styles Boost Motivation, Learning

Research Summary: Shipman and Shipman have verified that learning can require many approaches and that learners perform best in their own learning style. In study after study, (Carbo, DeBello, Della Valle, Hodges, Shea, Virotsko and White), research proves that when learners are taught in their own particular style, their motivation, initiative and results improve.   In fact, Mayberry and Sinatra suggest that the choice of learning styles actually affects the physical structure of the brain itself.

Wlodlowski says that the ideal method is to introduce the topic in the preferred learning style of the learner, and then, for maximum understanding, to engage the learner in many other processes, as time permits. Kroon says that after an introduction in the strongest learning style, it is best to then use the second strongest, and then the third. By creating a climate of greater student responsibility in learning, a teacher can often encourage learners to follow this sequence on their own. This approach seems to reinforce the learning very well and also leads to a greater likelihood that the learner will process a deeper synthesis of the material.

Researchers Douglass and Trautman found that learners scored "significantly higher" in a way that fits their own particular learning style. A report of the New York State Board of Regents' Panel on Learning Styles said that it is essential to alter the teaching strategies to meet a more multi-cultural global society.

Were you taught to present things in a logical, sequential order? Seventy-five percent of teachers are sequential, analytic presenters.   And 70% of all their students do not learn that way.   Blackman reports that the learners who are field-independent and have a reflective cognitive style are more likely to succeed in a traditional school context. Perhaps it is better to start with a more global overview, and then go to the sequential style. In order to reach both global and sequential types of learners, one must use both approaches.

Example: Think of a class you took in school.   Did you like it?   Did you learn a lot?   How did you feel about it?   Was it in your learning style?   How much you learned and how much you liked a class were often related to the teaching style that was employed.

Implications: Many learners who seem apathetic would be very enthusiastic if the learning was offered in their preferred style.

Action Steps: There are many ways to learn. For best learning, it is better to start with an experiential global approach, then move on to verbal and visual details. You might start with a concrete experience, explain it, role play it, then de-brief it.

Best Bet Resources: Books: *Righting the Educational Conveyor Belt,* by Michael Grinder,*Teaching and Learning Styles,* by Katherine Butler; *The 4-Mat System,* by Bernice McCarthy; *The Creative Brain,* by Ned Hermann.

Bandler-Grinder

Herrmann

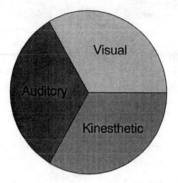

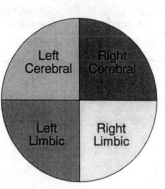

Dunn & Dunn

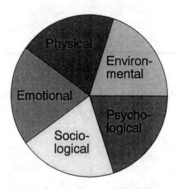

Gregorc/Butler

Concrete Random
Concrete Sequential
Abstract Random
Abstract Sequential

4-MAT System

What (abstract to reflective)
Why (concrete to reflective)
How (abstract to active)
If (concrete to active)

Pre-Exposure to Information Speeds Learning

Research Summary: Does prior exposure to information speed up the learning? Many researchers say yes. Ornstein says that pre-exposure to information makes subsequent thinking go more quickly. He likens this phenomenon to pre-consciousness.

Donchin found that the greater the amount of "priming" stimulus, the more the brain extracted and "compartmentalized" (lateralized) the information. He thinks the brain has a way of putting information and ideas into a "buffer zone" or "cognitive waiting room" for rapid access. If the information is not utilized over time, it simply lays unconnected and random. But if the other parts of the puzzle are offered, the understanding and extraction of meaning is rapid.

In one study, students were asked to name any fruit that starts with the letter A. Researchers measured the students' reaction time and the quantity of fruits named. Then the students were asked to name any fruit that starts with the letter P. Researchers discovered that students performed better on the second part of the assignment. The first question acted as a priming, or pre-exposure. It made more accessible the mental library of information.

Gazzaniga reports that in experiments done at Stanford, prior exposure to sentences led to quicker responses. Bower and Mann also found that learning and recall increased when a pattern was provided prior to exposure to the learning material. Subjects were shown sequences of letters that served as a priming and stimulus for the following information. He also found that providing "post-organizing clues" was useful. The clues related to past learning and provided a framework for recall.

Luiten examined 135 studies of the effects on learning of advance stimulation and organizers. He studied both acquisition and retention. His conclusions were that some form of "advanced organizers" are consistently positive. Stone also reviewed the research on the use of advance organizers. He found, in 29 reports on 112 studies, that the results were consistently higher learning and retention.

The research of Weil and Murphy says that the use of some kind of pre-exposure is very powerful. They say, "Advance organizers are especially effective for helping students learn the key concepts or principles of a subject area and the detailed facts and bits of information within these concept areas [the advance organizer idea]... is a highly effective instructional strategy for all subject areas where the objective is meaningful assimilation...."

Example: Several experiments were done to measure the timing for visual processing. One of them used the sentences below. Initially, respondents were quicker at recognizing and understanding sentence #4. Richer, more predictable sentence structure, maybe. But later, they were quicker to respond to sentence #1. This suggested that the content had been transformed into an association for faster meaning.

1. The boy kissed the girl.
2. The girl kissed the boy.
3. The boy was kissed by the girl.
4. The girl was kissed by the boy.

Lozanov used pre-exposure with positive visual suggestion by color-coding key items. Five hundred subjects showed much greater recall than subjects who did not get the color-coded material. Time had positive effect: consciously learned material went from 80% to 50%; the peripheral went from 85% to 91%. Even when the audience knows this method is being used, it works: scores from 600 people were 93% and 96%

Implications: Many students who seem like slow learners may simply need pre-exposure to lay the foundation for better comprehension and recall.

Action Steps: Pre-expose learners to your topic before officially starting it. Visually, you can prepare them with a note before the course begins, posted mind-maps of the topic or with preview texts and handouts. You can also get them ready with oral previews, examples and metaphors. Kinesthetically, you can offer role plays with similar experiences, simulations or games.

Flexible, Emerging Goals Optimal for Learning

Research Summary: The ideal experience of learner engagement is often referred to as being "in flow". Csikzentmihalyi defines this as a pattern of activity in which individual or group goals emerge (as opposed to being mandated) as a result of a pleasurable activity in interaction with the environment. In other words, a situation where learners "go with the flow" while enjoying themselves and increasing their own challenges as they see fit. This philosophy allows learners to discover what standards they want to achieve as they incrementally improve and enjoy. Another benefit of this type of experience is that creativity and learning are maximized.

Example: You start out learning to play an instrument, speak a new language, ice skate, play golf, jog or use a computer. At first, it seems a bit difficult. You are making an effort. Then, in time, mysteriously, it seems that you are not only getting better, but you are having fun! Time passes without your awareness, skills improve and you seem to learn without struggling.

Implications: Mandated, step-by-step instruction can work well for the initial stage of learning. It can create focus, belief and motivation. But once beyond that stage, learners can be stifled by it.

Action Steps: Assist your learners to get into the "flow" state by setting up favorable conditions for it. Set the challenge high, but keep stress low. Let the learners set the pace, then provide support to help them to continually improve and re-set goals. Probably the way you learned to ride a bike, use a computer, ski, swim, talk, use chopsticks or fix a household item engaged you in "flow".

Best Bet Resource: *Flow: The Psychology of Optimal Experience,* by Csikzentmihalyi.

Activating Prior Knowledge Boosts Learning

Research Summary: When prior learning is activated, the brain makes many more connections. Learning, comprehension and meaning increase. The research of Anderson revealed that the importance of discovering and relating to previously learned material is much greater than earlier thought. Additionally, "...[i]t is a better predictor of comprehension than is... an intelligence test score...."

Example: You're attending a new class. The instructor immediately starts in on new material. You're lost and overwhelmed in the first ten minutes. By the end of the first class, you're already worried about how you'll do in the class.

Implications: Many learners who should do well in a subject actually underperform because the new material seems irrelevant. Unless connections are made to their prior learning, comprehension and meaning may be dramatically lessened.

Action Steps: Before starting a new topic, ask the students to either discuss, do role plays or skits, or make mind maps of what they already know. Ask them what they'd like to learn more about.

Patterned Learning Maps Aid Understanding

Resource Summary: Neuroscientist Karl Pribram states that the brain's way of understanding is more through pattern discrimination than singular facts or lists. "The initial stages of processing are largely parallel rather than serial, and feature analysis results from patterns matching rather than feature detection."

Brain pioneer Hart says, "It can be stated flatly... the human brain is not organized or designed for linear, one-path thought.... [T]he brain operates by simultaneously going down many paths. We identify an object, for example, by gathering information--often in less than a second--on size, color, shape, surface texture, weight, smell, movement...."

Hart describes the importance of presenting material in larger patterns first: "Once we begin to look critically at this notion of teaching in a logical sequence, we can see that usually a further giant--and utterly wrong-- assumption has been made: that if a subject is fragmented into little bits, and the student is then presented with the bits... the student will be quite able to assemble the parts and emerge with the whole - even though never given an inkling of the whole!"

Several researchers who studied the use of graphic organizers like mind mapping, webbing or mindscapes have found that they do, indeed, help learners understand and recall information better. Armbruster found that students who were taught and using mapping boosted recall significantly. Some of the more interesting research was done by Chi on younger children, aged 4-8. But positive results were also found with adolescents and adults by Dansereau, Jones and Hagan-Heimlich.

Soloveichik reports on one of the most successful mathematics teachers in the world, Victor Shatalov. It seems that Shatalov has been using schematic organizers, like mind mapping, in his university level math classes for years. Students start the class by "mapping" what they understood from the previous class and then add to a new map as they learn the new concepts that day. Maps are color coded and revised to boost learning and retention.

In lectures around the former Soviet Union, Shatalov often would have overflow crowds of teachers, a thousand at a time, coming to hear him lecture on how he gets ordinary students and previously failed students to excel. Perhaps the most amazing quality of his students is their ability to perform complex and creative problems, often with great originality, indicating a true depth knowledge of the mathematics involved.

Example: Two groups of college students were given an essay-format post exam in a geology class. Those who had received instruction in conceptual mapping outperformed those who didn't.

In mathematics, most students have no concept of the "whole". All they get is an endless succession of facts, theorems and problems, each built on the previous ones. And none of them seemingly lead to a "whole" understanding of the subject. And, what's worse, if you miss any of the sequential steps, you lose out and are often lost for the term of the course because you can't pick up the understanding without a prior concept of the "whole!"

Implication: Many students who have done poorly in the past may have simply needed a larger "map" of the material.

Action Steps: A math teacher in New Zealand, Geoff Peterson, has tremendous success with his students because he provides those conceptual global maps before learning the specific problems. You may want to provide large graphic, conceptual maps of the whole subject before you begin teaching or learning. Utilize videos, mind mapping, mindscapes, murals, field trips, excursions and other overviews.

A more random pattern style presentation and note-taking system may be the best for the brain and learning, suggests Dr. Howe from Exeter University. "Key word notes personally made" (vs. fill-in blanks or another's notes) scored highest in understanding and recall compared to other non-patterned note-taking systems. Use a note-taking style most like a spider's pattern, a visual landscape, a web or mind map, says brain expert Tony Buzan.

Best Bet Resources: *The Mind Map Book,* by Buzan. There is also a book and video on the "mapping" techniques. These two resources are: *Mapping InnerSpace* and "Maps, Mindscapes and More," both by Margulies, available by catalog from Turning Point Publishing, see page 351.

Multiple Roles & Status Boost Learning

Research Summary: Research by Cohen at Stanford University and Pintrich and Garcia suggests that taking on many roles enhances learning. The optimal environment is one in which learners are at different times partners, teammates, individuals, and teachers. This diversity of roles provides for greater contextual, real-life immersion learning, and better ensures that the learning is integrated as real-world learning should be. And by designing the learning so that there are many roles and status levels to fill, instructors can insure that all learners will be able to find at least one contextually suitable activity that they can strongly invest in.

Example: A learner who thinks of himself as smart outside the classroom might find himself getting average or below average grades. He becomes frustrated by his lack of status, his self-image suffers, and he wants to drop out of school.

Implications: You may have many very smart learners, but in the absence of favorable circumstances, these learners may not be readily apparent.. All of us are gifted; the context provides the evidence.

Action Steps: There are many ways to utilize multiple status roles: Change the learner's status through the use of teams, peer tutoring, study buddies, multi-age projects, multi-grade projects. Involvement in the community or with co-workers, student-teacher partnerships and projects are other ways. Involve siblings, too.

Cross Lateral Activity Builds Better Brains

Research Summary: Most of us would say we feel better when we are healthy, exercise a bit or work out. But are our brains actually better? In a study on rats by Isaacs et al., research found that vigorous physical activity improves blood flow to the brain and increases synaptic and associated neuropil volume change.

Dennison goes further. He says that the use of cross lateral repatterning motions can have dramatic effects on learning. For students who are "stuck" in their learning, cross lateral movements can be the perfect and simple antidote to engage both sides of the brain for full advantage. This is particularly effective for students who are sleepy, overwhelmed, frustrated or experiencing a learning block.

Cross laterals are arm and leg movements that cross over from one side of the body to another. Since the left side of the brain controls the right side of the body and vice versa, engaging the arms and legs in cross over activities forces the brain to "talk to itself". A brain which is fully using more than just a small part is far more efficient and effective.

Example: When you go for a brisk walk or work out before coming to work, you feel better, happier. Learners who are active tend to also be more alert and learn more.

Implications: Building some physical activity into your daily learning schedule. may be preferable to leaving the activity up to the learner to do in a separate physical education class or on his own.

Action Steps: Take two minutes when you start your class to activate your learners. A short stretching, a brisk walk, some cross-lateral movements--all would do some good. Then make sure that you have some short but effective and well-timed breaks throughout the day. It will boost learner motivation. Your students will enjoy it, too.

Best Bet Resource: *Brain Gym: Teacher's Manual,* by Dennison, available by catalog from Turning Point Publishing, see page 351.

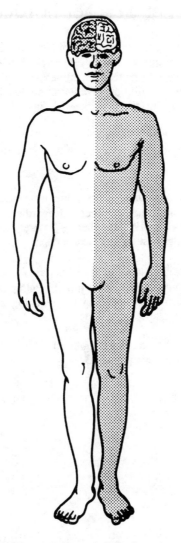

The right side of the brain
controls the left side of the
body. The left side of the brain
controls the right side of the body.

Positive Effect of Teacher Impacts Learners

Research Summary: Do the emotions of the teacher affect the learning of the students? Yes, according to Mills. He says that learners pick up on the particular emotional state of the teacher/trainer/instructor and it impacts their cognition. Teachers who use humor, give warm smiles, have a joyful demeanor and take genuine pleasure in their work will have learners who outperform those who do not.

Example: The days you are in a better mood, it seems that your learners mirror it back to you.

Implications: You may want to invest some time each day to make sure that you are at your best before teaching others. Regardless of the science of HOW it works, we know it does work. Teachers who are happier and more pleasant to be around bring out the best in their learners.

Action Steps: Take a few minutes each day for de-stressing. Listen to music that will help to put you in a great mood. Put up some kind of humorous cartoon or positive affirmation around your teaching area. Get into a good learning state before you start.

Best Bet Resource: For a FREE bulletin, "How To Get & Keep Your Student's Fullest Attention", see page 353.

Do Game Formats & Role-Playing Work?

Research Summary: The whole idea of taking academic learning and embedding it within creative expression or entertainment is centuries old. But does the method of re-contextualizing the learning really work? Yes, according to Bandura, Brophy, Malone and Leper, Bergin, and Csikszentmihalyi. One reason is that these creative presentations afford the opportunity for students to reach multiple goals (social, artistic, emotional, academic, etc.). But more important to students is the fact that in these contexts, learning becomes more enjoyable, learners exercise more choice and creativity, and there is minimal negative evaluative pressure.

Example: Many people learn history through a Jeopardy game show format.

Implications: Primary school students learn much more than they can consciously know when they work together to put on a school play. Adults are activating the brain on many levels when they engage in mock debates, "Jeopardy" shows, and humorous treatments of commercials.

Action Steps: Include creative and/or entertaining activities as a regular part of the learning process. Ideas include re-doing a popular commercial, presenting a debate, or role playing.

Best Bet Resource: *99 Energizing Activities,* available by catalog from Turning Point Publishing, see page 351.

Opposite Ear Listening Boosts Learning

Research Summary: Researcher Asbjornsen wondered if it matters whether learners use their left or right ear for listening to instructions. His staff conducted research with 40 right-handed females undergoing 36 trials with four different instructions. To insure complete data, he varied head and eye turns, together and separate, for both left and right sides, and he varied directions toward and away from the source of the voice. The results were a significant and clear *right ear advantage in all groups* during all conditions.

Music pioneer Don Campbell says that "half the people in the world change their voice response depending on which ear receives the information." He adds that if you have sequential, detailed information for your learners, position yourself so that you can address their right ear. That's the ear that has the first and fastest path to the left side of the brain.

In "Brain-Mind Bulletin", a report of research done at Cal State Fullerton in Los Angeles, California, explains that the ear choice used for listening was important. The study showed that when music (low volume baroque) was played into the opposite ear of the preferred hand used, learning increased. For right-handers, this meant music was played into the left ear.

Example: Watch your learners. You may have noticed that some of your learners constantly tilt their ear one way or another. It may be because they are appealing to the opposite side of the brain for best understanding.

Implications: Just as there are right and left handers, there are also ear dominances. It is unrelated to handedness, however. Some listeners may do better if they change position, if they "cup" their dominant listening ear, or if the person talking changes position in the room.

Action Steps: Make sure that you move around the room as you speak. You might redefine the "front" of the room. have students move into groups and teams each day or sit in different locations each week so that no one is disadvantaged.

Best Bet Resources: Contact Tomatis Center for Sound & Listening, 2701 E. Camelback Rd. #205, Phoenix, AZ 85016; Phone (602) 381-0086 or Fax (602) 957-6741.

Reframing Questions Vital to Brain's Thinking

Research Summary: The research of Wicker et al. discovered that the best way to help learners solve a problem may be to restate the problem. When they provided re-thinking training for 200 students in two separate studies, they found that flexible thinking was significantly more useful in problem-solving.

One of the groups used visualization to solve the problem, and their test results were lower. The conclusion was that visualizing may pigeon-hole thinking into a narrowed focus. By reframing and restating the problem, more creativity is unleashed and solutions arise that might otherwise have remained dormant.

Example: Students are asked to design a clock with no moving parts and no face. By visualizing, they may get stuck and come up with no answer. By re-framing the problem and asking new questions, however, they may come up with other solutions, such as a talking clock.

Implications: We have for so long stressed the importance of answers that we may have forgotten that it takes much more creativity and genius to come up with powerful questions. Answers are a dead end, since they stop the thinking. Questions open up the mind and get it going.

Action Steps: Give your learners a "reverse" test. You provide the answers and they provide at least two questions for each one. Then grade them on the quality of their questions. Or let them design the test. And use that as their grade.

Manipulation and Control Inhibit Learning

Research Summary: Research by Caine and Caine has shown that excessive control by teachers actually reduces learning. Caine says that learners "must have choice and variety." It all comes down to this simple concept that Caine explains so well: "If students are to be predominately self-motivated, they must be given the opportunity to focus on *their* areas of interest and to participate in activities *they* find interesting" (my emphasis).

In brief, unless learners have a real vote in determining the content and method of their learning, the learning becomes forced, rote, mechanical, short-lived and, eventually, distasteful. And, as Glasser notes in *Control Theory*, the more learners feel controlled, the more resentful they get. And resentment is either expressed or suppressed. It is expressed in the form of frustration, anger, rebellion, or lack of discipline. It is suppressed in the form of detachment, sabotage, apathy and cynicism about learning.

Example: You've had a manipulative and controlling teacher before. How did it feel? Teachers who enrich environments their way, use music their way, do their kind of stretching, design learning stations their way, can create a state of resentment and helplessness among their learners.

Implications: Even the best planned teaching can fail if it's too controlling. It's better to get student input or elicit learner responsibility for creating aspects like the environment, music, goals and activities.

Action Steps: Provide more options for learners, more choices in what they learn and how they learn it. Give students choices about the learning environment, the methods of instruction and types of assessment. Have discussion groups on the best types of student input. Utilize suggestion boxes, teams and expression areas. Students buy into and take pride in doing activities which they have helped to define and over which they have some control.

Best Bet Resource: *Making Connections: Teaching and the Human Brain*, available by catalog from Turning Point Publishing, see page 351.

Personal Learning Styles Can Be Expanded

Research Summary: In experiments by Torrance and Ball, student learning styles were assessed, and then the students were put through a course to expose them to other methods. Through exposure to right-hemisphere, non-linear learning strategies (imagery, intuition, brainstorming, metaphors, etc.), the learners were able to make more use of their existing capabilities and extend into new areas. The results also showed that the students were able to "change their preferred styles of learning and thinking through brief but intensive training."

Learners often change preferences for how information is presented to them based on the time of day. In a study by the University of Sussex in England, researchers found that detailed and literal learning was better in the morning, when performance was better on tests involving details and exact, precise information. In the afternoon, global learning improved, as did inferential and contextual material.

Another researcher, Grinder, says that while you might use several styles, your preferred (or dependent) style will stay with you for most of your life. Why? It's the one that you learned to use for survival as an infant, so your brain always gives it first priority.

Example: A fire breaks out in a room. Your immediate, first reaction will be one of the following: 1) visual (quickly size up the situation, looking for exits, others in need, etc.); 2) auditory (start yelling "Fire" or giving directions or screaming); or 3) kinesthetic (start running for the exits or grabbing others to help them out). While you may do all three, one will be an instinctual first reaction. That's your preferred learning style.

Implications: It may be better to think of learners as having preferences for certain learning styles, rather than fixed mandates.

Action Steps: Create options for your learners so that they can learn in the style of their first choice. Then expose them to a variety of other styles so that they may become flexible learners.

Best Bet Resources: *Righting the Educational Conveyor Belt*, by Grinder and a booklet titled, *Insider's Guide to Learning Styles,* available by catalog from Turning Point Publishing, see page 351.

Concrete, Vivid, Visual Images Most Powerful

Research Summary: What's the best way to convey motivating information to your learners? Is it through discussion, reading material or computers? None of the above, say the researcher teams of Fiske and Taylor and Nisbett and Ross. The most powerful influences on your learners' behaviors are concrete, vivid images. Neuroscientists might say that it's because 1) the brain has an attentional bias for high contrast and novelty; 2) 90% of the brain's sensory input is from visual sources; and 3) the brain has an immediate and primitive response to symbols, icons and strong, simple images.

Savvy advertisers and political strategists have known this for years. In the television medium, they use emotional shots, evocative visual images and real life events to persuade consumers and voters. And it works, say Petty & Cacioppo. Some argue that recent national elections have been decided by concrete, vivid images that made a lasting impression.

Example: From television, many recall quite vividly the Zapruder JFK film, the "Willie Horton" commercial, the CNN shots of SCUD missile attacks in the Middle East and starving children in Ethiopia and Somalia. The sight of an American soldier shot and dragged through the streets of Mogadishu is said to be the prime reason U.S. policy was changed towards Somalia.

Implications: As a teacher or trainer, a lot of talking, lecture or speeches may deliver content, but not be compelling or particularly memorable. For maximum impact, change the medium.

Action Steps: Use impactful videos, strong posters, mind maps, vivid drawings and symbols. Bring in things to show and tell. Ask students to generate the most evocative images they can, either through visualization or in the form of posters or murals.

Concrete Vivid Images

Learner Goal-Setting Well Worthwhile

Research Summary: Two researchers, Locke and Latham, surveyed nearly 400 studies on goals, and the results were definitive. They found that specific, difficult goals lead to better performance than easy, vague ones. They add that these "results are based on studies conducted in the U.S. and seven other countries... [on] more than 40,000 subjects, 88 different tasks, time spans ranging from one minute to three years, and many different performance criteria, including behavior change, quantity and quality outcomes and costs."

However, a few other criteria for goal setting are necessary, says Ford. First, the target has to be at an optimal level of difficulty - "challenging, but attainable". Then the goal-pursuing process will only be effective if the learners have: 1) ample feedback to make corrections; 2) capability beliefs to sustain pursuit in the face of negative feedback; 3) the actual skills needed to complete the task; 4) an environment conducive to success.

However, if goals are given too much attention, they can be counter-productive, according to Baumeister. Learners report that they feel self-conscious, make simple mistakes, and sometimes experience test anxiety and "choke" on material, forgetting things they should have known.

Example: If a sports team has a strong, clear goal of winning, and they have a "winning attitude", they are likely to have some success. And individual players who set goals often outperform those who don't. But the very best players, the ones at the top of their profession, set the goals, and then mentally set them aside while they do the task.

Implications: In the proper context, goal setting serves a function.

Action Steps: Let students generate their own goals. Have them discover whether their own beliefs can support them. Ask them about the learning environment. Is it supportive to achieving the goals? Do they have the resources to reach their goals?

Best Bet Resources: *Creating Your Own Future*, by Tad James; *Motivating Humans*, by Martin Ford.

Discussion Boosts Understanding & Action

Research Summary: Lewin, in USDA experiments, discovered that learners are more likely to integrate the learning and implement changes when lecture is followed by discussion. One group, the control group, was simply lectured to, then allowed to leave. About 3% of them actually changed their behavior based on the lecture. But in the other group, which stayed and discussed the lecture information informally, 32% changed their behavior. Research has proven, over and over, when participants make the learning *their own,* when they get to talk about it *their way,* without being manipulated and controlled, learning increases.

Example: When done poorly, class time consists of a teacher lecturing for 45 minutes until the bell rings and the students leave for their next class. When done well, there's discussion time built in to every class session. To produce better learning, share information, problem-solve and discover, then discuss.

Implications: Much of the problems in learning, teaching and training are not centered on the learner missing key information. The problem is that the learner has not made the information his own. The discussion of the information may allow the learner time to integrate, trouble-shoot and "buy-in" to more of the learning.

Action Steps: Provide consistent opportunities for learners to stop and discuss what they have learned. Let them talk about how it might affect them and what they could do about it. Many shorter discussions are just as powerful as single long ones.

Congruency Critical to Presentation

Research Summary: Research on the brain and our senses has shown that we are able to be conscious of only one incoming sensory message at a time. In other words, while you watch a movie, the sounds are reaching the nonconscious. While you are listening to a concert performance, the sights are reaching the nonconscious. European learning pioneer Lozanov describes teacher and trainer congruency as "dual plane messages", messages that are received by your learners on two levels, the conscious and the paraconscious. Your learners are aware of both your verbal and nonverbal communication, so that they are being influenced by messages that you, the presenter, may not even be aware of sending.

Example: You say to your learners, "I am very happy to be here today." But actually, your head is shaking from side to side as if to say, "I'd rather be elsewhere." While both messages are being received, the second one will have the greatest credibility.

Implications: Your learners are receiving a lot of mixed messages which undermine the content of your desired message and reduce your credibility. Lozanov calls this a loss of prestige and authority with respect to the course you are offering. Learners will learn more when the presenter communicates more congruently.

Action Steps: Practice your non-verbals. Videotape yourself and review it. Find the two or three areas you can improve the most and work on just those. Get feedback from others. Take an acting class. Practice in front of a mirror.

Best Bet Resource: *Present Yourself*, by Michael Gelb, available by catalog from Turning Point Publishing, see page 351.

Learner Chaos & Confusion Can Be Positive

Research Summary: Researchers Prigogine and Stengers, Gleik, and Doll have postulated that the learner climate of suspense, surprise, disequilibrium, uncertainty and disorder can lead to a richer understanding of the content. Prigogine even says that the brain is designed for chaos. He says, "Instability creates purposeful activity and direction."

In fact, these researchers say that the behavioristic, reward-punishment, super-ordered systems attempted in most learning contexts are actually the least likely to produce the desired results. Why? The most effective learning is either real-life or patterned after real-life. And real life can be suspenseful, surprising, uncertain and disorderly.

Green and associates found that when discrepant phonetic information is delivered both aurally and visually, the brain creates a whole new encoding for it. A typical experiment would feature the subjects watching videotapes of female presenters with a male voice dubbed over it. The reverse was also used. Even though there was an obvious gender incongruence, the learner was not only able to understand the material, but also created whole new meanings for it. In other words, it was so incongruent that it became novel and, hence, powerful.

According to Bigge, learner involvement "is at its best" when the learner is perplexed and confused, but not yet frustrated. He uses what he calls "positive dissatisfaction" to engage learners at peak levels of motivation and understanding. The designer of a higher order thinking skills computer-based program (HOTS) says that he purposely puts students into a state of "controlled frustration" in order to develop better quality thinking, patience and mental toughness.

Example: Learners are working on a play. An interpersonal conflict develops and two students want to quit. Instead of the instructional leader jumping in to "save the day" and solve the problem, the learners are simply encouraged to solve it for themselves in a way that everyone is happy. The chaos and controlled frustration becomes a learning tool instead of a way for the teacher to "take charge" and show how much he or she knows.

Implications: Much of what passes for "learning" is simply the rote memorization of surface knowledge. It's rarely integrated into real life. We need to allow for more variety and reality in our learning contexts. This does not mean that we should embrace thoughtless chaos, but rather that we should encourage a sort of "orchestrated disequilibrium" much more often.

Action Steps: Utilize learner-generated role-playing, simulations, theater, songs, experiments, field trips, extemporaneous speaking and meaningful project work in which chaos can occur. Allow the activity to run its natural course when possible. Minimize intervention.

Competition Reduces Motivation, Self-Worth

Research Summary: In the last several years, there's been a deluge of research about the advantages and disadvantages of competition in the classroom. Kohn argues strongly in his book, *No Contest: The Case Against Competition*, that competition has vastly undermined educational systems. Ames argues that the typical competitive learning environment is strongly detrimental to the learner:

> "[T]here is little, if any, viable evidence that a competitive goal structure in the classroom is associated with outcomes that are indicative of positive self-worth, continuing motivation, or quality of task engagement."

So, does the cooperative learning model fit for everyone? Among the pioneers of cooperative learning, Johnson et al. found that when positive cooperative structures were in place, some inter-group competition could exist without reducing motivation. Yet so many schools and businesses use only the competitive model.

Example: When participants cooperate successfully on a group project, the results are fantastic. They work without boundaries and often produce terrific quality.

Implications: When learners compete with each other, the goal is to win, not to produce quality. You'll often get high enthusiasm, but attention to deep meaning and creativity go downhill.

Action Steps: Form cooperative groups often. Mix them and reform new ones over time. When you use teams, never have them compete against each other unless they set up the competition.

Best Bet Resources: *TeamWork*, by Alyce Cornyn-Selby. (Available from Bench Press Publishing at (503) 232-0433, at 1928 S.E. Ladd Avenue Portland, OR 97214); *Learning Together and Alone*, by Johnson and Johnson.

Learning/Brain Style Profile Validity Varies

Research Summary: Most of us are familiar with theories on learning styles: left-brain, right-brain, abstract, experiential, etc. But Zalewski et al. found that one hemispheric assessment tool is highly inaccurate and unable to correlate to effective classroom teaching. The profile examined was a paper-and-pencil survey called, "Your Style of Learning and Thinking". The authors examined the instrument for 1) validity, 2) consistency and reliability, and 3) comparisons of healthy brains versus brain-injured subjects.

In the researcher's analysis it was revealed that the instrument was impaired by internal inconsistencies and low-to-moderate test-retest correlations. The construct validity was assessed by comparison with hemispherically dominant brain-injured subjects. With only one exception the analysis showed that "there were no significant differences". In other words, the instrument did not support the notion of preferred hemisphericity as measured in this way.

Yeap's research showed different results. He measured the psychological domain of the learner in terms of hemisphericity. He compared three levels of student achievement: low, moderate and high. His research showed no significant differences between the low to middle achievers. But between the moderate and high achievers, there was a "distinctly different" hemispheric dominance profile.

The Hermann Brain Dominance profile has been consistently proven valid. A doctoral dissertation by Ho asserted that the scores are consistent, statistically reliable predictors of personality and learning preferences. The Hermann model uses the quadrants of left and right, cerebral and limbic to identify personal profiles.

Example: You may be tempted to give your students a modality assessment profile for determining who is more visual, auditory or kinesthetic. But the very modality in which it is given is visual, with fine motor kinesthetic. By taking it, the learner may become biased towards making choices that might not ordinarily be made.

Implications: For many assessment needs, you may be better off if you simply use your personal experience of your learners. Watch, listen and engage them to learn as their own preferences dictate.

Action Steps: Avoid labeling learners. Instead, simply say to yourself, "That's how she is now", and know that learning styles can be contextually changeable. To determine who is more visual, watch your learners as you move around the room; they'll follow you with eye contact. To determine who is more auditory, soften your voice and watch who perks up their ears, or listen for those who talk to themselves. For the more kinesthetic learners, watch for movement in extremities and for positioning for comfort.

Best Bet Resource: *Booklet: Insider's Guide to Learning Styles,* available by catalog from Turning Point Publishing, see page 351.

Mental Practice Boosts Learning

Research Summary: An Oxford University study found that thinking before a learning activity improved learning. Elementary school children were asked to practice visualization, imagery and make believe. Then their performance was measured. The group that did the visualization first, then learned, scored higher than the other group who didn't.

Example: Before you went to your last job interview, chances are you rehearsed the interview in your mind many times over. This kind of practicing accesses the information, rehearses it and in a sense, "pre-exposes" your mind to itself.

Implications: In some cases, your learners may not be unmotivated, they may just need mental warm-ups. A few minutes invested early in the class could produce a big payoff later.

Action Steps: Create a daily routine for your students. Before you start, have them do both physical stretching and mental warm-ups, such as mentally rehearsing a role-play, asking questions, visualizing, solving problems or brainstorming.

Best Bet Resource: *How to Boost Visualization Skills,* available by catalog from Turning Point Publishing, see page 351.

Summary of Action Steps

1. Ask learners to set their own positive, specific and obtainable goals for today's class. You then need to provide the resources and learning climate to help your learners reach their goals.

2. Pre-expose learners to your topic before officially starting it: Prepare them visually, aurally, and kinesthetically. Before starting a new topic, ask the students to discuss, do role plays or skits, or make mind maps of what they already know.

3. Take two minutes when you start your class to activate your learners with a short stretching, a brisk walk, or some cross-lateral movements. Then make sure that you have some short but effective and well-timed breaks throughout the day. When the group energy seems to lag, ask your learners to stand up.

4. Take a few minutes each day for de-stressing with music or some kind of humorous cartoon or positive affirmation around your teaching area. Get into a good learning state before you start.

5. Assist your learners to get into the "flow" state by setting up favorable conditions for it. Set the challenge high, but keep stress low. Let the learners set the pace, then provide support to help them to continually improve and re-set goals.

6. Provide large graphic, conceptual maps of the whole subject before you begin teaching or learning, and continue to use impactful videos, strong posters, mind maps, vivid drawings and symbols during the teaching process. Ask students to generate evocative images as well.

7. Include creative and/or entertaining activities as a regular part of the learning process.

8. Give your learners a "reverse" test. You provide the answers and they provide at least two questions for each one. Then grade them on the quality of their questions. Or let them design the test, and use that as their grade.

9. Provide options for learners regarding their learning environment, instruction methods and types of assessment. Utilize suggestion boxes, teams and expression areas. Expose them to a variety of learning styles so that they will become flexible learners.

10. Provide consistent opportunities for learners to stop and discuss what they have learned. Let them talk about how it might affect them and what they could do about it. Several shorter discussions are just as powerful as single long ones.

11. Practice your non-verbals. Videotape yourself and review it. Practice in front of a mirror.

12. Utilize learner-generated role-playing, simulations, theater, songs, experiments, field trips, extemporaneous speaking and meaningful project work in which chaos can occur. Allow the activity to run its natural course when possible. Minimize intervention.

13. Form cooperative groups often. Mix them and reform new ones over time. When you use teams, never have them compete against each other unless they set up the competition.

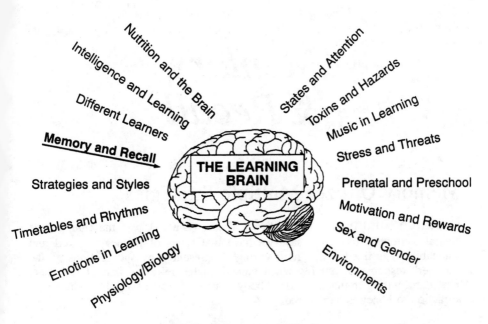

Nutrition and the Brain

Intelligence and Learning

Different Learners

Memory and Recall

Strategies and Styles

Timetables and Rhythms

Emotions in Learning

Physiology/Biology

States and Attention

Toxins and Hazards

Music in Learning

Stress and Threats

Prenatal and Preschool

Motivation and Rewards

Sex and Gender

Environments

THE LEARNING
BRAIN

Chapter Five

CHAPTER FIVE

Memory & Recall

Memory Utilizes Multiple Strategies

Research Summary: In *Memory's Voice*, Daniel Alkon, the chief of the Neural Systems Laboratory, says we have two types of memory: fixed and malleable. The fixed is the "hard wiring", represented by such actions as the knee jerk response of our leg when tapped on the reflexive part of the knee. The hard wiring remains in the body, encoded for survival. The bee's attraction to honey is hard wired.

The "soft wiring" is the created memory, like names, faces and addresses. To the honeybee, the location of a particular flower is in the soft wiring. Some of the bee's memory is fixed; some isn't. It is much like pre-determined value vs. undetermined value in our learning.

Neurologically, the hippocampus, amygdala and cerebral cortex are all involved in acquiring, storing and recalling human memories Memory record looks like altered molecular channels in neuronal membranes. Neuromolecular research revealed that a neuron's electrical signal remained charged for days and even weeks. This is what we call "short-term memory". Longer term memory is a different story. In it, our body converts electrical traces into verifiable physical-chemical traces.

Alkon says it's not unlike a tape player or CD Ram. A tape deck transforms a voice's sounds into patterns of magnetic force. A tape can be re-used, played back or removed from the machine. The brain makes a memory record; the record is preserved within the neuronal membrane by the alteration of potassium channels. Memory looks like electrical signals with a reduced flow of potassium across a membrane, much like the strokes of a painting.

Protein activates memory. Without protein, sensory cells cannot convert stimuli from the external world into electrical signals within the brain. The synapses do not function as well. The body's muscles are less able to execute the learned behavior. "Protein synthesis might be necessary in a variety of cells to permit learning and memory", says Alkon.

How does the brain know whether something is important or not? Simple. The answer lies in the body's total physiological response to the event. That means that the physical and emotional sides are at least as important as the intellectual side. Alkon says, "The emotional importance of what has been learned in critical periods determines its permanence."

Example: Traumatic events from your childhood are more easily recalled than the mundane.

Implications: What we eat influences memory. A lack of protein in our diet could have repercussions. Additionally, the emotional content of the material influences our memory of it as well.

Action Steps: Encourage your students to eat balanced meals, including 20-30 grams of protein daily. Whenever appropriate, make your learning as emotionally impactful as possible.

Complex Memory Strategies Boost Recall

Research Summary: In a review of the conceptualization of working memory, Schneider summarizes the research over the last 30 years. The theory that has become most validated and established is the connectionist model. In this model, three contributing factors to memory operations are identified.

The first factor is multiple region-based processing, meaning that memory is taking place in several areas of the brain. Horn says that "it is becoming increasingly clear that multiple memory systems may be a fundamental part of the design of the vertebrate brain." Secondly, there are efficiency and effectiveness trade-offs between fast and slow-connection changes in learning and memory.

Lastly, and maybe most importantly, there is a dramatic speeding of acquisition via multiple levels of learning. Schacter suggests that multiple memory systems are responsible for our best learning and recall. His research shows that different kinds of learning may require different ways to store and recall them, too. Any system utilizing two or more of the brain's natural memory processes is considered a complex strategy. It could involve the use of music, mnemonics, location triggers, intense sensory experiences, theater, motor manipulation or humor.

In one study by Fabiani et al., learners were asked to use either rote or elaborate strategies to memorize words. Those using the rote method had higher forgetfulness ratios and a lower recall performance. The rote method involved simple repetition, also called "taxon" memory or "list-related" memorization.

Example: Learners tend to remember much more when there is a field trip, a musical, a disaster, a guest speaker or a novel study location. Why? Multiple memory systems are activated.

Implications: Learners may seem to forget a great deal of what is taught, but the problem may be a reliance on singular memory system.

Action Steps: If something is worth learning, it's probably worth remembering. Activate multiple memory systems with a variety of teaching activities, such as reading, listening to a lecture and seeing a video. Then follow up with projects, role-playing, at-home assignments, music, discussion, field trips, games, simulations or drama.

Complex strategies boost recall

Greater Context Boosts Recall

Research Summary: Researchers at London University College tested two different groups of learners. The group who learned from print recalled much more than those who watched TV or videos, or who simply listened. Even for infants, the same rule holds true.

Boller and Rovee-Collier found that context dramatically improved memory. By learning about a subject in context, with a story, a map or something relevant, memory and recall improved. It also provided the framework for updating the memory by giving a kind of "revised edition" of the cognitive map.

Example: When you travel, you learn and recall much more than you do when you sit at home or in a training session or classroom. Why? Many reasons--but one of them is that the context is rich, meaningful.

Implications: Instead of putting most of the emphasis on memorization and recall, it may be smarter and more efficient to place more emphasis on the context in which something is learned.

Action Steps: Context provides more "hooks" and allows learners more time to make connections with what they consider to be important to them. Reading, hearing or experiencing the background on a topic aids understanding and recall. The placement of information being learned into a conceptual context, such as historical or comparative, boosts recall.

Best Bet Resource: *SuperMemory* by Ostrander and Schroeder, available by catalog from Turning Point Publishing, see page 351.

Memory Linked to Order and Novelty

Research Summary: Research has verified that an easy way to remember something is to make it new and different.   That's because our brains have a high attentional bias towards something which does not fit the pattern (novelty). Because it's immediately perceived by the brain as different and NOT fitting the pattern, the body's natural stress levels are raised.   If it's perceived as a negative threat, the body may release cortisol.   If it's perceived as a positive stress (challenge), then your body releases adrenaline.   McGaugh et al. say that these chemicals act as memory fixatives.   In fact, they proved that rats injected with adrenaline remembered far longer than those who weren't injected.

Once you have gone past the first item in a list or an experience, the novelty effect of it has eroded.   So the brain treats it differently and is less likely to re-release chemicals into the body as a response to the change.   This is why you remember the first and last moments of a learning experience more than the middle.   Psychologists refer to this as the BEM principal, (Beginning, End and Middle), the order in which you are most likely to recall something. There is a distinctly different mental set at the beginning of an experience (anticipation, suspense, novelty, challenge, etc.) than the middle (continuation, more of the same, boredom, stability).   And the ending mental set is much different, too (new anticipations, emotions, etc.).

Example: You often recall the opening or ending scenes from a movie or book, but not the last.   You remember how you felt and what you saw when you first arrived at a vacation spot for a holiday.   Those "beginnings" stay with you for a long time.

Implications: Your students may be able to remember much more of what happens if you provide more novelty (let them do much of it) and more beginnings and ends (and less middles).

Action Steps: Introduce short modules of learning instead of long ones. Break up long sessions into several shorter ones.   Have your students provide surprise introductions to new topics.

Best Bet Resource: *How to Boost Memory & Recall*, available by catalog from Turning Point Publishing, see page 351.

Is Contextual Memory The Brain's Best?

Research Summary: There are many ways to classify memory (e.g., short-term & long-term, positive and negative, etc.). One of the most useful is to talk about "contextual" and "taxon" memory. O'Keefe and Nadel conducted their initial experiments on rats and later extended their findings to humans. They discovered a critical biologically-based difference between the two ways we deal with new information: our brain sorts and stores information based on whether it is heavily embedded in <u>context</u> or in <u>content</u>.

"Contextual" is the term for the type of memory you use to remember effortlessly (e.g., "What did you have for dinner last night?"). It can be described as primarily based on location and circumstances, or context. Research discovered that it has unlimited capacity, forms quickly, is easily updated, requires no practice, is effortless and is used by everyone. This memory is context-dependent; it is based on your relationships and position in space and time.

The formation of this type of memory is motivated by curiosity, novelty and expectations. It's enhanced by intensified sensory input - sights, sounds, smells, taste, touch. The information can also be stored in a fabric or weave of "mental space", which is a thematic map of the intellectual landscape, where learning occurs as a result of changes in location or circumstances, or the use of thematic teaching, storytelling, visualization and metaphors.

"Taxon" is the type of list-oriented, sometimes rote, unnatural memory which requires rehearsal, is resistant to change, isolated from context, has strict limits, lacks meaning and is linked to extrinsic motivation. (e.g., She asks, "Remember that article you were reading last night? What was the name of the author?" He replies, "Gee, I don't remember. Why do you want to know?")

This type of information gathering and memory of content without a context is difficult. This type of learning is typified by school seat work (e.g., "Finish this set of ten problems in one hour. And no talking, please."), and homework ("Study for Friday's test by reviewing chapter six."). Information learned with the taxon method:

* is usually out of "real life" context, isolated and meaningless;
* is harder to update, change and revise;
* often requires extrinsic motivation.

Example: A trip to China would provide our brain with heavy "embedding" in context. Millions of information bits, all in context, would be remembered for years. A two-hour study session on China using a geography textbook is heavily embedded in content. And it all may be forgotten a day after the "big" test. Granted, the textbook is cheaper. But with some imagination, perhaps you could create more "context" for the learning.

Implications: There are profound consequences of applying this research. We may have been forcing many to learn in a very unnatural way. We have accidentally created generations of "slow" learners who easily forget what was taught. There may be a much better way to reach learners through the use of local memory, thematic mapping and interactive contextual learning.

Taxon learning does have its place, however. When you ask for directions, for example, you want the shortest route from A to B. You don't want to drive all over the city to figure it out (although that would create a stronger "locale map"). On the other hand, if you ask others what of significance they have learned in the last year, 90% of what they tell you will probably be contextually embedded information (vs. "rote" or "book learning").

There are dozens of implications of this research. It explains why we remember certain things and not others. Motor memory (e.g. riding a bicycle), musical memory (the melody of a favorite song) and sensory memory (smell of a flower) all fill the requirements of locale memory. More of these need to be used in teaching, training and learning. Linguistic and book work (lectures, reading, listening) are usually more taxon, although novelty, pattern changes and other variations can increase their impact.

For teachers concerned with discipline, there are significant implications (see also, "state-bound" learning). First, since students remember very well the location and circumstances in which they are disciplined, all forms of "heavy discipline" from the front of the room carry dire consequences. A student will remember how he felt and his brain's locale memory will link up that feeling with you, the classroom and the school. After only a few of these episodes, the student walks in the door of a classroom and immediately his locale memory tells him, "I feel badly in this room." That can only continue for so long until he starts missing classes. That, in turn, invokes more discipline.

Then, if he is required to stay after school or come to "Saturday School", his brain links up bad feelings with school again. Soon, being on campus triggers bad feelings everywhere he goes. Naturally, he hates how he feels while he's in school and drops out. An administrator or teacher says, "He just wasn't motivated." But the brain scientists know better. He was a victim of a school that failed to understand how the brain really works. Attach embarrassment, revenge, pain and discomfort to being in school and most any student will soon drop out just to avoid the pain.

Action Steps: This is one of the most important concepts of "brain-based" learning. It asks that you make a thorough analysis of your teaching and training to discover how much of what you do is "content embedded" and how much is "context embedded". Your own analysis may shock you.

Chances are, you'll want to reduce the amount of taxon memory required. Cut seat work by 90%. Give real world problems to solve in context. Give only homework which requires contextual learning, not lists, problems or pages of unrelated facts. Use whole language learning. Take advantage of the ease and thoroughness of the locale memory system to embed key ideas by using real life learning in real contexts, musicals, plays, role-play, real world excursions, on-the-job training, motor movement and intense sensory input. Use purposeful storytelling, thematic metaphors, directed visualizations and real-world problems. Be sure to review discipline policies. Eliminate any system that does behavior "score keeping". Stop actions which evoke the "bad dog!" feeling in students.

Best Bet Resource: *Making Connections: Teaching and The Human Brain* available by catalog from Turning Point Publishing, see page 351.

Memory Maps Dynamic, Not Replicative

Research Summary: Edelman says that our memory is changing all the time with new information and changes in beliefs and circumstances. Because we change, our perceptions of the event's circumstances change in relationship to our lives. Ordinarily (unless there is trauma), memory requires "repeated rehearsal in different contexts." It requires updating and new categorical input, as well as associations. This updating engages our creativity and thinking skills. That originates in the neo-cortex.

But much of our best long-term memory is supplied by the mid-brain, says Edelman and the team of O'Keefe and Nadel. This cortical appendage transforms short-term events by "ordering" and "charging" them. Without the hippocampus, whole "suites" of categorization in a time range between the immediate and the forever could not be linked. And without that, no long-term memory is possible.

Example: Each time we tell a favorite story of a summer vacation, wedding, celebration, traumatic event or family experience, the context of the telling affects how we tell it (who is there listening, what are the unique circumstances of that day). And we tell the story differently depending on our age, too. By telling the story, our memory increases. With our students, once they learn the material, unless they continually create "dynamic maps" of the their understanding, the "replicative maps" lose meaning and repeating the material becomes much less powerful.

Implications: Some students say that as soon as a test is over, they've forgotten all that was on it. The so-called learning was simply replicative and not dynamic.

Action Steps: There are many ways to keep the memory of learned information alive in your learners. Have students do peer teaching and peer review on a weekly basis. Have students re-create the material with mind maps, and then do presentations on it. Encourage the use of murals, mindscapes and student projects.

Best Bet Resources: *Mapping Inner Space,* by Nancy Margulies, available by catalog from Turning Point Publishing, see page 351.

OLD VIEW
Replicative Memory

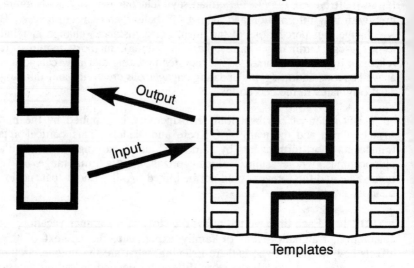

Templates

NEW VIEW
Dynamic Memory

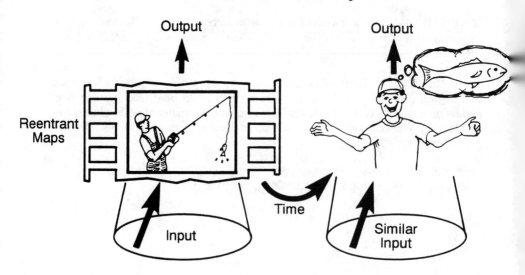

Is It Real or Is It Your Imagination?

Research Summary: Researchers have identified that some memories actually do physically exist in our brain. Lavond, Kim and Thompson have made an important distinction, however. While biological substrates have *not* been found for *all types* of memory, researchers have positively identified essential memory traces from classical conditioning (stimulus-behavior, repeat: stimulus-behavior, repeat...) These neurobiological substrates have been localized and indicate that some sort of memory engram does exist. Nonessential memory, useful for association and adapting, has not been localized in substrates so far.

Example: You've driven on a road to a destination so often, you can drive on "auto-pilot". You kiddingly say, "My car even knows the way." The truth is not that far off. Your brain not only knows the way, the knowledge is physically embedded! Chances are, there is in your brain some physical substrate from that conditioning.

Implications: When learned behaviors are repeated numerous times, the brain creates a physical manifestation of the behavior, called a biological substrate.

Action Steps: If there is a behavior that you want to have truly automatic in your students, then repetition is, indeed, the secret to skill.

Summary of Action Steps

1. Encourage your students to eat well, including sufficient amounts of protein, which promotes learning and memory. Whenever appropriate, make your learning as emotionally impactful as possible.

2. Make sure that what is learned is embedded in unique contexts. The best way to insure long term memory is to provide context cues, not content clues.

3. Introduce short modules of learning instead of long ones. Break up long sessions into several shorter ones. Have your students provide surprise introductions to new topics.

4. Activate multiple memory systems with a variety of teaching activities, such as reading, listening to a lecture and seeing a video. Then follow up with projects, role-playing, at-home assignments, music, discussion, field trips, games, simulations or drama.

5. Reduce the amount of taxon memory required. Cut seat work substantially. Give real world problems to solve in context. Give only homework which requires contextual learning, not lists, problems or pages of unrelated facts. Use whole language learning. Take advantage of the ease and thoroughness of the locale memory system to embed key ideas by using real life learning in real contexts, musicals, plays, role-play, real world excursions, on-the-job training, motor movement and intense sensory input.

6. Keep the memory of learned information alive in your learners by having students do peer teaching and peer review on a weekly basis. Have students re-create the material with mind maps, and then do presentations on it. Encourage the use of murals, mindscapes and student projects.

7. The use of emotions in learning is a consistently powerful strategy. Engage students in suspenseful activities, competitive debates, emotive storytelling, challenging projects or thrilling drama.

8. Review discipline policy. Eliminate any system that does behavior "score keeping". Stop actions which evoke the "bad dog!" feeling in students.

9. Use purposeful storytelling, thematic metaphors, directed visualizations and real-world problems.

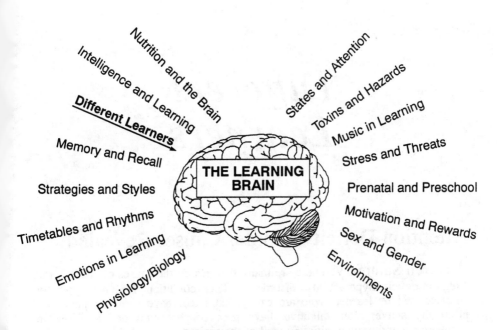

Nutrition and the Brain

Intelligence and Learning

Different Learners

Memory and Recall

Strategies and Styles

Timetables and Rhythms

Emotions in Learning

Physiology/Biology

States and Attention

Toxins and Hazards

Music in Learning

Stress and Threats

Prenatal and Preschool

Motivation and Rewards

Sex and Gender

Environments

THE LEARNING BRAIN

Chapter Six

CHAPTER SIX

Different Learners

Attention Deficit Disorder Causes Revealed

Research Summary: There are many theories on the causes of ADHD, the attention-deficit hyperactivity disorder. This condition is most typically characterized by learners who are easily distracted, have short memory, are physically active, often talkative, have poor concentration and are low in achievement and productivity. Several of the brain researched theories, but not all of them, are mentioned here. At this time, each has their promoters and detractors.

The brain stem and limbic systems regulate attention, say LeDoux and Hirst. Our brain's ability to pay attention is regulated by complex variations in the efficacy of chemical neurotransmitter molecules. Norepinephrine and dopamine (both catecholamines) are the principal neurotransmitter systems that process attention. Sylwester and Cho say that an insufficient number of these molecules may cause hyperactivity. Learner attentiveness may be optimized with a "normal middle level" of these catecholamines. Stimulant drugs like Ritalin™ work to normalize the brain's reaction to distracting stimuli, improving concentration and focus. While the drug seems to work miracles, some parents are concerned about the principle behind prescribing behavior-altering drugs at an early age. Others are concerned about side-effects.

Another point of view comes from Barkley. He says that the disorder is a combination of a "rule-following disorder", (a dislike of following rules), a linkage in the linguistic-motor system created by a genetic disorder(words and actions match up poorly), and a high motivational threshold (it takes a great incentive for seemingly simple tasks). But, he adds, the disorder is so situational, we may want to redefine what attention deficit it really is. In other words, take an ADHD child out of school and put him in a different setting, and his symptoms often disappear.

Levinson says that although 3-10% of the population supposedly has it, millions of others are undiagnosed. In fact, he says, from 10-27% may have ADHD. More than 80% of the cases are caused by a malfunction within the inner ear system. That area regulates our balance and sensory motor responses, and affects vision. He says that 90% of all problems can be treated successfully by one to four years of drug therapy. While sometimes vitamin B-6 works, Ritalin™ and Cylert™ are the most popular.

The research of Hynd et al. on morphology may turn out to be critical. By using MRI scans, they discovered that ADHD children had a smaller corpus callosum, particularly in the region of the genu and splenium and its anterior. Hynd says that "subtle differences may exist in the brains of children with ADHD and that deviations in normal corticogenesis may underlie that behavioral manifestations of this disorder." That's a fancy way of saying that "children with attention deficit disorder may suffer from a right hemisphere syndrome". Put simply, the left and right side of the brain don't talk to each other as well as they should.

McGuinness, a neuropsychologist, says that since most hyperactive behavior disappears in boys over time, it's a dubious sex-based label. She says that if you factored in the differences in male developmental stages, most boys would not be labeled a problem. There is, in fact, a considerable movement developing worldwide that wants to create more appropriate gender-based learning.

Grinder says that some students diagnosed as hyperactive may, in fact, simply be expressing their particular learning styles. A kinesthetic learner may want to move around, touch, tap, hit, try out and engage his body in almost everything. If the teacher is visual, the movement may be attention-getting and, at times, annoying. To the teacher, this is a "problem student" when, in fact, the student may be normal.

Perhaps the most promising research on hyperactivity and dyslexia comes from researchers who have made strong correlations to inner ear problems. It seems that infection-related fluids (effusion) interferes with hearing which interferes with auditory perception and processing. Levinson's double-blind studies and research led him to discover a 96% incidence of cerebellar-vestibular dysfunction in dyslexics. He has successfully treated many dyslexics with motion-sickness drugs and repatterning exercises.

Other researchers, mentioned elsewhere in this book, refer to a host of other contributing causes. Research correlates the disorder to excessive lead in the water supply, emotional problems stemming from inadequate family stability, food additives (especially red dye, aspartame, preservatives and artificial flavors), excess sugar, a couch-potato lifestyle, refined carbohydrates, and excessive television watching. Whichever turns out to be the cause, it will be some time before we know for sure. There is an understandably enormous difficulty in isolating specific behaviors and testing with all the variables.

Example: A student continually gets into fights and can't sit still for more than a minute. The student rarely does any class work, is distracted easily and has few friends. This student may have ADHD, or may not. The truth is uncertain. One doctor identifies a student as ADHD whom another would call "normal".

Implications: Many learners are just normal and they have been misdiagnosed and put on drug therapy. Many have serious other problems and the drug therapy is masking the real problems. For some, the drug therapy is a miracle cure. At this time, there is no consensus about the singular or true causes of ADHD.

Action Steps: Start with the simplest things first. Begin eliminating variables. Discover if the student is more kinesthetic or has a rule-following cognitive disorder. Then focus on diet changes. Stay open-minded about symptoms and treatment. If one method of treatment is not working, it's not a hopeless case. Switch to another professional and switch methodologies.

Is Language-learning Hormonal or Genetic?

Research Summary: Research by Tallal et al. on families with language and learning disorders has shown a high male statistical dominance. Tallal's study unexpectedly found that when the mother was affected, she had three times as many sons as daughters. And this language or learning impaired mother is likely to have FIVE times as many impaired sons as daughters. This indicates a strong hormonal (testosterone) influence, as well as an obvious genetic link.

Example: You may have had a student in your class with a problem. And their parents may also have had the problem. That may not be a coincidence.

Implications: Knowing a bit about the family history of learners may enable you to diagnose problems more quickly. In the interest of keeping an open mind, it may be better not to know the history at the start, but certainly, if things are not working well, history can provide some insight.

Action Steps: If a student seems to be having a learning problem, check the family history for evidence of the same problem in other family members, and for insights into finding solutions.

Best Bet Resource: *All Kinds of Minds,* by Mel Levine, available from Educator's Publishing Service, 75 Moulton St., Cambridge, MA 02138-1104.

Recent Dyslexia Treatments Assessed

Research Summary: Several researchers have reported on various different strategies for dealing with dyslexia. Each uses recent brain research to help the learner to manage the disability and learn successfully. Right now, there is no scientific consensus about how to deal with this troubling reading problem.

Livingstone says that our brain processes sensory information on two separate parallel paths. The faster sensory system notes the location in the background. The slower system, in the foreground, processes what the objects are. In dyslexics, the faster system is sluggish and doesn't delete quickly enough the previous word or words seen. As a result, when eyes move from word to word, the reader experiences blurring and fusing of words. He says that special colored lenses (called Irlen) can help the reader successfully deal with this problem.

But Cotton & Evans disagree. They say that the supposed benefits of tinted lenses are unsubstantiated. The literature is either unpublished or difficult to obtain. They also contend that recent experiments have proven that the intervention of colored lenses is insupportable.

Frenchman Guy Berard reports that 85% of dyslexics have hearing difficulties, and that's the real source of the problem. Why? A hearing defect in the range of 500 cycles per second prevents hearing the quieter, more easily-confused voiceless consonants, such as M, N, P and B. The left hemisphere is specialized for hearing clicks and other closed sounds, while the right is more sensitive to vowels.

Since dyslexics are frequently right hemisphere dominant, they miss out on many key sounds. In addition, a split second delay in the routing of information within the brain, when it has to cross hemispheres twice, creates a time delay in understanding oral instructions. This makes super-attentive listening a requirement for dyslexics. But that can get exhaustive when it has to go on for more than a few minutes. As a result, the child tends to lose attention, and gets further behind in learning.

Davis, on the other hand, says that the problem has to do with spatial orientation. He defines a point of perception in space which he calls the "visuo-awareness epicenter". The location of this epicenter varies among individuals. For example, a boxer's epicenter is 16 feet above his head; a race car driver's, 30 feet in front of him. For best reading, the epicenter may need to be within inches of the head--above and behind. By retraining the brain to be in control of this roving center of awareness, reading improves dramatically. Davis said

112

his method is "not a panacea but a learning process". It takes about 35 hours of training and counseling to implement his method. He claims an 80-90% success rate.

Hynd et al. reviewed the Balance Model, which states that hemispheric stimulation may be beneficial in treatment. In this model, many of the problems of dyslexia are treated by proper stimulation of the left hemisphere. In fact, Galaburda of Harvard says that the brains of dyslexics have different patterns of cell organization from those found in normal brains.

Some researchers have made strong correlations to inner ear problems. It seems that infection-related fluids (effusion) interferes with hearing which interferes with auditory perception and processing. Levinson's double-blind studies and research led him to discover a 96% incidence of cerebellar-vestibular dysfunction in dyslexics. He has successfully treated many dyslexics with motion-sickness drugs and repatterning exercises.

Obler's research agrees. Furthermore, he states that these differences occur prenatally during key times of cell migration. Certain groups of neurons end up in the "wrong" areas, causing poor reading but encouraging mechanical or creative abilities. In fact, many of the most creative artists, composers, producers, athletes, singers, and musicians will tell you that they are dyslexic.

Example: Many celebrities including Cher, Muhammed Ali, Madonna, and Dustin Hoffman are dyslexic.

Implications: Never give up on learners who are having a tough time. A majority of those learners who have dyslexia can be successfully treated.

Action Steps: Do some research to find local resources that are successful in treating dyslexia. Print a list of these resources and make it available to parents or students.

Best Bet Resources: For information on dyslexia and hearing difficulties, write: Berard: 28 rue Royale, 74000 Annecy, France; for the Davis Treatment, involving a "visuo-awareness epicenter", contact: RRC, 1799 Old Bayshore Hwy. Burlingame, Calif. 94010, (415) 692-8990.

Forced Silence & Inactivity Impairs Learners

Research summary: Many learners are asked to remain in their seats and to remain quiet for optimal learning. But research by Della Valle et al. says that may not be a good idea. Among adolescents, 50 % of the learners needed "extensive mobility while learning". Of the remaining 50%, half of those (25%) needed occasional mobility and the remaining needed minimal movement opportunities.

Example: You're talking to a group and the majority of them begin to get drowsy and listless.

Implications: Some learners are paying little attention to your message. Others seem low in energy or curiosity. Both of them may need some mobility. What may seem like a boring topic or bad time of the day may simply be a product of learners who are restless and need some activity.

Action Steps: Schedule a "Stand up and stretch" break every 20 minutes. Create a diversity of activities so that learners get to move into teams, go outside, work with partners or do simple activities that get the circulation going and keep active learners happy. You may want to do cross-lateral movements, offer water, create a more active learning process or simply let them stretch and take in some deep breaths.

Best Bet Resources: *Office Biology* by Edith Weiner and Arnold Brown, and *Sitting On The Job* by Scott Donkin.

Forced silence and inactivity impair
learners choices for input and processing

Blind Learners Have Great Imaginations

Research Summary: If you think being blind prevents visualization and creativity, think again. Researcher Paul Torrance found that it doesn't. He tested 182 students, aged 10-21; half were sighted and half were blind. He used words to stimulate their imaginations and asked them to respond. The blind learners scored significantly higher than the sighted ones in creative imagery. Torrance says, "Being blind may, in fact, be an advantage on a creative imagery task."

Example: One successful educator, Californian Bill Schmidt, has been blind since age three. But Bill went on to complete his college education, became a successful teacher, creatively remodel his home and become a top administrator. He is often cited by his peers for his creativity and imagination.

Implications: Those who are labeled as "disabled" are really "differently abled". We may have been underestimating the abilities of those who are, on the outside, different.

Action steps: Avoid putting limitations on others. Let others prove what they can do by giving them the opportunity to be creative.

Best Bet Resource: For more information on Paul Torrance's research, contact: College of Education, Old Dominion Univ., Norfolk, VA 23508.

Deaf Mutes Can Learn to Hear & Speak

Research Summary: Kotulak reports groundbreaking research on deaf mutes by Dr. Mary Joe Osberger et al. at Indiana University. Children deaf and mute from birth were hearing and speaking for the first time by using surgically installed devices called the Cochlear implant. "I couldn't believe it," said Osberger. "We thought we might be putting sounds like pops, buzzes and clicks into their brains. But their brains hear them as words, and as words, they came out.... These are children who are not partially deaf, they are totally deaf. Until now, their ability to speak was zero, no matter how intensely they were trained."

Michael Merzenich of the University of California at San Francisco says, "The first thing that the implant does is start changing their brains.... The fact that the implants work at all is amazing... miraculous, actually."

A child can now learn a language by simply hearing it. Somehow the brain can assemble the most complex syntax, ideas and emotions without ever learning to read or write. Apparently, the previously unactivated brain cells are so eager to do their job that they are easily activated at the sounds of the human voice. These medical miracles are possible up to age ten. After that, the brain cells responsible for hearing and speech lose their receptivity to that particular type of neural activation. They either look for other signals to process (like visual stimuli), or they die off.

There is some controversy over the effectiveness and appropriateness of Cochlear implants. Some say that they merely provide "vague representations" of what a non-impaired person hears. Others call them nothing short of a miracle. There are also some members of the deaf community who refuse to use them. They say that deafness is a natural part of their life and that it's not a handicap any more than it is for a normally sighted person to be unable to see ultraviolet light. There is much more to the argument (some of it embedded in "political correctness") than space permits here.

Example: The fact that the brain cells responsible for hearing and speech are no longer receptive after age 10 explains why adults learning a foreign language often have a tough time. Unless, that is, they have been introduced to it early in life. It also sheds light on why, for example, Japanese people who learn to speak English after age 10 often have such a strong accent and have difficulty pronouncing the letter "r". There's nothing genetic about pronouncing the letter. After all, Japanese who are raised by English-speaking parents speak perfect English. Anglos who learn Spanish late in life are usually unable to pronounce the Spanish "rolled r". Yet those who learn Spanish early in life find it easy.

117

Implications: Never give up on students who are language or hearing impaired. You may be able to direct some to a specialist who can access a Cochlear implant. They may be able to be helped.

Action Steps: Introduce foreign languages to children at an early age. It's a global world and children should be getting a global education. All elementary school children should be introduced to at least two or three languages--not grammar, but conversational speaking skills. When children have learned just 100-500 words in another language, the rest of the language will be learned much more easily later on.

Hyperactivity Linked to Environmental Lead

Research Summary: Extensive research by Trites in Canada and Needleman et al. in Boston was done on over 16,000 children. It dramatically linked their classroom hyperactivity to lead. In Ottawa, when teachers completed surveys on the quantity of symptoms among their students, a city-wide map was created showing where in the city were the low and high levels of hyperactive children. The map showed a large corridor of hyperactive behavior running through the center of the city which exactly matched the main road, the Queen's highway. Follow-up studies on the soil and water confirmed that the lead content was much higher near all of the major arteries.

In Boston, teachers completed surveys on their students without knowing the studies done on the children. The surveys asked questions: "Do you consider this child hyperactive? Is your child distracted easily? Is he frustrated by difficulty? Is he disorganized? Can he follow directions? Is he over-excitable and impulsive?" The amazing results were clear-cut: for every questionnaire completed, the higher the correlates to hyperactivity, the higher the concentrations of lead found in the children.

Example: You may have a student who seems to be smart, but he just doesn't focus and stay attentive. Many of the students from lower income areas are also living near highways, power lines and industrial sites. These are the areas where there are more likely to be toxic hazards.

Implications: There are many complex factors which lead to the success of a learner. The more obvious ones are nutrition, parental support and school quality. But the geography of a student's home may also be a factor.

Action Steps: Inform your students and parents about potential environmental dangers. Be straightforward and truthful. Avoid being an alarmist. Simply let them know that some studies have shown that environmental lead can impair learning. In some cases a drinking water check may be appropriate.

Some Misbehavers May Be Superb Learners

Research Summary: Rosenfield says that, in its search for meaning, our brain is constantly sorting out incoming data to find patterns. This pattern-detecting allows the brain to make cognitive maps. O'Keefe and Nadel says that our brain needs to register something familiar and yet is simultaneously motivated and intrigued by novelty. James says that the brain either "matches" up with (familiar) data or it "mis-matches" (different-ness, exceptions) with it (and combinations in-between).

What does all this mean? A learner may learn by similarities (familiarity) or differences (novelty) in varying amounts Virtually no one does either type of learning 100% of the time, but that there are tendencies. James says that 50% of Americans match and mismatch evenly--they do both with the same frequency. He adds that 10% of the population mismatches constantly and that 40% are habitual "matchers". The matchers work at the same job for years, keep the same friends, eat at the same restaurants and do many of the same activities year after year. They use generalizing phrases like "everyone, always, we, never, all". They make generalizing patterns quickly.

The "mismatchers" tend to prefer changes over sameness. They try out new things, go to a different restaurant, take a new route home, and experiment more. They find exceptions to the rule, they use phrases like, "but..." and "not always..." If a sign says "NO Trespassing" a matcher will obey. A mismatcher will wonder "What's in there?" By the way, mismatchers are distinctly different from:

1) divergent thinkers (who tend to be more exploratory and creative, but not as contrarian);
2) skeptics (who tend to question things consistently but often keep their same beliefs);
3) age-related "phases" (most all two year-olds say "NO!" to nearly everything, but it's not a mismatch--it's often a developmental stage);
4) delinquents (who simply want to be "bad" because of domestic problems, peer pressure, low self-concept, etc.).

The degree to which a nation's population or particular culture (urban, rural, men, women, etc.) matches or mismatches is entirely culturally reinforced. In some cultures, like Japan, it's simply bad etiquette to mismatch, so you have a nation which has a higher percentage of matchers. In Israel, the culture encourages asking questions, finding exceptions and mismatching. Australia has a higher percentage of mismatchers not because it was used as a penal colony by England. It has what is known as the "California greener grass syndrome". That means those who emigrate are often self-selected as being "different thinking" and wanting a change. In America, more matchers live in the Midwest than any other part of the country. States with relatively high percentages of mismatchers include Vermont, Oregon, California and Washington.

Example: Walt Disney was a mismatcher, as is Michael Milken, who was convicted of insider trading in the bond market. The difference between the two is that Disney used his mismatching to break the rules of social conformity and establish what he thought was missing (family entertainment). Milken used his mismatching tendencies to break the rules, too, but for illegal trading on Wall Street.

Mismatchers in the classroom tend to focus on differences, exceptions and what is missing. You say to a group that you'll be done in ten minutes. After some time, a learner raises his hand and says "It's been eleven minutes." You pass out some paper. A student, having found the only misspelling on the handout, raises his hand and says, "How come this is spelled wrong?" You ask your students to begin an activity. One says, "Why aren't we doing this the way Mr. Jones's class did it last year?"

Or let's say you set up rules for discipline. Most students respect the rules, but one keeps breaking them, almost as if he is obsessed with trying to find out the answer to the question, "I know the rule, but is there an exception to it?" This kind of response is typical of that made by a mismatcher.

Implications: We may have labeled countless learners as troublemakers when, in fact, the way they learn is simply by trying to establish a pattern for meaning. Think of the question, "Is this person filling the mold (matching) or trying to break (mismatch) the mold?"

Action Steps: Learn to recognize learners as "matchers" and "mismatchers". Those who are matchers tend to:
* agree with you more often
* prefer the familiar, tried and true
* be uncomfortable with novelty
* follow rules, stay with the group
* learn by similarities
* do what is expected by others

Those who are mismatchers tend to:
* disagree more often
* prefer novelty, change, a bit of risk
* sometimes ignore rules and boundaries
* need differences to understand

To deal with those who are mismatching:

1) Don't try to "fix" them; they're not broken.
2) Appreciate and respect their alternative point of view ("Thanks for pointing that out. I hadn't thought of that.").
3) Make sure that they follow the same rules as everyone else. Avoid labeling any learner, since they may vary preferences, depending on stress levels or circumstances. It's best to use "matcher" and "mismatcher" as active, flexible verbs (e.g., "He was mismatching me again," or, "Good mismatch."

Best Bet Resource: *Insider's Guide to Learning Styles,* available by catalog from Turning Point Publishing, see page 351.

Left Handers Often Face Learning Obstacles

Research Summary: Research by Dr. Paula Tallal, Co-Director of the Center for Molecular and Behavioral Neuroscience at Rutgers University, found that those with learning disorders were more likely to have a balanced size cerebrum and neocortex. Both left and right hemispheres were of equal size and had an equal amount of activity.

That is a problem, because in order to properly process speech, the left hemisphere needs to be slightly larger and faster than the right hemisphere. It takes 8/1000 of a second for normal children to process language. But in those with learning disorders, it may take up to one-third of a second to distinguish one sound from another. Slower processing from less active or smaller hemispheres means the brain is unable to keep up with the rapid pace of language.

Example: You may have noticed left-handers encounter more academic difficulty. More left-handers have learning problems than right-handers. Because handedness is related to stress and testosterone levels during pregnancy, boys outnumber girls four to one in learning disorders. Ninety percent of right-handers process speech and language dominantly in the left hemisphere.

Implications: An important question is, "Does the handedness cause the disorders or does the propensity towards the disorders create handedness?" Therefore, can and should earlier intervention be used? Many parents think that's not fair to a child. Others disagree. The actual usage of a particular hand may still be up to the individual child, but the knowing parent can influence greatly.

Action Steps: As a parent or teacher, it is certainly worthwhile to encourage and even direct the child to use the right hand. You also may want to provide extra resources, support and attention to those who are left handed, if it's appropriate.

Summary of Action Steps

1. In working with learners with ADHD, start with the simplest things first. Begin eliminating variables. Discover if the student is more kinesthetic or has a rule-following cognitive disorder. Then focus on diet changes. Stay open-minded about symptoms and treatment. If one method of treatment is not working, it's not a hopeless case. Switch to another professional and switch methodologies.

2. If a student seems to be having a learning problem, check the family history for evidence of the same problem in other family members, and for insights into finding solutions.

3. Do some research to find local resources that are successful in treating dyslexia. Print a list of these resources and make it available to parents or students.

4. Schedule stand up and stretch breaks every 20 minutes. Create a diversity of activities so that learners get to move into teams, go outside, work with partners or do simple activities that get the circulation going and keep active learners happy.

5. Introduce foreign languages to children at an early age.

6. Inform your students and parents about potential environmental dangers. Be straightforward and truthful. Avoid being an alarmist. Simply let them know that some studies have shown that environmental lead can impair learning. In some cases a drinking water check may be appropriate.

7. Learn to recognize learners as "matchers" and "mismatchers". Those who are matchers tend to:

> To deal with those who are mismatching:
> 1) Don't try to "fix" them; they're not broken.
> 2) Appreciate and respect their alternative point of view.
>   ("Thanksfor pointing that out. I hadn't thought of that.")
> 3) Make sure that they follow the same rules as everyone else.
>   Avoid labeling any learner, since they may vary preferences,
>   depending on stress levels or circumstances. It's best to use
>   "matcher" and "mismatcher" as active, flexible verbs (e.g.,
>   "He was mismatching me again," or, "Good mismatch,
>   Tim").

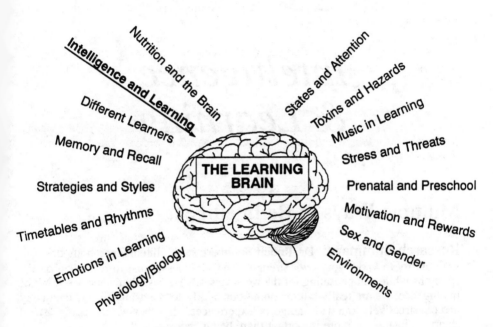

Nutrition and the Brain

Intelligence and Learning

Different Learners

Memory and Recall

Strategies and Styles

Timetables and Rhythms

Emotions in Learning

Physiology/Biology

THE LEARNING BRAIN

States and Attention

Toxins and Hazards

Music in Learning

Stress and Threats

Prenatal and Preschool

Motivation and Rewards

Sex and Gender

Environments

Chapter Seven

CHAPTER SEVEN

Intelligence & Learning

Multiple Ways to Be Intelligent

Research Summary: Dr. Robert Sternberg says, "Intelligence boils down to your ability to know your own strengths and weaknesses and to capitalize on the strengths while compensating for the weaknesses." He says that when we think of intelligence, we are really talking about our ability to react intuitively, creatively and constructively to a wide range of experiences. In other words, being "street smart" is just as, or more important than, being "book smart".

The work of Harvard Graduate Professor of Education, Howard Gardner led to the conclusion that there is not just one way to be smart, there are over 200 ways! Gardner researched the nature of intelligence and defined it as the ability to: 1) use a skill, 2) fashion an artifact, or 3) solve a problem in a way that is valued by the particular culture of that individual. In other words, a Wall Street stockbroker and an Australian aborigine can both be considered highly intelligent--in their own culture. If they switched roles with each other, both would have a difficult time surviving (although I suspect the aborigine might last longer).

126

Gardner grouped the array of human intelligences into just seven categories. Instead of having one single figure or mark that assesses our intelligence, he says that each of us has our own unique combination of these intelligences and that they can and do change over a lifetime. The seven categories are:

1) Mathematical-logical: the ability to solve problems, do math, fix, repair, troubleshoot, understand order, program and do puzzles.
2) Spatial: one's relationships to objects and others; dance, sports, packing, parallel parking, driving a truck or bus, ice skating, flying a plane.
3) Bodily-kinesthetic: mime, acting, sports, performance, dramatics.
4) Musical-rhythmic: clapping, drumming, composing, playing music.
5) Verbal-linguistic: use of words, language, reading, writing, word puzzles, speaking, arguing, jokes, explaining, debating.
6) Interpersonal: reading other people, social skills, cultural bonding, rapport-building, empathy, building relationships.
7) Intrapersonal: introspection, self-assessment, reflection, goal-making, journal writing, vision, planning, knowing weaknesses and strengths.

Example: In a mathematics class, a learner who is average in mathematical-logical intelligence, but low in interpersonal or verbal-linguistic skills, may be poor at explaining or expressing what he knows. Yet if he is strong in intrapersonal skills, he may be able to assess his own progress and troubleshoot for mistakes. If he's strong in spatial, he may be able to make a graphic of what he knows. And if he's strong in musical-rhythmic, he could express ideas with sound.

Implications: Many intelligent learners have been labeled as stupid, average or slow because: 1) the presentation style of the teacher did not tap into all seven intelligences, or 2) the assessment was so narrow that it never allowed the learner to demonstrate what he really knew.

Action Steps: Learn more about multiple intelligences. Two areas for immediate action are presentations and assessment Use all seven intelligences in your instructional design at least once every five to seven hours. For assessment, make sure that your learners have choices on how to express their knowledge.

Best Bet Resources: *Seven Kinds of Smart,* by Armstrong; *Seven Ways of Teaching,* by Lazear; *Teaching and Learning Through the Multiple Intelligences,* by Campbell; *Multiple Intelligences Made Easy,* available by catalog from Turning Point Publishing, see page 351.

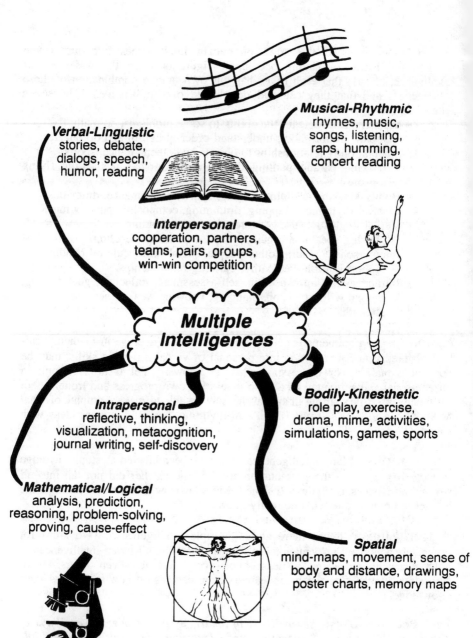

Musical-Rhythmic
rhymes, music,
songs, listening,
raps, humming,
concert reading

Verbal-Linguistic
stories, debate,
dialogs, speech,
humor, reading

Interpersonal
cooperation, partners,
teams, pairs, groups,
win-win competition

Multiple Intelligences

Bodily-Kinesthetic
role play, exercise,
drama, mime, activities,
simulations, games, sports

Intrapersonal
reflective, thinking,
visualization, metacognition,
journal writing, self-discovery

Mathematical/Logical
analysis, prediction,
reasoning, problem-solving,
proving, cause-effect

Spatial
mind-maps, movement, sense of
body and distance, drawings,
poster charts, memory maps

Are Patterns Key to Learning & Intelligence?

Research summary: A summary of research by Hart and Nummela-Caine tells us that learning has much to do with the creation of meaningful patterns and programs of experience. For example, you have a regular routine (program) that you go through each morning as you get up and get ready for the day. But optimal learning occurs when, Nummela says, "external sensory input challenges the student's brain to 1) 'call up' the greatest number of appropriate programs, 2) expand an already existing program, and 3) develop new programs." In other words, an environment of challenge, novelty and relevancy.

Yet, all of this has to take place in an environment of low or no threat for the brain to be at it's best. In fact, Caine says, the optimal circumstances for learning would have the following: 1) no threat 2) thoughtful orchestration of multi-dimensional teaching strategies 3) real-life experiences. To summarize the importance of patterns, Caine asks:

"Why, with our magnificent ability to detect patterns, make accurate approximations, speak multiple languages and create limitlessly, do we still break reality into bits and pieces . . . and fail to help learners understand the interconnectedness . . . into which the fragments fit?"

Example: Here's how it might work in your teaching situation: Have your learners develop an in-house consumer database of information about where to shop, services, foods, movie reviews and leisure activities. This project might take weeks and involve all seven intelligences. It is certainly relevant, challenging and novel.

Implications: Many learners may have been underperforming because the learning environment was not optimal for the brain.

Action Steps: Field trips and excursions followed by discussions and debriefings can be quite valuable. Larger, longer, complex projects that have immediate personal or practical value to the learners are also optimal.

Best Bet resource: *Making Connections: Teaching and the Human Brain*, by Caine and Caine; *Human Brain, Human Learning*, by Hart; *Pattern Thinking*, by Andrew Coward.

Color Stimulation Improves Reading Skills

Research Summary: How does the brain respond to color? At Oregon's Pacific University College of Optometry, says that colored light stimulation for 20 minutes a day dramatically improved reading in a group of learning disabled students. All of the learners were two or more years behind in reading and were divided into three groups. One group looked into lime green light and deep red light for 10 minutes each, 16 times over five weeks. One control group did typical vision exercises and the other looked into white incandescent light.

The colored light group improved visual field size by 220% and parents reported improved reading, greater self-esteem and even improved athletic ability. The vision exercise group improved slightly, an average of 8%. But the other control group, the white light group, showed a dramatic 48% decrease in visual field size. They reported headaches, nightmares, and lost appetites, and some parents asked to have their children dropped from the study.

Kaplan says that visual stimulation alters brain activity. These perceptual changes then affect the hypothalamic, pituitary and pineal regions of the brain. In fact, the whole sympathetic nervous system may be brought into play. There is some controversy over the efficacy of this method.

Example: Optometrist Jack Liberman did his own study of 18 problem learners and a control group. The test group had 24 colored light sessions over six weeks. Their visual field improved 300%, attention span increased 400%, visual memory increased 700% and auditory memory 160%. Parents said that "withdrawn children came out of their shell" and "hyperactive children calmed down". Two were taken off Ritalin and 75% improved in school.

Implications: It may be important to measure visual fields. Tunnel vision is more common than earlier thought, especially with children who have reading disabilities. Boring classroom settings with little stimulation may be, in fact, starving learners' brains for stimulation.

Action Steps: Be aware of the possibilities for eyesight problems. Know whom to refer your students to, if needed.

Best Bet Resource: Contact: Liberman: 10651 N. Kendall Dr. #100, Miami, FL (305) 595-6605.

Can Spinning Merry-Go-Rounds Help Brain?

Research Summary: David Clark of the Ohio State University College of Medicine has discovered that children's spinning games can be good for the brain. Games like merry-go-rounds, ring-around-the-rosy, spinning while in a swing and other circle spinning games affect the semicircular canals of the inner ear. That, in turn, affects physical balance and even helps the eye maintain stable images on the retina. The learners in his studies improved alertness, attention, balance, reflexes, and motor coordination. The spinning also calmed some learners enough to reduce hyperactivity and boost self-esteem in just two weeks.

Example: Students come in from active play and are excited, but ready to learn. It may be the "merry-go-round effect".

Implications: Some play may be great for the brain. After all, Piaget said, "A child's work is his play." Now, let's get even more creative: what other toys and games are there that are good for the brain and learning?

Action Steps: Encourage the use of brain-boosting games, especially those involving spinning. Research others and build your own repertoire.

Best Bet Resource: *Awakening Your Child's Natural Genius,* by Thomas Armstrong. For follow-up on topic's research, contact: David Clark, Anatomy Dept., Ohio State University, College of Medicine, Columbus, OH 43210.

Video Games Sharpen Elders' Brains

Research Summary: A study reported by Dustman showed that activity, activity and more activity is best for the brain, aging or not. Research on older adults aged 60-79 found that they could sharpen their mental abilities and improve their reaction time by playing video games over two months.

Example: Learners in this survey were given 11 weeks of video games. They outperformed the other two groups, one of which watched old movies and the other of which did nothing. Active and stimulating pastimes other than the video games used in this study were also just as powerful in boosting mental powers.

Implication: Never give up on the elderly just because they are physically less able.

Action Steps: Offer opportunities for challenge and novelty well into old age. These can include hobbies, sports, jobs, activities, social interactions and yes, even video games.

Best Bet Resource: Contact person for study: Robert Dustman. *Journal of Gerontology*, Veterans Affairs Medical Center of Salt Lake City, Utah.

Can Wrong Answers Boost Learning?

Research summary: A Canadian researcher, J. W. Powell, says that by analyzing a learner's "wrong" answers, we can discover meaningful information. Often the wrong answers fit a pattern or reveal something important about the type and style of the learner's processing. Because teachers often listen for the expected answer, they can miss out on the more interpretive and qualitative possibilities. Powell discovered that "profoundly informed people often read more ambiguity into a question than had been intended."

Example: A student completes a multiple choice test. Wrong answers usually get a zero and are 100% wrong. Yet the student may have a more profound understanding of the topic than the score indicates. There's just no opportunity for it's expression.

A physics teacher has a test question: "Using a barometer, how can you tell the height of this building?" The "proper" answer is to say, "Measure the air pressure at the bottom of the building and then compare it with the air pressure at the top of the building. Then use a prescribed formula to compute the difference in feet or meters." But a student who got the answer right was marked wrong because he found other, more creative, ways to calculate the right answer. After all, you could: 1) Tie a string onto the barometer and throw it out the top of the building. Then when it lands, measure the length of the string needed. 2) On a sunny day, use the shadow cast by the barometer and the building as a comparison and compute the ratio. 3) Go to the stairwell of the building. Using the barometer as a ruler, count how many times you need to flip it end over end to get to the top. Multiply that number by the length of the barometer. 4) Take the barometer to the building inspector, engineer or architect. Offer to trade the barometer to that person in exchange for the exact height of the building.

Implications: We have been missing out on a huge opportunity for learning about our learners in the depth diagnosis of so-called wrong answers from the assessment instruments.

Action Steps: Allow learners to work in groups to self-assess their tests. Let them formulate rules for the patterning and understanding of the experiences and information. Have them share and shape their discoveries instead of being evaluated by a "superior" who tells them what is right and what is wrong.

Best Bet Resource: For a FREE bulletin, "Best 7 Ways to Use Multiple Intelligences" see page 353.

Do Better Questions Produce Better Minds?

Research Summary: Berliner reports that the better the quality of the questions asked, the more the brain is challenged to think. The Socratic Method may have more than history going for it; it may be best for our brains. In study after study, (Redfield), learner performance scores improved when the questions asked of the learners improved in depth.

Example: Instead of asking students questions which require a statement of fact or a "yes" or "no" answer, ask more thought-provoking ones. Instead of: "What is it called when things keep falling back towards the earth?" ask, "What theories are there about gravity, which ones do you think are true, and why?"

Implications: Most of the question-answer interactions in a typical learner environment are of minimal, if any, benefit to the learner.

Action Steps: Have your learners make up the test questions instead of answer them. Let students do all of the lower-level quizzing of each other on simple-answer questions. As the teacher, you can put more attention on the more complex and provocative questions.

Study Skills Boost Brain Power & Learning

Research Summary: When learners are taught learn-to-learn skills, their ability to process new information can rise substantially. Researchers Weinstein and, in another study, Segal et al., confirmed the importance of what we knew: that teaching study skills can have significant positive impacts on the learner. Key ingredients in study skills mastery?

The following suggestions were taken from ten of the top sources, including *Becoming a Master Student* (Ellis), *Study Skills Program* (NAESP), *How To Study* (Standley), *SuperStudy* (Wade), *Dancing With Your Books* (Gibbs), *Mastering the Information Age* (McCarthy), *Getting Straight A's* (Green), *Use Both Sides of Your Brain* (Buzan), *Student Success Secrets* (Jensen).

* Proper nutrition, good environment
* Set a goal, develop a purpose
* Browse the material, build "perceptual maps"
* Develop maps on paper and ask questions
* Read for best comprehension, writing & thinking
* Summarize what's been learned, reflection
* Act on the learning, make tapes, build models, projects

Example: In schools, homes and businesses where study skills are learned, the results have been positive.

Implications: A worthwhile investment in time would be to make sure that your learners have the learn-to-learn skills necessary to succeed.

Action Steps: Make sure that your learners have access to either the actual instruction or the resources to become excellent learners.

Best Bet Resource: *Student Success Secrets,* and *The Student Success System,* by Eric Jensen; *Quantum Learning,* by DePorter. available by catalog from Turning Point Publishing, see page 351.

Brain Promotes Own Intelligence

Research Summary: Gazzaniga says that developing nerve nets in the brain can use their own "unique ability to perform logical operations to structure their own development. In short, the brain can use its own intelligence to promote its own development." The brain can simply order itself to build, change and otherwise promote its own development of neural networks. These neural networks are often thought of as strategies for intelligence-building. As the brain becomes more complex, it can make itself even more complex .

Example: It seems like those whom we consider very intelligent just keep getting smarter. In fact, it's true that so-called "smarter" people *are* able to make themselves even smarter. By contrast, we see others who apparently have no interest in self-development. The less they develop themselves, the harder it is to develop themselves.

Implications: If the brain can actually make itself smarter, then the smarter we get, the more capable we are. In fact, there may be no limit to our own ability to induce intelligence.

Action Steps: Multi-status and multi-age groupings can help to establish role models that set high standards and give strong messages about what the brain can do.

Best Bet Resources: For primary schoolers: *Thinking, Changing, Rearranging* , by Jill Anderson. For adult learners, *The Everyday Genius,* by Peter Kline*Boost Your Brainpower* by Michaud, *Awaken the Genius* by Patrick Porter, *Pumping Ions,* by Tom Wujec; *How to Be Twice as Smart,* by Scott Witt, *Learning To Learn* by Trinidad Hunt and *Creative Growth Games,* by Eugene Raudsepp.

Learning May Be Brain's Re-Discovery

Research Summary: Cell biologists have differing views on what exactly is learning, at the cellular level. Gazzaniga says that our new knowledge about the brain may solve an age-old riddle on instruction vs. selection: Is the brain a blank slate, a tabula rasa? Or is it more like what French Nobel laureate Jaques Monod proved when he showed that so-called adaptive enzymes are, in fact, induced by preexisting genes.

Is learning merely confirming? Yes and no, says the research. We shape the environment, then the environment shapes us. Our genes provide a menu of choices from which we learn and hence, do, in a way, select our future. Researchers say we are learning from the built-in options our genes have provided-- we do not or cannot modify them at this point in time. In other words, we do have choice over our own learning destiny. But it's much like a stacked deck in a card game, or like ordering from a menu at a restaurant where the chef will not make custom meals.

Researcher Monod says that, while in our everyday learning, "much of what happens to a person appears to be the result of instruction, at the molecular level we consistently see signs that selection is operating." That means that our very nature may contain much of our learning possibilities, pre-programmed. Gazzaniga adds, "It is quite possible that we humans are living in a delirious frame of mind about what influences what and what we can do about it."

Example: Some adults go to workshop after workshop for self-improvement. And, after thousands of dollars, they seem to be no different. Is it lack of motivation, laziness or just the genes?

Implications: Maybe much of what we learn is simply rediscovering what we are "pre-programmed" to know.

Action Steps: Do something that you think is not in "your pattern." Try something outside of your usual personality. How did it feel? Would you do it again? Or are you really just fulfilling your genetic blueprint? Just for fun, start asking yourself if what you do each day is totally predictable, your pattern, or if it is truly spontaneous.

Can Stuffy Nose Affect Learner Performance?

Research Summary: Research by Shannahoff-Kalsa at Salk Institute proved that we tend to breathe more through one nostril for ninety minutes to two hours, then switch. But something more important emerged: when breathing through the left nostril, your right brain is dominant and vice versa. Research by Block revealed that spatial and verbal processing is affected by nostril breathing. It does matter whether you are breathing more through the left or right nostril, or through both. He found that right-handed males excel in verbal tasks during left nostril breathing and spatial tasks during right nostril breathing. Right-handed females were the reverse, scoring higher in spatial during left nostril breathing.

Researchers concluded either that unilateral nostril breathing differentially activates hemispheres or that "attempts of the brain to control the nasal cycle unilaterally interfere with performance." Research tells us that this occurs in most learners every 1-3 hours.

Example: You have a cold or the flu. You're sitting at your desk, struggling with paperwork or reading. You get up to blow your nose and come back to your chair refreshed. Suddenly you're breathing better. Your work immediately improves.

Implications: Some of your learners may be underperforming, simply because of the way breathing affects learning.

Action Steps: Tell your learners about this. Make tissues available. In some content areas, it may be worthwhile to repattern the brain's thinking by a few minutes of single-side nostril breathing. For example, by altering to the left side of the brain before doing very sequential, linear tasks.

Maps & Patterns: Brain's Keys to Learning

Research Summary: Edelman says that "[t]he brain constructs maps of its own activities, not just of external stimuli, as in perception...." The brain areas responsible for concept creation contain structures that categorize, discriminate, and recombine the various brain activities occurring in different kinds of global mappings.

Such structures in the brain, instead of categorizing outside inputs from sensory modalities, categorize parts of past global mappings according to modality, the presence or absence of movement and presence or absence of relationships between perceptual categorizations. They must be able to activate or reconstruct portions of past activities of different types of global mappings, for example, those involving different sensory modalities. They must also be able to recombine or compare them.

Researcher Nummela-Caine states the importance of patterns to learning. The neocortex is both a pattern-maker and pattern-detector. The ability to make meaningful sense out of countless bits of data is critical to understanding and motivation. Since the brain's craving for meaning is automatic, patterning occurs all the time. Each pattern that is discovered can then be added to the learner's "perceptual maps" and the brain can then leave that state of confusion, anxiety or stress. It "maximizes" again and is ready for more challenges.

Every pattern that the brain is able to create means that it can then relegate that new "blueprint" to the nonconscious. From a survival point of view, it is critical to create patterns as quickly as possible. The process of creating a pattern or perceptual map utilizes both the conscious and nonconscious brain.

In this process of establishing a map, the brain is less able to generate other parallel maps and is "thematically distracted". To the brain, there is a certain survival risk and vulnerability while a pattern is being created. But in the long term, that's what the brain must do and is best at.

Example: You are working on something in the kitchen or garage. You are learning something or trying to figure something out or thinking about other things while you are working. After a while, you discover that you have cut yourself, but just now are feeling the pain or seeing the bleeding.

While concentrating and learning, your brain was making a "map". You did not know that you had hurt yourself. That's good for pattern-making, but it's a reminder that the brain is just as dedicated to map-making as it is to your own survival.

139

Implications: Two things: 1) the importance of pattern-making and, 2) the importance of tying into past learnings. The past learnings are part of the learner's perceptual maps. Therefore, the learner needs to integrate into the new learning what he or she knows, or it may not be "accepted."

In regard to patterns, there's much room for change. Maybe learning ought to consist less of the formalized start-a-topic and finish-a-topic format, and more of an informal, multi-level, pre-exposure with an on-going process of creating and eliciting maps. We could provide learners with patterns of the material to be learned in the early stages.

Action Steps: There are many ways to provide more patterning for learners.

1) Before beginning a topic, give global overviews using overheads, videos/disks, and posters.
2) Before actually starting a topic, pre-expose learners with oral previews, applicable games in texts/handouts, metaphorical descriptions,and posted mind-maps of the topic.
3) Help learners to form patterns during a particular topic by allowing them to discuss the material (unstructured talking), or putting them in teams to create models, mindmaps or pictures.
4) When you finish with a topic, make sure that you allow learners to evaluate the pros and cons, discuss the relevance, and demonstrate their patterning with models, plays, and teachings.

Best resource: *Making connections: Teaching & The Human Brain,* available by catalog from Turning Point Publishing, see page 351.

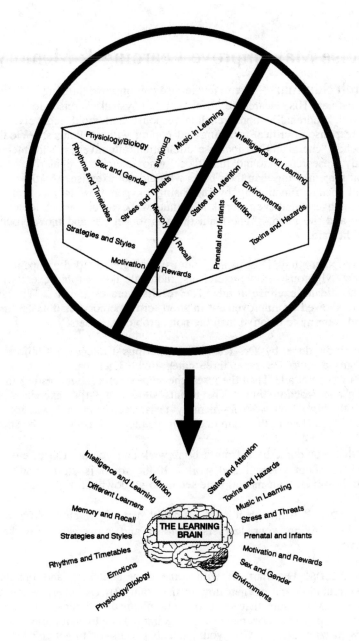

Our brain wants the pattern, not just the data

Exercise May Improve Learning & Memory

Research Summary: Aerobic exercise can improve thinking and learning, says Dienstbier. His research confirms that "...physical exercise alone seems to train a quick adrenaline-nonadrenaline response and rapid recovery." This adrenal response is critical to facing and coping with challenges. Wlodlowski recommends "energizers" to increase circulation, attentiveness and interest. In one study, researchers found that those who exercised regularly were "far better" at remembering than their peers who did not exercise. Aerobic exercise improved mental functioning by increasing oxygen flow to the brain. Dr. Hermann suggests that even a brisk 20 minute walk can be enough to serve both the body and the mind. "The main thing is to get out and move your body around," he said.

In another study, Dustman, a Utah psychologist, divided groups into three categories: vigorous aerobic exercisers, moderate non aerobic exercisers, and those who did no exercise at all. The results were clear cut: "The aerobic exercisers showed an improvement in short-term memory, had faster reaction times and were more creative than the non aerobic exercisers."

A study done by Dr. Kushner at Scripps College in California also divided groups into the same three categories. Each had various levels of exercise or none at all. Then the researchers spent three hours testing memory, reasoning and reaction time. The results were that "[t]he exercisers scored significantly higher on working-memory tests, reasoning and reaction time." Increased blood flow to the brain does help you to think better and be smarter.

Example: You come back from a brisk walk and you are full of energy and feel positive about yourself and work. If the room is stuffy and you are lethargic, however, your mental state seems to go downhill, right along with it.

Implications: Although it's not officially part of the curriculum or your lesson plan, giving your learners exercise and movement may be very productive.

Action Steps: 1) Start off with some slow stretching and breathing to increase circulation and oxygen flow to the brain 2) Use energizers every 20 minutes 3) Make sure that some of your planned activities have a built-in component of physical movement such as going outside to do a project, working on jigsaw puzzles, etc. 4) Give your students permission to get up on their own to move around, stretch or do an errand, so that they can monitor and manage their own energy levels.

Brain Growth Enriched by Continued Learning

Research Summary: Can the brain continue to grow after birth? Research by Diamond documents the positive effects of enriched environments on rats. But can we apply these studies to humans? A research team headed by Jacobs verified that we can. His research on cortical dendrite systems in 20 neurologically normal right-handed humans (half male and half female) evaluated:

* total dendritic length
* mean dendritic length
* dendritic segment count
* proximal vs. ontogenetically later developing distal branching

These variables have been known to relate to the complexity of the brain, the ability to solve problems, and overall intelligence. Jacobs' measurements investigated several independent variables: gender, hemisphere and education. The results of his research uncovered the following:

Gender: Females had greater dendritic values and variability than males.

Hemisphere: Left hemisphere had greater overall dendritic measurements than right, but the results were not consistent with each individual.

Education: Level of education had a "consistent and substantial effect" on dendritic branching: the higher the level, the greater the measurements.

Example: The group of graduate students who were involved in challenging activities, showed over 25% more "brain growth" than the control group.

Implications: Learning does, indeed, grow a better brain in humans than allowing the mind to remain inactive, wasting time. And while our life's goal may not be to grow a better brain, we need better thinking and problem-solving skills in order to be contributing members of society, and to help our planet survive.

Action Steps: Enrichment comes from many sources. Three areas are: 1) positive, engaging, social contact (use of partners, teams, cooperative projects), and 2) high-challenge, low-stress novelty exercises (continual variations of student-generated experiences) and 3) real-life experiences in novel situations (travel, cultural events, etc.).

Best Bet Resource: *Enriching Heredity,* by Diamond.

Problem-Solving is Brain's Favorite Exercise

Research Summary: University of Wisconsin psychology professor Dr. Denney says that "[p]roblem-solving is to the brain what aerobic exercise is to the body." It creates a virtual explosion of activity, causing synapses to form, neurotransmitters to activate and blood flow to increase.

Her studies indicate that your brain will stay younger, smarter and more useful by working out with these mental weights. Especially good for the brain are challenging, novel and complex tasks requiring multi-tasking and think time.

At Harvard University, a researcher conducted a study of the elderly. First he divided them into two groups. One group was asked to sit and reminisce about the old days, when they were younger. The other group was asked to play act, pretending to be in the year 1959. They listened to old radio programs, watched old speeches, watched old TV shows, and did activities they used to do. They acted, thought, talked and role-played being years younger. The results were spectacular. After just one week, the role-playing group showed a dramatic increase in their scores on intelligence and reaction times. The other group showed no improvement.

Dr. Schaie, Director of Pennsylvania State University's Gerontology Center, confirms that these results are duplicated in countless other studies. She says that withdrawal from the world and reduction of stimulation will be certain to bring on senility. Activity, challenges, novelty and stimulation are best, she says.

Example: In class, many learners want it all done for them. They have not been taught to think, have forgotten how to think or are out of the habit. Heavy television watchers and drug users are less interested in learning than those who purposely challenge their minds.

Implications: Learners who spend all of their free time "doing nothing" can get out of shape--not just physically, but mentally. Television is not exercise; active thinking and problem-solving is. We, as instructional leaders, have to set the example and provide the climate to make it happen.

Action Steps: Get some resources that can provide a variety of mental "workouts". Make sure that you are not just teaching or training, but that you are "growing better brains". Use visualization, problem-solving, debates, projects and drama. Reduce lecture time, seat-work and other rote activities. Challenge your students' brains, and also give them the resources to meet the challenge.

Feedback is Vital Key to Boosting Intelligence

Research Summary: While enriched environments and both mental and physical activity are important, something else is equally critical. Research by noted brain expert Santiago Ramon y Cajal has emphasized that the brain needs feedback from its own activities for best learning and growth.

Other researchers such as Moore, Anderson and Wenger have verified that one of the best ways to boost thinking and intelligence is by describing your own perceptions and recording your own observations onto audio tape or disk. This examination of one's own thinking, sensing and organizing language provides a powerful vehicle for the brain's development as a problem-solver and thinker.

Since different areas of the brain process different activities, the question is: what does one area of the brain do with the activity once it processes it? If it does nothing with it, some of the potential is lost. Intelligence is often the ability to bring together many diverse bits of information to create new thinking, to maximize potential and provoke solutions. The brain needs a large number of circuits and connections to make the best possible decisions. These are called "phase relationships" because they tie together simultaneous stimuli. By providing more consistent feedback, better quality feedback and tying it all together, the brain integrates the information into higher quality relationships and patterns.

To do this, it takes a strategy known as "pole-bridging". This word, coined by Wenger, describes the way the brain connects information and processes both the front and back and the left and right side of the brain. To "pole-bridge," simply talk about what you do while you do it. While you *can* write it down later in a journal, the best results have come from recording it "in the moment". By talking deliberately, perceptively and purposely, you'll find that the learning and thinking go up dramatically. Studies collected by Wenger have documented gains from one to three I.Q. points *per hour* of "pole-bridging" practice. Some have increased intelligence up to 40 points in 50 hours of work.

Example: Most "great" thinkers of history like Leonardo Da Vinci have kept elaborate journals of their work. That was their self-feedback. As a child, you had plenty of environmental stimulation, but you also got the all-important feedback. When you first learned to ride a bike, you experienced immediate and conclusive feedback: either you stayed up or fell down. Imagine trying to learn to ride a bike without knowing how you're doing until a month later. You'd still be trying to learn!

Implication: We all may be accidentally retarding thinking, intelligence and brain growth, and ultimately creating "slow learners", by the lack of feedback and the large lag time we have built into the typical learning environment.

Action Steps: Make sure all of your learners get consistent and conclusive feedback. Allow them to talk themselves through their thinking, out loud. Have them keep a journal. Have them pair up with other learners and teach the new material to them.

Best Bet Resources: "Some Principles for the Design of Clarifying Educational Environments", in *Handbook of Socialization Theory & Research*, ed. David Goslin. Best contact person is Win Wenger. For more information on these techniques, call (301) 948-1122 or write to him at: Project Renaissance at Box 332, Gaithersburg, MD, 20884-0332.

Summary of Action Steps

1. Make sure that you always activate, integrate and coordinate activities for both sides of the brain. Set up activities for the right brain and then follow up with the left brain processing.

2. Make sure that you are not just teaching or training, but that you are "growing better brains". Provide a variety of mental workouts with visualization, problem-solving, debates, projects and drama. Reduce lecture time, seat-work and other rote activities.

3. Learn more about multiple intelligences. Use all seven intelligences in your instructional design. For assessment, make sure that your learners have choices on how to express their knowledge.

4. There are four great times for "energizers" in your work:
   1) Start off your class with some slow stretching and breathing to increase circulation and oxygen flow to the brain
   2) During the class, every 20 minutes or less, make sure your students get up for a stretch break.
   3) Make sure that some of your planned activities have a built-in component of activity (moving outside to do a project, jigsaw, etc.).
   4) Give your students permission to get up on their own to move around, stretch or do an errand.

5. Expose learners to patterning opportunities:
   1) Give global overviews before beginning a topic using overheads, videos/disks, posters.
   2) Pre-expose learners to topic before actually starting it with oral previews, games in texts/handouts, metaphors, posted mind-maps of the topic.
   3) Allow learners to have unstructured discussions about current material; put them in teams to create models, mindmaps or pictures.
   4) when you finish with a topic, make sure that you allow learners to evaluate the pros and cons, discuss the relevance, and demonstrate their patterning with models, plays, teachings.

6. Enrichment for brain growth can come from: 1) positive, engaging, social contact (use of partners, teams, cooperative projects), and 2) high-challenge, low-stress novelty exercises (continual variations of student-generated experiences).

7. Field trips and excursions followed by discussions and debriefings can be quite valuable. Larger, longer, complex projects that have immediate personal or practical value to the learners are also optimal.

8. Let students do all of the lower-level quizzing of each other on simple-answer questions. As the teacher, you can put more attention on the more complex and provocative questions.

9. Offer opportunities for challenge and novelty well into old age, including hobbies, sports, jobs, activities, social interactions and even video games.

10. Make sure all of your learners get consistent and conclusive feedback. Allow them to talk themselves through their thinking, out loud. Have them keep a journal. Have them pair up with other learners and teach the new material to them.

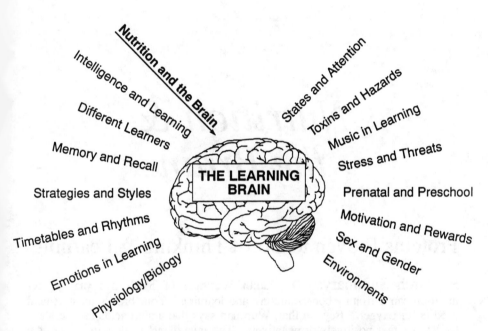

Nutrition and the Brain
Intelligence and Learning
Different Learners
Memory and Recall
Strategies and Styles
Timetables and Rhythms
Emotions in Learning
Physiology/Biology

States and Attention
Toxins and Hazards
Music in Learning
Stress and Threats
Prenatal and Preschool
Motivation and Rewards
Sex and Gender
Environments

THE LEARNING BRAIN

Chapter Eight

CHAPTER EIGHT

Nutrition &
the Brain

Proteins Proven to Boost Thinking & Learning

Research Summary: Dr. Judith Wurtman of MIT says that proper nutrition can definitely boost thinking and learning. Your brain's most critical need is for oxygen. Beyond that, Wurtman says that amino acids set the stage for you - either positively or negatively. The ingredients in protein are critical to the brain. Tyrosine and tryptophan are two examples. The first enhances thinking; the latter slows it down.

Your brain uses tyrosine to make the neurotransmitters dopamine and norepinephrine, two electrically charged chemical messengers that are critical to alertness, quick thinking and fast reactions. These neurotransmitters can help your brain to perform calculations, increase attention span and increase conscious awareness. Tyrosine is found in proteins. Wurtman is currently studying the effects of tyrosine supplements in several areas.

But how much is enough? It depends on your weight, age and activity levels, but 15-30 grams per day is sufficient, say the experts.

Example: Low-income learners typically have carbohydrates for breakfast (toast, breads, cereals) and this may impair thinking. Middle and upper-income learners often have the more costly yogurt, eggs, cottage cheese, fresh fruits or lean ham, which provide the nutrients that can enhance learning.

Implications: Possibly you or your learners may be underperforming if the foods eaten are slowing down the brain.

Action Steps: To boost your alertness and mental performance, include a natural source of tyrosine in your diet by eating protein. The best foods high in protein are eggs, fish, tofu, pork, chicken, and yogurt. Eat just three to four ounces, since eating more than that does not further increase alertness. Talk to your learners about the positive role nutrition can play in performance, thinking and testing. Set an example: Try a "brain-rich" diet for 60 days and determine whether you feel sharper, more alert. If so, keep eating the same foods.

Best Bet Resources: *Managing Your Mind and Mood Through Food,* by Wurtman; *The "Almost Genius Diet",* available by catalog from Turning Point Publishing, see page 351.

Is There an Exotic, Mysterious Brain Potion?

Research Summary: There are already many readily obtained substances which can boost learning. Countless studies have already been done on mammals which prove that they can boost alertness, learning, intelligence and memory. Many are already used as anti-aging, anti-disease drugs which have hundreds of clinically-proven studies to back their efficacy. Although most are totally safe and non-toxic, even in large doses, the FDA, for suspicious political motives, has continued to threaten and intimidate the new generation of "smart drug" users.

Some of the more well known of these mind drugs include: choline, lecithin, ginko biloba extract, DMAE/Deanol, Hydergine, Ginseng, Vasopressin/Diapid, Piracetam, Lucidril and others. Very few physicians will prescribe these for brain-boosting. Most doctors, fearful of being branded or liable, understandably, take the conservative path of "not me."

Example: One day you feel exceptionally alert and your learning seems to go quickly. Was it something you ate, without knowing that it was "brain food"?

Implications: Foods that your learners eat may be affecting their thinking dramatically. Researchers have discovered some possible "brain boosters," but what other, simple, safe, natural nutrients are there that can boost alertness, learning and memory? More research is needed.

Action Steps: Educate yourself regarding what everyday food nutrients are excellent for improving memory and learning. Encourage your learners to be attentive to the foods they eat. You may want to experiment with some commercially available products.

Best Bet Resources: *Mind Food and Smart Pills* by Ross Pelton and *Smart Drugs (1 & II)* by Dean, Morgenthaler and Fowkes, available by catalog from Turning Point Publishing, see page 351.

Excessive Carbohydrates Linked to Problems

Research Summary: In study after study, convicts and inmates who had diets low in refined carbohydrates had significant reductions in disciplinary behavior claims, report Harper and Gans. There were fewer fights, more self-discipline and fewer problems in general reported to the wardens. The complex carbohydrates and proteins in their diets seemed to be a positive factor.

An experiment by Simeon and Grantham-Macgregor with 9-11 year-olds showed that they became impulsive and had a shorter attention span when they skipped breakfast. In another study, children with low glucose levels actually remembered more than those who ate breakfast. Why? What they remembered were more of the materials from spatial memory (presumably out of anxious glances around the room) and less of the essentials from the teacher's lesson.

Example: There are strongly fluctuating levels of blood sugar among the Qolla Indians of Peru, who are known as one of the most violent and aggressive tribes in the world.

Implications: Students showing behavior problems or weak learning skills may actually be exhibiting dietary problems.

Action Steps: Inform your students about the effects of carbohydrates and blood sugar levels on behavior and learning. Encourage your learners to be more attentive to the foods they eat. Experiment on your own diet.

Growing Brain Especially Vulnerable to Sugar

Research Summary: In studies by Connors at the National Institute of Mental Health, diet affected children's attention spans, their ability to focus and their activity levels. Researchers already knew that sugar affects behavior; the news from this study was that when sugar was eaten with carbohydrates, the effects on the learner were much worse. And when the sugar was eaten with protein, the sugar was beneficial to the brain and learning. Apparently, sugar is utilized differently by the brain when "carried in" with protein. Possibly the brain has "windows of receptiveness" to sugars based on the growth spurts of the physical brain.

Harper and Peters found that "consumption of single meals of protein-deficient diets will elevate brain serotonin concentration...." In other words, protein helps counteract the serotonin effects. In studies by Goldman, Milich and Prinz, sugar intake was found to strongly affect the child's behavior. Research shows that the younger the child, the more sugar affects their learning. Older learners seem to eat better balanced diets with more protein and, hence, the effects on them are lessened. Bolton confirmed that low levels of blood sugar led to greater approval and justification of violent acts among college students.

Carbohydrates are essential to the brain, but only when part of a well-balanced diet. Sugars are not good or bad - they are both. It's all a matter of what you have with the sugars. The protective role of protein prevents overloading in the brain by various sugars and carbohydrates.

Example: A student is sleepy and lethargic. Are your afternoon (or morning) learners fatigued? If a student comes to your class and seems tired, work is poor and his participation is below average, it could be due to a sugar problem.

Implications: Learners should only have sugar and carbohydrates before a learning situation if protein is also eaten - preferably first. Many students underperform due to improper diet.

Action Steps: Educate yourself in what everyday food nutrients are excellent for improving memory and learning. Encourage your learners to be attentive to the food they eat.

Best Bet Resource: *Feeding the Brain,* by Connors; *Managing Your Mind and Mood Through Food,* by Wurtman.

Nutrients Can Boost Learning, IQ & Genes

Research Summary: In a well-designed, rigorous study, Benton and Roberts reported that 90 teens (12-13 year-olds) who took multivitamin supplements showed a significant rise in IQ over those who took a placebo. This IQ test, given a year later, was divided into two parts, verbal and nonverbal. The largest score increase appeared in the nonverbal area. The study also showed that 16% of the teens were deficient in thiamin. This nutrient may be able to increase visual acuity, reactive time and intelligence.

A German study documented that high vitamin B doses can improve fine motor control. In a controlled eight-week study, top marksmen were given B-1, B-6 and B-12 supplements. The control group received a placebo. The vitamin group improved from a 181 to 191 average score, about a 5% gain. The control group showed no gain.

Maguire reported that at the Maudsley Hospital in London, Dr. Richard Levy experimented with Alzheimer patients to boost memory. Since the neurotransmitter acetylcholine seems to be important to memory and Alzheimer patients seem to be deficient in it, why not try supplements? He did, and there was memory improvement. The supplements were comprised of natural sources of lecithin, found in egg yolks and wheat germ. In his study, over half of his patients showed significant memory improvement after drinking two milkshakes daily containing 35 grams of lecithin, an acetylcholine-booster.

In recent studies by the University of Helsinki in Finland and University College in Wales and England, folic acid and selenium were discovered to reduce depression and boost learner performance.

Studies in Germany also confirmed that subjects deprived of folic acid experienced sleeplessness, irritability and forgetfulness. Folic acid is found in leafy green vegetables, beef liver and beans.

Subjects who had selenium deficiencies were more anxious, tired and depressed than those who had the supplements. Researchers suspect that selenium may act as an antioxidant, slowing the aging process and protecting us against disease. Selenium is a mineral found in seafood, whole grain breads, nuts and meat. The best sources are white meat tuna and the motherlode of selenium, Brazil nuts.

In a recent study by the U.S. Department of Agriculture, reported by Carper, boron supplements improved mental activity. The experiments were done at the USDA's Human Nutrition Center in Grand Forks, North Dakota. Subjects on a low boron diet had consistently more sluggish mental performance. When the subjects got a 3 mg. supplement, performance picked up. The trace mineral boron is found in broccoli, apples, pairs, peaches, grapes, nuts and dried beans.

In a study on autistic children, massive doses of vitamin B6 improved learner behavior and increased speech patterns. A control group was used and they were given a placebo, but 70% of the time, the panel of judges correctly guessed which had been on the B6 therapy. While the daily recommended dosage of B6 is usually about two milligrams, Dr. Rimland used from 75-3,000 mg. daily. He says that the problem is usually not a matter of vitamin deficiency, but rather, a major metabolic dysfunction.

Carper reports that researchers at the University of Texas Medical Branch at Galveston and the USDA reported that both men and women improved test performance with zinc supplements. There was also improvement in short term memory and attention span. When the men were on a low daily zinc intake (1-4 mg.), their mental skills lagged. But when supplements boosted the daily intake to 15-20 mg. per day, performance improved. Researchers noted that daily doses over 25 mg. can be toxic. Zinc can be found in fish, beans, whole grains and dark meat turkey.

One of the most amazing discoveries recently is on the power of nutrition to affect our offspring. Campbell and Schurman, Professors of Nutritional Biochemistry at Cornell University, are emphatic when they talk about "the ability of nutritional factors to control gene expression." What you eat does more than affect your mood and mind; it is now known to affect your genes. This dramatic news means that we are biochemically changing ourselves with the possibility of measurable nutrient-generated gene changes from generation to generation.

Example: A student comes to your class and seems tired and stressed out. His work is poor and his participation is below average. Is it nutrition or another factor?

Implications: We may have been ignoring how important diet is in the learning process. It's clear that optimal nutrition increases brain performance.

Action Steps: Educate your learners about the components of healthful, performance boosting nutrition. Explain the dietary sources and benefits of vitamins and minerals. Send home to parents a listing of nutrients that can boost learning.

Best Bet Resources: For nutritional influences on genes, contact Dr. Colin Campbell and Dr. Jacob Gould Schurman, Professors of Nutritional Biochemistry at Cornell University, Ithaca, New York.

Water Enhances Optimal Brain Function

Research Summary: Researchers Dennison, Ward and Daley asserts that the average learner is often dehydrated. This dehydration leads to poor learning performance. Hospitals have reported improved patients when they are encouraged to drink up to 20 glasses a day. Athletes have learned to boost water consumption for peak performance. Performers in theater have learned to keep a pitcher of water nearby for their best effort. More and more educators have found that pure water does help learner performance.

Brain specialists recommend from 8-15 glasses per day, depending on your body size, weather and your activity level. Nutritionists recommend pure water to insure that it is free of contaminants. It's also better to have pure water than coffee, tea, soft drinks or fruit juices. This is because the caffeine and alcohol found in many of them serve as diuretics and your body needs even more water to make up the deficit.

Example: Teachers have found that in classrooms where students are encouraged to drink water as often as needed, behavior improves, as does performance.

Implications: Students who are bored, listless, drowsy and who lack concentration may, in fact, be dehydrated.

Action Steps: Talk to your students about dehydration and the value of water. Remind learners to get a drink of cool, fresh water before entering a class. Allow learners to bring a container of water into the learning area. If you have tests or classes which last over 45 minutes, allow students to bring water or leave the room to get water. Let them leave to get a drink if they feel dehydrated.

Best Bet Resource: *It's All in Your Head,* by Barrett; *Learning to Learn,* by Ward and Daley.

Brain Runs Better On "Nibbling Diet"

Research Summary: A study by Jenkins et al. published in the *New England Journal of Medicine* took subjects with normal eating habits and divided them into two groups: One group ate the traditional three meals a day; the other had the identical food, but spread it out over 17 snacks per day. The subjects followed the diet for two weeks. The results were that the "nibblers" maintained a better insulin level, had lower cortisol levels and better glucose tolerance. These indicators can lead to better cognitive functioning, fewer discipline problems and an enhanced sense of well-being.

In another study in Mexico, Cravioto reported that well-fed learners rated higher in communication skills and did better in the classroom. The students on even marginally deficient diets produced 300% more "poor" performances. This study was interesting because the diets were only slightly worse. Yet, the performance was much worse.

In MacMurren's research, adolescents were given a choice of either snacking and nibbling during a test or not eating at all. Those who were permitted to eat the snacks (popcorn or raw vegetables) achieved "significantly higher" scores than the group who was not allowed to nibble.

Example: Students usually eat a snack at recess and return to the classroom energized.

Implications: Many typical learning problems may represent cases of undernutrition. Too much food or the wrong kinds of food can cause lethargy and drowsiness. Too much time in between eating can cause loss of concentration and decreased alertness.

Action Steps: Make sure your learners are given several opportunities to eat nutritious snacks throughout the day.

Best Bet Resources: For a FREE bulletin, "The Almost-Genius High-energy Learning Diet", available by catalog from Turning Point Publishing, see page 353.

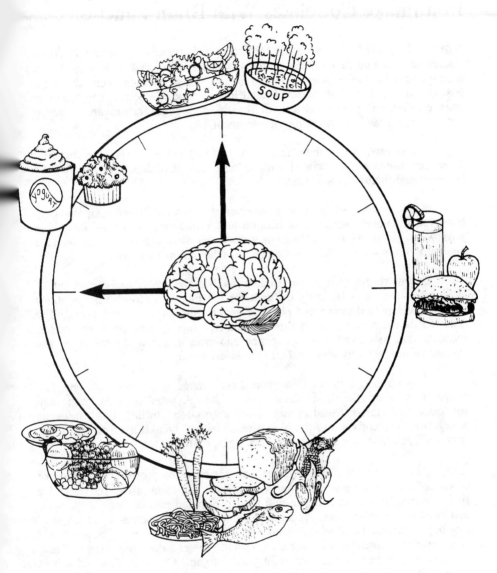

Brain runs better on a "nibbling diet"

Iron Intake Correlates With Brain Function

Research Summary: Research by Tucker and quoted by Connors describes studies of the brain's electrical activity which verify that low iron levels correspond with lower activity in the brain. Most affected were the right posterior hemisphere and the left frontal lobes. Studies document that anemic learners often score lower on tests of general intelligence, attentiveness, motor coordination, speed and muscular development.

Prasad reports that there is a large body of evidence showing that iron deficiency states are associated with reduced cognitive function, maladaptive behavior and motor development.

In an Indian study, iron supplements to female learners significantly improved attention, memory, perception and visual-motor coordination. The girls were given 60 mg. of ferrous sulfate for two months. The benefits gradually diminished in the few months after the treatment ended.

The interesting part of the research involves the analysis of dietary intake of iron. It seems to be fairly difficult for the blood to absorb the quantities needed, especially during rapid physical growth, menstruation and stress. The other foods eaten at the same time as iron-rich foods(dark-green vegetables, meat, beans, fish, poultry, eggs, grains and rice) make a difference in the amount of iron actually absorbed into the bloodstream.

For example, vitamin C sources (like orange juice, broccoli and bell peppers) enhance the iron absorption, while phytates (cereals, bran and soybeans) and tannin (found in tea) inhibit absorption. In fact, **five times as much** iron is absorbed into the bloodstream with a breakfast of orange juice, fruit and eggs as it is with cereal or bran, eggs, coffee or tea.

Example: A menstruating teenager may not have the proper combination of foods necessary for maximum iron absorption. But think about the diet of a typical teenager: it is low in iron-rich foods. Supplements do not get the same results as the complete diet. As a result, the teenager feels stressed and fatigued. She begins drinking coffee, diet drinks or tea to pep herself up. The additional stimulants then interfere with her brain's ability to get a deep physiological rest. She now experiences further irritability and fatigue. Concentration and school work suffer.

Implications: Inadequate diets for teens can have profound consequences, manifested by under performance in school. Optimal nutrition is the key to improvement. Since iron levels are linked to learning, stress and fatigue, its deficiency may explain certain behaviors. Many important nutrients are often not found in your typical learner's diet.

Action Steps: Educate your learners regarding the importance of iron in their diets. This information is especially important for females.

Best Bet Resources: The Indian study mentioned above was reported by Purnima Kashyap in the *1988 Nutrition Research 7: 1117-1138.*

Polyunsaturated Fats Best for Learning

Research Summary: At the University of Toronto, Dr. Greenwood found that although the brain needs fats in order to be at its best, the kind of fat eaten is important. In one of her studies, animals on a diet of polyunsaturated fats learned 20% faster than those on a saturated fat diet. And they also retained the information longer.

Other research confirmed these findings from a biochemical approach. Research by Bourre states that while the brain's development is primarily genetically developed, certain nutrients are critical. These nutrients are polyunsaturated fatty acid (PUFA), lineolic acid (LA) and alpha-lineolic acid (ALNA). Feeding animals diets low in these nutrients reduced only slightly motor function and activity, and dramatically impaired learning. The recovery rate for brains with an improved diet was extremely slow.

Bourre also found that the presence of ALNA conferred a greater resistance to certain neurotoxic agents, such as lead. Experiments have also shown that there is a linear relationship between dietary intake and brain levels of ALNA. The same results were found for excesses of LA.

Implications: If you've made lots of suggestions about nutrition and none have helped, maybe the problem is related to fats in the diet. Most learners have no clue about the effects nutrients can have on the brain and learning. As a result, many students underperform in relation to their actual capabilities.

Action Steps: Be aware of the dietary sources of saturated and unsaturated fat. Diets rich in polyunsaturated fats include safflower, sunflower or soybean oils. Encourage your learners to be attentive to the kind of fat that is in the foods they eat.

Carbohydrates Calm Learner Tension

Research Summary: Maguire reports on Dr. Fernstrom's work done at Massachusetts Institute of Technology. He says that a potato, bran muffin, bagel, chips or even a candy bar might reduce anxiety. But it doesn't directly help learning.

How does this happen? Tryptophan is the amino acid strongly present in high-carbohydrate foods. It stimulates the production of the neurotransmitter serotonin, a chemical messenger that slows thinking, induces sleep and weakens reactions. This natural sedative also makes you more calm and enables you to better withstand pain. If you are having trouble sleeping or are anxious about an upcoming test, eat carbohydrates, especially at night. However, right before test time you may want to eat proteins, since they help to trigger the release of the neurotransmitters most responsible for clear, fast thinking.

What if you eat a meal with both proteins and carbohydrates? Whichever gets to the brain first gets the dominant reaction. By the way, most foods have combinations of amino acids, so we are talking about the dominant or prevailing one, not the only one.

Example: Your student eats a candy bar. He experiences the "sugar high" right away, then becomes lethargic. That's because the brain first processes the sugar for more energy, and then the carbohydrates in the candy bar trigger the serotonin, which leads to slowing down.

Implications: It's not only what you eat, but in what order you eat it that seems to make a difference.

Action Steps: If you eat carbohydrates early in the day, balance their intake with protein. And eat the protein first, so it gets into the bloodstream right away.

Best Bet Resource: *The "Almost Genius" Diet,* available by catalog from Turning Point Publishing, see page 351.

Summary of Action Steps

1. To boost your alertness and mental performance, include a natural source of tyrosine in your diet by eating protein. The best foods high in protein are eggs, fish, turkey, tofu, pork, chicken, and yogurt. Talk to your learners about the positive role nutrition can play in performance, thinking and testing.

2. Educate yourself regarding what everyday food nutrients are excellent for improving memory and learning. Encourage your learners to be attentive to the foods they eat. Explain the dietary sources and benefits of vitamins and minerals.

3. Talk to your students about dehydration and the value of water. Remind learners to get a drink of water before entering a class; allow them to bring a container of water into the learning or testing area.

4. Educate your learners regarding the importance of iron in their diets. This information is especially important for females.

5. Make sure your learners are given several opportunities to eat nutritious snacks throughout the day.

6. Encourage your learners to be attentive to the dietary sources of saturated and unsaturated fat. Diets rich in polyunsaturated fats include safflower, sunflower or soybean oils.

7. Inform your students about the effects of carbohydrates and blood sugar levels on behavior and learning. If you eat carbohydrates early in the day, balance their intake with protein. And eat the protein first, so it gets into the bloodstream right away.

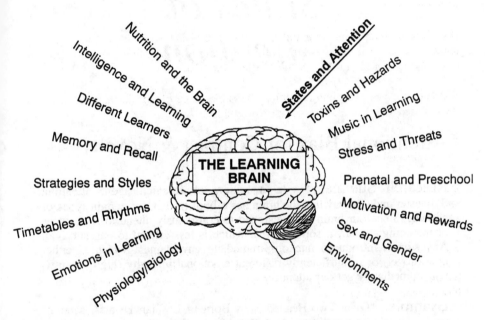

Nutrition and the Brain

Intelligence and Learning

Different Learners

Memory and Recall

Strategies and Styles

Timetables and Rhythms

Emotions in Learning

Physiology/Biology

States and Attention

Toxins and Hazards

Music in Learning

Stress and Threats

Prenatal and Preschool

Motivation and Rewards

Sex and Gender

Environments

THE LEARNING BRAIN

Chapter Nine

CHAPTER NINE

States of Attention

Attentional Bias for Contrast & Novelty

Research Summary: In a review of research about attention, Sylwester and Cho say that the brain has a built-in bias for certain types of stimuli. Since our brain isn't designed to consciously attend to ALL types of incoming stimuli, it sorts out that which is less critical to our survival. Any stimuli introduced into our immediate environment which is either new (novel) or of sufficiently different emotional intensity (high contrast) will immediately get our attention.

Example: "Giant Two Headed Baby Born to Lesbian Dwarf", screams the sexist tabloid headlines. And "Double murder with a shocking twist-- news at eleven", teases another. What gets your attention on television is the "shock effect". Even the commercials for the shows are played into our brain's bias for high contrast and novelty. A passing glance over a crowd of people will pick up what's different (any familiar faces), any sudden changes in movement, familiar voices or emotional overtones.

Implications: Your learners can become jaded and "over-shocked" by constant high contrast stimuli. As a result, in a sedate learning environment, they may become bored, listless and detached. Teachers who capitalize and use this part of the brain's tendency can get and keep attention longer. But that's only useful for the short term.

It makes more sense for the teacher to be less of the "show". Capturing the learners' attention then becomes less of an issue. Giving the learners more control and allowing them to choose complex, interesting life-like projects will focus their attention on their learning instead of on their daydreams.

Action Steps: Use the brain's bias for high contrast--be outrageous and different. But also focus more on designing learner-generated projects so that you don't have to be a shock-show to run a class. Then the novelty and variation of other learners provides much of the attentional bias needed.

Best Bet Resource: For a FREE bulletin, "How To Get & Keep Student's Fullest Attention", see page 353.

Does Learning Fuel Awareness States?

Research Summary: Our body perceives pain quite differently depending on whether we are enjoyably engaged or bored by the activity. Karkowski et al. gave 52 women subjects, in two groups, two different types of tasks. Both were pre-assessed for pain perception. One group was given a boring and repetitive task; the other, a fun, creative task. The assessment sessions were long and both groups reported fatigue at the end. Then, each subject was again given a pain perception activity (finger pressure). The group that had the more boring task felt less pain than the group with the creative one. The researchers speculated that doing challenging, enjoyable work may lead to states of "hyper-arousal", where one becomes more acutely aware of sensory input. On the other hand, boring, repetitive work seems to deaden the senses.

Example: When you're out on a wonderfully romantic date, the moon seems brighter, the stars prettier, the champagne tastier and the kisses sweeter. When you've just gotten a raise or promotion, the sky is bluer, the people are friendlier and flowers seem more colorful.

Implications: When you are engaged in what you're doing and really enjoy it, the whole world around you seems more vibrant, alive.

Action Steps: Use your awareness of your senses as a barometer of your learning. The more engaged you are, the more vibrant and sensitive you'll be.

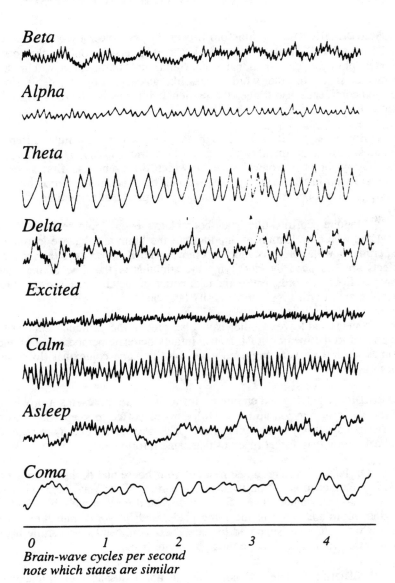

Beta

Alpha

Theta

Delta

Excited

Calm

Asleep

Coma

0   1   2   3   4
Brain-wave cycles per second
note which states are similar

Learning Embedded in Location & States

Research Summary: Stanford University psychologist Gordon Bower and Howard Erlichman of New York City University confirm that each mental, physical and emotional state "binds up" information within that particular state. In other words, states like anxiety, curiosity, depression, joy and confidence also trigger the particular information learned while in that state.

Bower says, "It is as though the two states constitute different libraries. . . a given memory record can be retrieved only by returning to that library, or physiological state, in which the event was first stored." Learners who hear a lecture while a certain baroque music composition is playing will test better if that same music is re-played at exam time.

Maguire confirms this "state-bound knowledge" brain research, also. How and where we learn is as important to the brain as what we learn. In experiments with color, location and movement, Kallman says the recency effects are enhanced by identifying the stimulus at the time of the state change. In other words, pause and take notice of the circumstances of your learning and it will trigger more easily later on.

Shields and Rovee-Collier have also proven the particular context to be critical to the memory of infants. Infants better remembered faces and sounds when they were triggered again by the same contextual (location) cues.

Example: Studying and cramming for a final exam presents a problem. If you study in a hyped-up mood with cups of coffee to keep you awake, you're in a specific psychological state. The next day, while more relaxed and calm, you may forget much of that same information.

Or, let's say you're in one room of your house and decide to go get a book in another room. You walk three-quarters of the way there and you forget what you wanted to get. So what do you do? You walk back to the original room and stand in the same place, and let your brain remember what it was you were supposed to get. Then, confidently, you stride back to the other room and retrieve the appropriate book.

Implications: There are hundreds, if not thousands, of inferences. Many learners may actually know the material they are being tested on, but may not demonstrate it well during exam time. If they study under low stress, then take an exam under high stress, their brain will not retrieve as much as if they study AND take the exam BOTH under moderate stress.

Obviously, it's unlikely that an exam would be a low stress experience; studying that way is less useful.

The fact that information is "state-bound" also lends credibility to role plays, simulations and acting out learning. This may explain why the physical, concrete learning done when learners act out the learning better prepares them for the actual event. Pilots use simulators for training, the military creates mock war situations and theater groups do rehearsals. In formalized learning situations, an increase in the amount of role playing may increase the applications of the learning.

Action Steps: Role playing is most productive when the same physiological, emotional and mental states are rehearsed that would be needed for the real situation. Fire drills, safety and health emergencies may be best rehearsed under deadlines. Business and social role-plays may be best done with the same intensity as real-life. Learners may want to coordinate their study time, environment and state of mind with the exact time, place and state that may be present at the final exam.

Best Bet Resource: *The Care & Feeding of The Human Brain,* by Maguire, *Brain States* by Tom Kenyon, both available by catalog from Turning Point Publishing, see page 351.

Attention Span Has Internal-External Shifts

Research Summary: Research about the brain and its attention-processing mechanism suggests that it is critical to understand the E-I (external-internal) shift. Sylwester and Cho say that our brain frequently shifts its focus between external learning events and our internal stored memories and present interests. This shifting of focus seems to be a critical element in: 1) maintaining understanding; 2) updating long-term memories; and 3) strengthening our neural networks.

This shift can happen non-consciously or consciously, through recalling and telling stories. When we do recall or retell our memories, they serve to enhance and enrich our own brain's networking system. The best and simplest way to describe this learning pattern is that learners alternate their focus between the external source of learning and their own internal processing. Some students need equal time for external and internal time and others may need a 5-1 ratio, meaning they have a longer attention span.

Example: You see a good student in the class who is not paying attention. It may be that something he just learned has triggered his internal memories or has shifted to internal processing.

Implications: It may be that keeping students' attention is a moot issue. Maybe you shouldn't have their attention all the time. Maybe they need more time than we think to internalize information. The learner who we think is not focused may be simply re-thinking things in light of new information.

Action Steps: Provide thinking time and group and partner discussion time. Avoid long lectures. Give frequent breaks. Provide end-of-class reflection time.

Positive Learner Expectancy Pays Off

Research Summary: Gratton and fellow researchers were interested in finding out why, when, and how the learner's brain responds to visual and auditory information. They were also curious about whether it matters if the information presented is made during a focused phase (directed learning) or parallel phase (peripheral and diffused learning). In addition, they questioned if it matters whether or not the learner thinks that the material is going to be useful later on. The answer was "yes" to each of these. The results of their experiments indicate that "expectancies about the relative utility of the information extracted during the parallel and focused phases" was *the key determiner* in how successfully they responded.

Example: Your so-called "top" learners often expect to get the most out of a class--and they usually do. Those who learn less often expect to learn less.

Implications: You may want to affect your learner's expectations about your course or class. How much learners get may be affected profoundly by how motivated you get them, how much relevance the material has for them, and how much they think they will learn.

Action Steps: Can you send a note to the students before the course begins to generate positive expectancy about the value of the course? Have students generate their own high expectations of the learning: What's the best that they could learn, how could it help them, how easy will it be to learn? As the instructional leader, you can help set up the learners to learn more with your own enthusiasm and positive expectations.

Your Optimal Learning States Revealed

Research Summary: Csikszentmihalyi, Caine and Singer suggest that there are optimal states for the learner. These are mind-body states that are affected by our fears, environment, expectations, nutrition, personal goals, controlling agencies (teachers, institutions, etc.), emotions and circumstances. The ideal learning takes place when the following conditions are met:

* High challenges, intrinsically motivated
   (not too easy, not too hard, your own relevant choice)
* Low stress, general relaxation
   (not NO stress, just minimal stress)
* Immersed "flow" state: attention on learning and doing
   (not self-conscious or evaluative)

While many possible physiological states can lead to learning, some are significantly better than others. Csikszentmihalyi describes the optimal state as "flow". That's when your skills, attention, environment and will are all matched up with the task. But you can't just "will" yourself into flow. Millions have tried. There are some ways to make it more likely, though, such as starting with an easy task and upgrading the challenges until it's just right. Your performance anxiety can be reduced by switching your focus to a particular part of the task.

Example: You get a new computer, open it up and start it. You begin to play around with it, getting used to it. Time passes, you keep learning new things. At a certain point, the phone rings or you realize it's dark outside. You discover you've been at it for almost three hours, but it felt like a half hour! That's being in a state of "flow".

Implications: Getting and keeping your students in a state of "flow" may be one of the most important roles you have. In that state, learning is enjoyable and learners are highly internally motivated.

Action Steps: It is fairly easy to get learners into optimal learning states if you remember what gets *you* into that state. Have your learners design a complex project that is relevant to them, and then vary the resources to keep the task appropriate to their ability levels. Make it exciting, use teams, simulations, technology, and deadlines, but without too much pressure.

Brain's Code for "Convincing" Itself

Research Summary: The work of Bandler reveals that our brain has three criteria which must be filled in order for it to "know what it knows". These criteria give the brain its "self-convincers" and they vary from person to person. Learning is one thing; the brain must get verification for it in order to truly believe it. The criteria are: 1) your dependent modality: it must be in either visual, auditory or kinesthetic; 2) frequency: you must get it a certain number of times, from 1-20 depending on the person; 3) duration: you must have the validation process last for a certain length of time, often from two seconds to as much as a minute. When these three things occur, you have a feeling that *what* you know, you REALLY know.

Example: You leave the house and go for a drive. Ten minutes away, you suddenly wonder, "Did I lock the door? Did I unplug the iron? Did I turn on my answering machine?" These are examples of you not knowing whether you actually did something. Similarly, when you write or type out a familiar word, you sometimes look at it and wonder, "Is that word spelled right?"

We've all heard someone say, "I'll believe it when I see it." That's a case of a visual learner who HAS to see it. Another might say "I saw it, but I just don't believe it." They call their neighbor first and find out whether they get agreement, then they decide. And a third might say, "If I can touch it, hold it or be there first hand, I'll believe it." These three examples represent modality variables: visual, auditory and kinesthetic. In addition, a frequency variable defines how much repetition, ranging from one to ten times, each learner requires before believing something. And a duration variable indicates the length of time learners need for affirming information, ranging from as few as a couple of seconds to an entire minute.

Implications: There are far-reaching and profound implications. Some learners access the self-convincer state on their own. They simply know how to convince themselves of what they know. They tend to have more self-confidence, often even arrogance or gullibility. A learner must "know what he knows," or he'll leave the room thinking he hasn't learned anything. He goes home and his mother asks, "What did you learn today?" And he says, "Nuthin'" although he actually did learn a lot.

In general, "at-risk" learners have more complex and difficult self-convincer strategies. In other words, they don't know what they know and have little self-confidence. On the other hand, the so-called "gifted"

175

learners are often better at self-convincing. As a result, they tend to have more self confidence.

Multiply that scenario over a thousand times and you have learners with little or no self-confidence, motivation or love of learning. Too easily self-convinced, and you are gullible. Too hard to self-convince, and you're a skeptic.

Action Steps: To make sure that all your students leave your class in a state of "knowing what they know", provide activities that give them a chance to validate their learning. They might have to teach a peer, put on a role play, write in their journal, do self-assessment or teamwork. Do these activities at the end of the learning, so that students can discover what they know and if what they know is "right".

For those who "self-convince" too easily, and think they "know it all" long before they really do know it, there's another solution. These are usually the more contextual-global learners. Give them a checklist of the specific criteria for what is to be learned. Tell them that they are ready for assessment when they have completed each of the items on the checklist. That will help insure more in-depth, true learning.

Best Bet Resources: *SuperTeaching*, a 288 pg. book, or a shorter affordable booklet *How to Boost Learning by 30%*, available by catalog from Turning Point, see page 351.

Chemicals Affect Attention Span

Research Summary: LeDoux says that our brain's ability to pay attention is regulated by complex and predictable variations in the efficacy of chemical neurotransmitter molecules. Norepinephrine and dopamine (both are catecholamines) are the principal neurotransmitter systems that process attention. These "attentional molecules" increase in the human system from 6-8 a.m., causing many to wake up. They begin to decline in the afternoon and reach their lowest level after midnight. An insufficient number of these molecules may cause hyperactivity and excessive amounts may lead to schizophrenia. Learner attentiveness may be optimized with a "normal middle level" of these catecholamines.

Example: Your students are most alert in the morning, slower in the afternoon.

Implications: Mid-afternoon drowsiness may be occurring on a molecular level. Maybe the Latin idea of a "siesta" is even more practical than earlier thought.

Action Steps: Schedule more global and less specific, detailed activities in the afternoon. Make these afternoon activities interesting to help counteract the fact that the brain's attention molecules are lower than in the morning. Optimal dietary intake for best levels of catecholamines are unknown at this time. We do know that low levels of carbohydrates and caffeine, and moderate levels of protein and natural stimulants like Ginko tea can induce stronger states of alertness.

Relaxation Improves Learning & Memory

Research Summary: Researchers at the Stanford University School of Medicine did a study on 39 men and women. Members of one group were taught to relax every muscle in their body, from head to toe. The other group was simply given a lecture on positive attitudes. Then, each group attended a 3-hour memory training course. The researchers then tested the two groups. The group that had consciously practiced relaxation before the test scored 25% better than the other group.

Example: Your students are worried about an upcoming test or some tension around the school or at work. They underperform. Maybe it's you that is tense, stressed and uptight. You rush off to a meeting or a class. Your performance is a bit below your usual high standards.

Implications: Physical relaxation may be more important to learning than just having the will to learn.

Action Steps: Teach your students about the benefits of relaxation. Even better, make it part of the daily routine.

Best Bet Resource: *How to Boost Memory & Recall*, available by catalog from Turning Point, see page 351.

Is 99% of All Learning Nonconscious?

Research Summary: How much of what you learn is from formal instruction? Not much, it turns out. Dr. Emile Donchin at the University of Illinois says that more than 99% of our learning is non-conscious. That means we simply absorb the experience and our brain adds it to our perceptual maps. Learning is going on all the time. The question is whether or not we're aware of it. Donchin notes that while being aware of taking in one type of sensory information, you're unconsciously taking it in through the other four senses as well.

Example: When you listen to a speaker, you hear the words and see the non-verbals. But to which one are you paying more attention? The answer is, both--but not consciously, at the same time. Either you listen attentively and "happen" to take in the non-verbals, or you watch the non-verbals and just "happen" to take in the speech.

Implications: Most of what is learned is not in the lesson plan or course design. Learners are very aware of more than you usually are. While you put up an overhead transparency, they are listening, too. When you have something clever, articulate and important to say, they are watching your facial expressions and other non-verbals.

Action Steps: You may want to become more aware of your non-verbal messages, since research verifies that it is being absorbed by the non-conscious minds of your learners. Practice your presentation in front of a mirror to improve the non-verbals. Or, videotape your presentation and critique yourself. You may also want to get some "coaching" from a colleague.

Physiology Plays Key Role in Learning

Research Summary: Teachers have long known that posture affects the learner. A contracted, slumped over student will learn less than an alert one in an upright posture. But how much does learner physiology affect the learning? A great deal, it turns out. But sufficient breath and upward eye patterns have been found to be critical to learning.

Grinder reminds us that a slumped over posture impairs optimal breathing and directs the eyes downward (accesses feelings). Where your eyes look directs the brain to access certain senses. For 90% of right-handed learners, looking up and to the left allows you to access stored pictures (visual recall). Looking up and to the right is where your eyes usually go to create new pictures. Looking ahead, eyes to the left best accesses stored sounds (what was said or heard) and to the right, creating new sounds.

Looking down and to the left is for internal dialogue (talking to yourself) and down and to the right is for feelings. Left handers often use opposite patterns. It's most important to check out each learner individually by asking questions that require that type of answer. For visual recall: "What are the colors of your furnishings? Your car's interior?" For visual creativity: "What would you look like in a clown suit? How would your car look with stripes on the side and dots on the front?" Be alert and you'll catch the eye movements.

Researchers at a Florida University have found that dolphins (oxygen breathing mammals) exchange nearly 90% of their lung's capacity each time they surface. That means most all of the "stale" air is exhaled and replaced with fresh oxygen. That may not seem like a great deal until you compare it with humans. In one study, it was found that classroom learners exchange between 10% and 25% of their lung's capacity with each breath taken. The human brain, which thrives on oxygen, is often starved for it! Even changing posture can assist in increasing blood flow and oxygen. One study showed that there's a 10% increase in blood flow (and oxygen) to the brain while standing up (versus sitting down).

Example: A student whose eyes are roving at test time may actually be searching within his brain for the answers. It takes eye movement to get the internal information. Ask a colleague the question, "Where did you park your car?" If you're quick, you'll catch the eye movements that tell you they used the part of their brain linked up to visual recall.

Have you ever seen a dolphin short of energy? Of course not! They oxygenate their systems quite well. Students who are standing are much more alert and ready to learn than those in a poor sitting posture.

Implication: A student who is constantly told to "Keep your eyes on your own paper", may actually be moving his eyes to get a picture or sound in his brain. And when it comes to posture, many of the learners who are having difficulty are sitting in slumped-over postures, getting insufficient oxygen and blood flow.

Action Steps: At test time, allow students to move their chairs away from other students. Then let their eyes rove around. Provide leadership by conducting stand and stretch breaks every 20 minutes. Offer stretching, "Simon says" or movement activities. Keep your learners alert with movement, stretching and water breaks.

Best Bet Resource: *Sitting On The Job* by Scott Donkin

Brain Activity in States of:

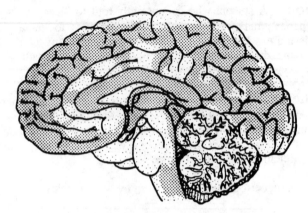

High Challenge, Low Stress

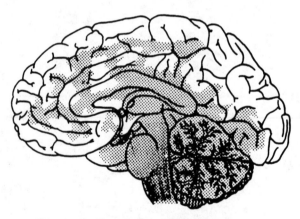

Stress, Anxiety, Threat or
Induced Learner Helplessness

Learner-Induced Helplessness Affects State

Research Summary: Helplessness can devastate even the best learners. Giving the learner control over his environment, however, can definitely improve his attitude, according to Breier. There is evidence showing that giving learners control can boost their learning. And this effect happens whether the control is real or illusory. In an experiment on noise and control, two groups were put into a noisy room. The subjects used were in good mental health. One group had no control over the noise and the other had a placebo control knob that they thought gave them control over the loud noise. The subjects reported their moods before and after each 100 decibel session.

Neither group actually did have control over their environment, but one had the perception that it did. After the group who perceived no control ended their sessions, subjects reported increases in depression, anxiety, helplessness, stress and tension. After the other group's session ended, with exactly the same level of noise, they reported being affected very little.

Example: Your learning environment is cold. But you give the learners control over monitoring the temperature. Their perception of having some control changes their attitudes about learning. On the other hand, if you ask a learner to complete an assignment, and he doesn't know how to do it, he experiences induced helplessness.

Implications: Participation and motivation are boosted by inclusion, ownership and control. They are impaired by autocratic insistence.

Action Steps: Think of three aspects affecting your learners that they can control. For example, it could be their environment, the content of their work and the work processes. Rotate the emphasis, so that they get to control one factor at any given time. You'll find that participation and motivation goes up.

Can Hope Change Learner's Brain?

Research Summary: The work of UCLA psychiatrist Dr. Lewis Baxter has proven that carefully chosen words can activate the same areas of the brain as a highly prescribed drug used for behavior changes. He asserts that this may indicate an equivalent response for both methods. The therapeutic value of language now indicates that words can, indeed, heal.

So, can hope change the brain? The dualist-interactionist (those who agree with Nobel-prize winning physicist David Bohm) answer is that thoughts are indeed things, and that *hope can fire a neuron.* Hooper and Teresi say, "If a thought affects us, it must *do something* to neural tissue...." Naturally, if neural tissue is affected, we would have to say that the brain is, too.

Example: Many years ago a public elementary school in the Bronx area of New York held a graduation ceremony. The commencement speaker was a former graduate, Eugene Lang, who had become a multimillionaire businessman. He was about to give his traditional speech exhorting the theme of "work and study hard and you can make it in the system," when he realized that his audience didn't need that message.

The school was located in an area ravaged by hopelessness, poverty and drugs. They needed a different message. They needed hope. So, Lang boldly offered a college scholarship for every qualifying child that graduated from secondary school. Something special must have happened because years later, the high school had its highest ever percentage of graduating seniors. Hope is very powerful.

Implications: For many learners, if there is no hope of climbing the ladder of success in life, nothing else matters. Without hope, most academic learning seems irrelevant. We may have been trying far too many costly and complex systems and strategies for helping the at-risk learner. Maybe we ought to start with hope first.

Action Steps: Let students work with partners. Give them a second chance. Tell them success stories. Build self-confidence first. Make tutoring available. Let students express their learning in multiple intelligences. Provide for revision opportunities. Break down the work into small pieces. Start with immediate successes. Make complete and specific references to career options available to those who master the content of your teaching. Let students make up one or two test questions. Make teaching a journey in itself so that they enjoy the process, too.

Summary of Action Steps

1. Role playing is most productive when the same physiological, emotional and mental states are rehearsed that would be needed for the real situation. Learners may want to coordinate their study time, environment and state of mind with the exact time, place and state that may be present at the final exam.

2.. Use the brain's bias for high contrast--be outrageous and different. But avoid over-doing it. Focus instead on designing learner-generated projects so that you don't have to be a shock-show to run a class.

3. Use your awareness of your senses as a barometer of your learning. The more engaged you are, the more vibrant and sensitive you'll be.

4. Schedule more global and less specific, detailed activities in the afternoon. Make these afternoon activities interesting to help counteract the fact that the brain's attention molecules are lower than in the morning.

5. Have students generate their own high expectations of the learning: What's the best that they could learn, how could it help them, how easy will it be to learn? Have them design a complex project that is relevant to them, and then vary the resources to keep the task appropriate to their ability levels. As the instructional leader, you can help set up the learners to learn more with your own enthusiasm and positive expectations.

6. Getting and keeping your students in a state of "flow" may be one of the most important roles you have. In that state, learning is enjoyable and learners are highly internally motivated.

7. To make sure that all your students leave your class in a state of "knowing what they know," provide ending activities that give them a chance to validate their learning, such as teaching a peer, role playing, writing in their journal, doing self-assessment or working in teams.

8. Provide thinking time and group and partner discussion time. Avoid long lectures. Give frequent breaks. Provide end-of-class reflection time.

9. Teach your students about the benefits of relaxation and make it part of the daily routine.

10. You may want to become more aware of your non-verbal messages, since research verifies that it is being absorbed by the non-conscious minds of your learners. Practice in front of a mirror, videotape your presentation and critique yourself, or get some coaching from a colleague.

11. At test time, allow students to move their chairs away from other students. Then let their eyes rove around. Provide leadership by conducting stand and stretch breaks every 20 minutes. Offer stretching, "Simon says" or movement activities. Keep your learners alert with movement, stretching and water breaks.

12. Think of three aspects affecting your learners that they can control. For example, it could be their environment, the content of their work and the work processes. Rotate the emphasis, so that they get to control one factor at any given time.

13. Tell students success stories, build self-confidence, make tutoring available. Let students express their learning in multiple intelligences. Provide for revision opportunities. Break down the work into small pieces. Start with immediate successes. Make complete and specific references to career options available to those who master the content of your teaching.

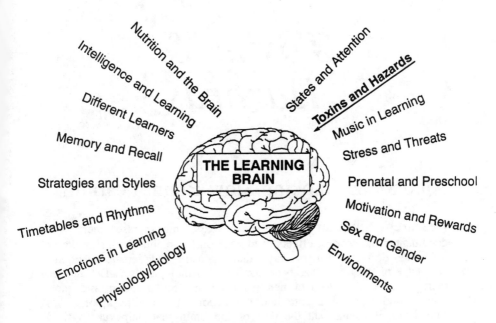

Nutrition and the Brain

Intelligence and Learning

Different Learners

Memory and Recall

Strategies and Styles

Timetables and Rhythms

Emotions in Learning

Physiology/Biology

States and Attention

Toxins and Hazards

Music in Learning

Stress and Threats

Prenatal and Preschool

Motivation and Rewards

Sex and Gender

Environments

THE LEARNING BRAIN

Chapter Ten

CHAPTER TEN

Toxins &
Hazards

Alcohol & Smoking Slow Brain, Learning

Research Summary: Over the years, many researchers have documented the adverse effects of alcohol on the brain. In his studies of moderate drinkers, Harper says that in male and female alcoholics, shrinkage of the brain "has been confirmed pathologically." He adds that there is a selective loss of neurons from the frontal region and motor region, and from shrinkage and "retraction of dendritic arbor. . . ." Translated, it means that the part of the brain that helps us to think, remember and make connections is getting smaller. According to researchers at the National Institute on Alcohol Abuse and Alcoholism, even low doses of alcohol can impair learning. They reduce the ability of the brain to make connections and remember efficiently.

Fein says that even after the drinking has stopped, the impairment continues. His study shows that 50-67% of all recovering alcoholics exhibit cognitive impairment during the first months of detoxification and residual effects lasting for years in some patients. The most severe deficits have been in the following areas: perceptual-motor integration, visuo-spatial abilities, abstract reasoning and new learning. The severity and duration of the effects seem to be linked to age and recency.

In another study, Van Dyke and Fox review data on fetal exposure to PCP and cocaine. He says that there is a growing body of evidence linking exposure to these drugs to "abnormal brain patterns, short-term neurological signs, depression of interactive behavior and poor organizational responses to environmental stimuli." Nadler et al. report that prenatal exposure to alcohol produces "irreversible pathological changes in brain function. . . ."

Smoking also impairs learning. It constricts arteries and reduces blood flow to the brain, says Dr. Hermann. In studies with both smokers and non-smokers, the non-smokers had better recall and higher test scores.

Example: We have all heard about or seen on television infants born to a mother addicted to cocaine. They often are anxious, learning impaired, prone to violence and depressed. Significant damage has also occurred when the mother uses alcohol or tobacco.

Implications: Some things are in our control and others we can only influence. This is an important area, through education, for us all to be influencing agents.

Action Steps: Set a good role model in your own behavior. We may want to step up our education of young people on the dangers inherent in these substances. We may need to be better trained in recognizing drug and alcohol related problems in our learners. We also may need to have lists of resources for treatment.

Food Additives May Impair Brain Function

Research Summary: After two decades of experimentation with the effects of food additives, the results are in. When food additives (coloring, preservatives, thickeners, etc.) are removed from the diet of most children, learning improves. The man who first proposed a link between food additives, behavior and learning was Dr. Feingold. His best-selling book, *Why Your Child is Hyperactive,* made him the foremost advocate for natural, additive-free foods and gave him guru-like status among parents.

In the turbulent years that followed, many other studies attempted to duplicate his own or build on them, with mixed results. Out of the 18 major studies, nine of them were unconvincing and nine of them confirmed his earlier research. The fact that half of the studies confirmed his research speaks strongly for his basic premises.

A summary of all the research revealed three things. First, the greatest improvement in results came with preschoolers. It could be an especially receptive time for the brain. Second, the most improvement came after the first hour of food ingestion. Thirdly, the best results came in conjunction with optimal diets using good nutrition.

Researchers tend to dismiss a theory unless it works 100% of the time. But given all the variables that were worked with, the difficulty of isolating diet, lifestyle, parents, peers and the placebo effect, it may be that getting positive results in half of all studies (the nine that validated Dr. Feingold) is statistically significant. Dr. Keith Connors of the Duke University Medical School, who reviewed tomes of research, says, "Scientists may discount the significance [of the studies]... but if the child were my three year old, it wouldn't matter. I would choose to eliminate artificial colors."

In another study in Wisconsin by the Nutrition Foundation, there was no link found between an additive-free diet and hyper kinetic children. The spokesperson said that there *may exist a subset of hyperactive children who actually are negatively affected,* "but that sub-set is very small." One may want to keep in mind, however, that the Nutrition Foundation is funded by the food industry which makes and uses the same food dyes that it was investigating.

Example: A student is constantly hungry, misbehaving and ready for the next meal. He has a tough time concentrating and focusing. His work is poor and his work is below average.

Implications: Some students may underperform based on the additives contained in the typical learner's diet.

Action Steps: Encourage your learners to be attentive to the ingredients in the foods they eat. Find out what they eat. Have them share any unpleasant symptoms they have experienced. Give them some information or guidelines for eating. Reduce or eliminate the additives in your own diet to find out if you are also affected. After a two month trial period, evaluate your vitality and assess your results.

Best Bet Resource: *Feeding the Brain,* by Keith Connors

Electromagnetic Fields Affect Learning

Research Summary: The results of the Carnegie Mellon University report on electric and magnetic fields by Morgan have confirmed that *humans are affected by both industrial and household electromagnetic fields.* But the extent of the risk is still unknown and it currently falls within the "acceptable risk" range. The three-year research project involved interviews with experts, extensive field testing and the examination of hundreds of studies.

Many researchers disagree. Jauchem, Kavet, and others say that there is no evidence to link any risk for disorders, cancer or reproductive problems. Jauchem dismisses the studies which do link problems with the EMFs (electromagnetic fields). He calls them biased, deficient and flawed. Kavet calls the contradictory studies inconsistent.

While more research is needed, two things are true: 1) it is difficult to find willing subjects for long-term, double-blind experiments, and 2) the thorough and long-term Carnegie-Mellon Report did not dismiss the claims as frivolous, but instead recommended that we act with "prudent avoidance." At this time there is some evidence that electromagnetic fields can and do promote cancer, birth defects and "various neurological effects." Among them is chronic depression. It is not impossible that a school located near 500KV transmission lines or in an area laced with 60Hz fields may find its students underperforming, just as an individual might in certain situations.

Morgan advises that with regard to the risks associated with the fields, we should exercise "[p]rudent avoidance." This means that you may want to take simple precautionary steps. Life carries risks; the fact that automobile accidents kill thousands of motorists each year does not mean we should ban them. So, we have learned to use seat belts, avoid alcohol, drive carefully, service our brakes, buy cars with dual airbags and be courteous. The same level of "prudent avoidance" may be appropriate for electromagnetic fields.

Example: You probably know someone who has recently gotten cancer or died of it. Why is it that in this world where we all take precautions, people are still getting this disease? There are many reasons. Some of them may be as commonplace as the computer terminal or the electric blanket.

Implications: There are invisible forces at work on the learners you work with. It is difficult, if not impossible, to establish a definite "cause and effect" relationship between many of these forces and impaired learner performance. Yet that relationship may, in fact, be valid.

Action Steps: "Prudent avoidance" is the most common sense approach when considering the risks derived from exposure to high electromagnetic fields. These steps may include putting away the electric blanket, moving a motor-driven electric clock away from your bedside, limiting time on a computer or keeping the VDT screen a safe distance from your body.

Many recommend reducing or eliminating the use of electric razors (there's a 250% higher likelihood of cancer) and women's hair dryers, both of which have strong electric currents. You may not want to live near overhead power lines or send your child to a school which is located underneath them. These strategies may be all that are necessary to reduce your risks to an acceptable level.

Best Bet Resource: *"Electric and Magnetic Fields,"* published by Carnegie Mellon University, Pittsburg, PA 15213.

Microwave Towers May Impact Discipline

Research Summary: Janet Healer was the research head of the Federal Electromagnetic Radiation Advisory Council. She stated that recent findings indicate a link between exposure to microwave radiation and behavior disorders. More dangerous than TV sets and microwave ovens, the powerful transmitters from over a quarter of a million television, telephone and radio wave towers may alter the brain biochemically. In both human and rat experiments, there were increases in violent and aggressive behaviors and higher than normal white blood-cell counts.

Example: In some cases, you'll have learners who seem to have good nutrition, positive attitudes and a learning styles which you are successfully addressing. But for some otherwise unexplained reason, they are aggressive and violent.

Implications: Many learners are handicapped by the invisible terrorist-electrical fields. Around the world, it is estimated that over 20 million people live within a too close proximity to these radiation fields.

Action Steps: Educate your learners about the effects of radiation on the brain. You may want to ask learners about their residence location.

Caffeine Overdose Muddles Learning

Research Summary: A study at the University of Leicester in Britain revealed that the alertness associated with caffeine may backfire. The study, done on 32 university students, measured thinking, calculations and other mental performances after they were given beverages. In this blind study, one beverage had the caffeine found in one cup of coffee (125 mg.), another had the caffeine level of two cups of coffee (250 mg.), and the third had no caffeine.

In most of the basic parts of the test, the scores were the same. As soon as the test had questions with ambiguous, confusing and numerical information, the differences were huge. The group who had no caffeine did fine. The middle-level group did worse and the two cups of coffee group had the very worst scores, with twice as many errors as the no caffeine group.

In another study, a psychologist with the U.S. Army Research Institute in Natick, Massachusetts, found that low doses of caffeine did improve mental alertness - but only for a short time. He used dosages from as low as 32 mg. in soft drinks to that from two cups of coffee (256mg.). The results showed that the low dosages worked as well as the larger doses and that the effects of the caffeine lasted for about an hour. The men in the survey improved test performance, boosted concentration and sped up reactions.

Interestingly, in another study, Silverman, et al. and Smith found that there are gender differences in the body's response to caffeine. Using double blind tests with a placebo, females were affected more by ingestion of caffeine and subsequently performed better on the assigned recall tasks.

While too much caffeine can impair learning, a small amount seems to be ideal. Wurtman says that "caffeine can and does play an important role in elevating morning brain power. It is a role similar to that of the protein foods, which induce the brain to manufacture more of the alertness chemicals dopamine and norepinephrine...." What is the ideal amount? While some subjects can notice the effects in doses as low as 10mg., Silverman says the averages of the lowest dose which subjects reported improved task scores with self-discrimination was 100 mg. (about one cup of coffee).

Fortunately, the body's reaction to caffeine does not wear out after prolonged usage. A study at the University of Health Sciences in Bethesda, Maryland, proved that the body's reaction to coffee stayed the same, day after day, without a diminution in effect   Silverman says, "Persons who consume low or moderate amounts of caffeine may have a withdrawal syndrome after their daily consumption of caffeine ceases."

Example: You drink two cups of coffee in the morning. You're alert and "wired" but make mistakes on details.

Implications: Too much stimulation and too much instant stimulation is bad. Better to let the foods that you eat slowly bring the brain up to alert stages. Or at least, be careful about the amount of caffeine ingested.

Action Steps: Reduce your coffee intake in the morning down to one cup. Or, you may allow the natural energy from fresh fruit to give your brain the charge it needs without over stimulating it. Be aware that there may be other effects of caffeine on the body, particularly the heart rate. The research mentioned above focused entirely on the effects on the brain and learning.

Food Dyes Impact Learner Performance

Research Summary: While any one dye may not dramatically affect a learner, often the synergistic effect of several dyes can. A Hayward, California psychiatrist named Buckley and allergist Hawley say their research has confirmed that many children are dramatically sensitive to aniline food dyes. Buckley believes that the region most sensitive to allergens and food dyes is the mid-brain (limbic) area.

Typical dietetic allergic reactions to these chemical intrusions include impaired learning, hyper kinetic behavior and attention deficits. The reactions range from modest to none at one end of the scale, to dramatic and serious at the other. Removing these allergens from the diet can improve learning, concentration and patience in learners.

Dr. James Swanson at the University of Toronto, Canada, has done research at the Hospital for Sick Children. He tested 40 children with an average age of ten. Half of the children were classified as hyperactive. He first tested them with a regular diet containing no dye. That gave him a baseline. Then he divided the 40 into two groups, half getting a placebo and half getting a federally approved food dye (Red No. 3) in amounts at the high end of daily normal consumption for 5-12 year old children.

The children were tested throughout the day, three times with picture and number learning and memory associative tests. In the study, 17 of 20 hyperactive children performed worse after the dye, while only 2 of 20 in the placebo group performed worse. Because the effects of the dye lasted more than 30 minutes, scientists label the effects "behavioral" and not "allergic".

Example: After a morning food break or lunch break, you have a learner or group of learners who change behaviors--for the worse.

Implications: There are many factors working on your students' brains. Additives can be a problem for some learners. Know the symptoms.

Action Steps: Educate your learners about the possible effects on the brain of food additives. Some people are completely unaffected, but in many cases, specific additives and dyes will affect an individual. Recommend to those with unsolved learning difficulties to see professionals who know how to do testing for food allergies.

Lead Exposure Damage Estimates Worsen

Research Summary: Feldman and White reviewed recent studies of the effects of lead exposure on the development of the nervous system and the brain, and on subsequent learning. The damage is even more pronounced than earlier believed. Feldman concludes the following: 1) the effects are not only on prenatals; they continue through to adolescent and adult learners; 2) toxic lead damage on the brain remains *after* removal from the exposure; 3) sufficient evidence exists to show that even low levels of lead damage behavioral and intellectual performance, which results in learning disorders; and 4) the allowable toxicity for lead is much lower and worse than earlier thought.

Canadian researcher Trites and Needleman et al. in Boston researched over 16,000 children. In Ottowa, teachers completed surveys on the quantity of symptoms among their students. The surveys asked questions: "Do you consider this child hyperactive? Is your child distracted easily? Is he frustrated by difficulty? Is he disorganized? Can he follow directions? Is he over-excitable and impulsive?..."

Their studies dramatically linked classroom hyperactivity to lead. The survey results were clear-cut: for every questionnaire completed, the higher the correlates to hyperactivity, the higher the concentrations of lead found in the children. A dramatic city-wide map was created showing where in the city were the low and high levels of hyperactive children. The map showed a large corridor of hyperactive behavior running through the center of the city which exactly matched the main road, the Queen's highway. That road was known to have high levels of automobile and truck exhaust, industrial pollutants, toxic waste and other lead sources. The follow-up studies on the soil and water confirmed that the lead content was significantly higher along that road and near all of the other major arteries. Lead, indeed, was the single common factor.

Example: The problem is so great that the U.S. Government was alarmed by the recent research. After deliberation, the Center for Disease Control has just redefined the lead threshold for intervention from the previous level of 25 micrograms/dl to just 10 micrograms/dl. You may have a student who seems to be smart, but he just doesn't focus and stay attentive. Many of the students from lower income areas are also living near highways, power lines and industrial sites. These are the areas where there are more likely to be toxic hazards.

Implications: There are many complex factors which lead to the success of a learner. The more obvious ones are nutrition, parental support and school quality. But the geography of a student's home may also be a factor. The damage already done will stay with them and they'll be tougher to reach. With millions worldwide living near toxic dumps and contaminated underground water supplies and soil, we'll have problems for years.

Action Steps: Inform your students and parents about potential environmental dangers. Be straightforward and truthful. Avoid being an alarmist. Simply let them know that some studies have shown that environmental lead can impair learning. In some cases a drinking water check may be appropriate. Educate your learners about the risks of lead in the water, soil, food and air. For some learners, it may be appropriate to recommend toxicity testing for lead residues. Encourage students to drink purified water if testing shows a need for it.

Can Artificial Sweeteners Blur Thinking?

Research Summary: The primary ingredient in Nutrasweet™ is aspartame. It is produced, packaged and consumed by hundreds of millions of people worldwide. Is it safe? Not according to a top biochemist of Massachusetts Institute of Technology, Dr. Richard Wurtman and researchers Ritter-Walker and Connors.

Before the Food and Drug Administration (FDA) hearing, over 80 studies were cited on aspartame's toxic side effects, including its linkage to cancer. At the official hearing, its approval was declined by the FDA. But later, the director of the FDA overturned the board's decision unilaterally. Within 30 days, he resigned his post and accepted a paid position with the food industry - the very same food industry that wanted FDA approval so badly.

Aspartame is most widely used as a sweetener for diet drinks, but is found in hundreds of desserts, drinks and restaurant foods around the world. Drs. Richard and Judith Wurtman of MIT are two of the nation's most respected researchers on nutrition and additives. The Wurtmans' research has led them to the following conclusions about the effects of aspartame:

* Some individuals may be genetically more susceptible than others; small children and women are most at risk.
* The effects may show up only after months of usage, so the user may never suspect the real source of the problems.
* The actual effects of the additive include insomnia, headaches, tremors, confusion, memory loss, dizziness, irritability, drowsiness and restlessness, hearing loss, depression, slurring and even seizures.

Example: Teenage girls, who are among the largest consumers, often have difficulty staying focused. They are also most prone to depression, headaches and irritability.

Implications: Much of the difficulty in reaching learners may be because of diet.

Action Steps: Become an informed consumer as well as an instructional leader. Educate your learners regarding the possible effects of aspartame on their health.

Best Bet Resources: *Managing Your Mood and Your Mind Through Food,* by Judith Wurtman; *Endangered Minds: Why Our Children Don't Think,* by Healy, available by catalog from Turning Point Publishing, **see page 351.**

Are Computers and Other VDTs Safe?

Research Summary: There is mixed evidence at this time regarding the safety of VDTs (video display terminals, such as computers). Some, including Kavet, say that they are completely safe. Others, including Cardinali, Horowitz, and Sarkin, insist that we may want to exercise "prudent caution."

In Kavet's summary work, he found that 9 of 10 studies concluded that VDTs do not predispose pregnant operators to spontaneous abortion. He states that studies of fetal resorptions in mice have been inconsistent. Researchers may well be asking why other symptoms were not researched besides the triggering of a spontaneous abortion. Females do seem to have a higher risk for VDT-related problems.

Horowitz says that the problem is that VDT-related work may also mean that the subject is exposed to 1) electrostatic ambient air negative ion depletion (the electrical charge of the atmosphere is changing); 2) the radiation itself; and 3) eye strain and postural stress.

There are different emission standards of radiation for computer screens and most of them follow the less stringent U.S. ones, the MPR and MPR II. The more rigorous Swedish standard, TCO measures the radiation from a closer distance, 30cm.(instead of 50 cm.). None of the largest selling screens meet the higher Swedish standard, although most meet the MPR II standard. Is that a problem? It's difficult to tell. Studies are usually conducted by interested, invested parties and over a short term. In other words, unbaised research is tough to come by. More research will need to be done.

Example: Someone you know who is otherwise healthy, with no genetic predisposition towards cancer, suddenly develops a tumor. They also happen to work in front of a VDT all day, every day.

Implications: There may be some evidence of risk, but more controlled studies need to be made.

Action Step: You may want to exercise "prudence" in the location (keep it two or more feet away), frequency, duration (never more than an hour at a time) of VDTs in your work and home life.

Best Bet Resources: *Videoclear,* an interference device which neutralizes the harmful effects of EMF from computers & TV. Available from Gateways at 800-477-8908 or fax 805-646-0980

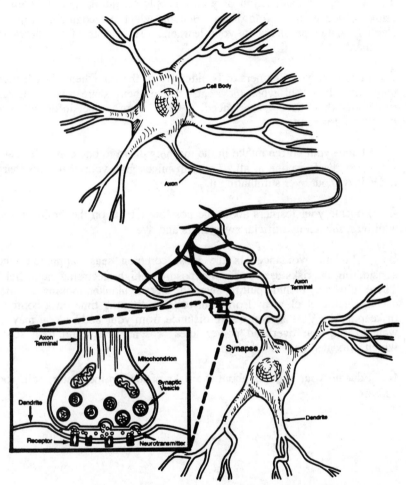

Enrichment helps our cells grow dendrites. Learning occurs when the dendrites create new neural pathways and connect with other dendrites. The synapse is a chemical reaction that occurs at the moment of connection.

Summary of Action Steps

1. Step up your education of young people on the dangers inherent in drinking alcohol and taking drugs. Become adept at recognizing drug and alcohol related problems in your learners. Have lists of resources for treatment.

2. Encourage your learners to be attentive to the ingredients in the foods they eat. Find out what they eat. Have them share any unpleasant symptoms they have experienced. Give them some information or guidelines for eating.

3. Reduce your coffee intake in the morning down to one cup. Or, better yet, go to decaf or none at all. Let fruit juices give your brain the charge it needs without over stimulating it.

4. Educate your learners about the possible effects on the brain of food additives, including artificial sweeteners and dyes.

5. "Prudent avoidance" is the most common sense approach when considering the risks derived from exposure to high electromagnetic fields. These steps may include putting away the electric blanket, moving a motor-driven electric clock away from your bedside, limiting time on a computer or keeping the VDT screen a safe distance from your body. You may not want to live near overhead power lines or send your child to a school which is located underneath them.

6. Educate your learners about the risks of lead in the water, soil, food and air.

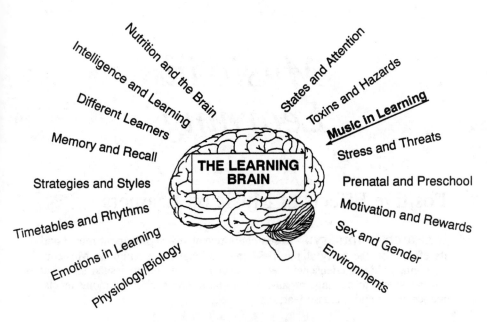

Nutrition and the Brain

Intelligence and Learning

Different Learners

Memory and Recall

Strategies and Styles

Timetables and Rhythms

Emotions in Learning

Physiology/Biology

States and Attention

Toxins and Hazards

Music in Learning

Stress and Threats

Prenatal and Preschool

Motivation and Rewards

Sex and Gender

Environments

THE LEARNING BRAIN

Chapter Eleven

CHAPTER ELEVEN

Music in Learning

Positive Effects of Music on Learners

Research Summary: Researchers revealed insights about music and its effects on the body at the 1984 international symposium on Music in Medicine held in Ludenscheid, West Germany. The report issued said that "Music seems to massage organs, entrain biorhythms, alter hormone levels, reduce stress and increase learning."

In an interview with Campbell, learning pioneer Dr. Jean Houston says that regarding the use of music in learning, "it's hard to talk about any specific miracle story.... I see this[miracles] all the time in my work." Dr. Houston says music "raises the molecular structure of the body...."   She may not be far off. The body resonates at a stable molecular wavelength. Music has its own frequencies, which either resonate or conflict with the body's own rhythms. When both are resonating, you feel powerfully "in synch", and more aware and alert.

Music carries with it more than just feelings. It can be a powerful vehicle for information. Webb says, "Music acts as a premium signal carrier, whose rhythms, patterns, contrasts, and varying tonalities encode any new information...." The use of music as partner, point-counterpoint or sound surfer can be a powerful way to carry a large volume of content. In fact, according to Lozanov, a "well-executed concert can do 60% of the teaching work in about 5% of the time."

How does music do this? It activates more than the right brain. It elicits emotional responses, receptive or aggressive states and stimulates the limbic system. The limbic system and subcortical region are involved in engaging musical and emotional responses. But more importantly, research has proven the limbic part of the brain is responsible for long-term memory. This means that when information is imbued with music, there's a greater likelihood that the brain will encode it in long-term memory.

Example: In Japan, one group of anesthetized surgery patients listened to music on headphones while another group did not. The "music" group had lower stress levels in the blood, which is positive. In your classroom, you may have found that when you play relaxing music or Baroque in the major key, your students tend to settle down and focus.

Implications: We may be under utilizing music. We rely so much on our own voices to deliver meaning. Yet music is a terrific carrier of meaning and it is readily available for learning.

Action Steps: If you're not using music in your teaching, it may be a good time to start. If you are already, it may be time to expand or enhance your collection.

Best Bet Resources: For beginners: *How to Use Music in Teaching and Training,* For intermediate and advanced levels: *Trainer's Manual for Accelerated Learning with Music,* available by catalog from Turning Point, see page 351.

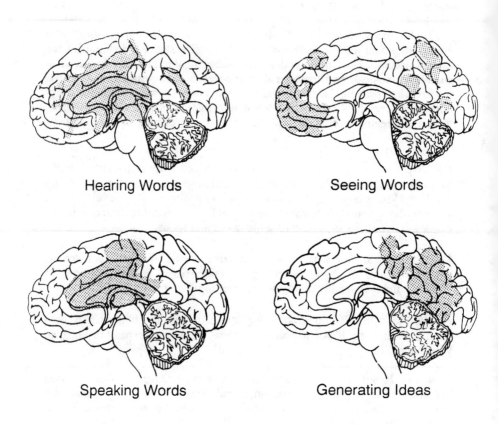

Hearing Words

Seeing Words

Speaking Words

Generating Ideas

PET (positron emission tomography) scans reveal
which part of the brain is being activated by greater blood flow
during specific learner behaviors (individuals may vary)

Musical Ability Linked to Hormone Levels

Research Summary: A study was done by Hassler on the biological basis of special musical talents. The experimenter's study included composers, instrumentalists, musicians of varying ability, and painters, with an equal number of boys, girls, and non-musicians. Salivary testosterone levels were measured in both adolescents and adults.

The most creative musical behavior was associated with very low testosterone values in males and high testosterone levels in females. Hassler speculates that while there may be a complex interaction of social and biological factors, "an optimal testosterone range may exist for the expression of creative musical behavior." Interestingly enough, he adds, "Exceeding the range in the course of adolescence may be detrimental for musical creativity in boys."

Example: One of the best students in music also had the lowest levels of testosterone. It may also explain why there is such a stigma attached for boys who play for the school band instead of a contact sport like football. Other boys tease them about not being interested in "contact sports".

Implications: If hormones affect our learning potential in music, what other hormones affect what other skills and abilities?

Action Steps: Avoid labeling learners who have low or high ability in music. It may be as much a matter of hormones as it is choice.

High Frequency Music Boosts Learning

Research Summary: How does sound affect the brain? French physician Dr. Alfred Tomatis says our ears may do much more than just perform hearing and equilibrium functions. They may, in fact, be the keys to energy, vitality and dynamism. The Tomatis approach is profound. He says that changes in hearing change our speech. His work strives to improve listening, attention, and awareness through self-monitoring.

Hearing defects between 500 and 1000cps make music appreciation impossible. Defects in hearing between 1000-2000cps keep one from singing in tune and defects from 2000 and up make the voice flat and monotonous. His dramatic research also proved that you can charge the brain's energy levels with sound because the inner ear acts as a receiver for the frequencies that creates a compatible brain resonance.

Tomatis says that the middle ear has more receivers for high than for low frequencies, and the high ones have the positive, "charging" effect. He recommends Mozart as an example of beneficial, therapeutic music. Tomatis says that depressed learners who listened to "charged" music reported increased motivation, memory, concentration, and competence, and reduced fatigue. His research found that when he filtered out the low frequencies (2000Hz), benefits increased. He claims that 8000 Hz is the optimal frequency for recharging the "brain's batteries."

Example: Many of the people who have flat, monotone voices also are poor at hearing. And often those who have no singing voice are poor at hearing a range of voices or music.

Implications: The best way to help many learners with their speaking skills may be to improve their listening and hearing abilities.

Action Steps: Students who mumble, speak in monotones and are doing poorly may be candidates for a hearing test. The two may be related.

Best Bet Resource: *Super-Memory* by Ostrander and Schroeder. Or, contact Billie Thompson, Tomatis Center for Sound & Listening, 2701 E. Camelback Rd. #205, Phoenix, AZ 85016   Phone (602) 381-0086 Fax (602) 957-6741.

Many Music Types Enhance Learning State

Research Summary: Halpern says, "Important new evidence shows that not only is the study of... music beneficial in itself, but the introduction of [it] into a school's curriculum causes marked improvement in math, reading, and the sciences." He adds that the absence of art and music "can retard brain development in children." From his personal experience and exposure to others in the field, Halpern has become convinced of the necessity of music in learning. He says, "Ideally, sound and music should be used educationally throughout the curriculum." The benefits he cites are:

> * Relaxation and stress reduction (stress inhibits learning)
> * Fostering creativity though brain wave activation
> * Stimulating imagination and thinking
> * Stimulating motor skills, speaking and vocabulary
> * Reducing discipline
> * Focusing and aligning energy as a group
> * Patterned concert readings (using music as a background to presentation)

Researcher King did experiments that were designed to determine if a particular selection could evoke a particular neurophysiological response. He says that there is no statistically significant difference between using Baroque and New Age music in the effectiveness of inducing alpha states for learning. King used music from the artist Kenny G, "Duotones", but speculated that other similar music types may work as well. Multiple independent tests were performed for all samples, and King concluded that either New Age or Baroque music could be used to enhance learning.

Researcher Felix says that the following summary can be made about the role of music in teaching, training and learning:

> "Significant positive effects of music during learning have been reported. Positive effects of music played during testing are not as consistently supported.... There are also a small number of studies which report no significant effect of background music during learning or testing.... Studies reviewed lend support to claims for the effectiveness of music from the baroque and classical periods.... [O]ther styles of music... may also be effective."

There's clear evidence that music affects brain waves and our physiological states. There is also an abundance of anecdotal and experiential evidence that the purposeful and well-planned use of music can positively impact learners. And this can come in many forms.

Dr. Patrick Pillai of The Acupuncture Foundation and Niels Primdahl of Electro Medica in Toronto have pioneered a breakthrough sound wave generator. This device emits frequencies in 10,000hz range and has been found to be as effective in healing as traditional needle acupuncture! Sound can indeed affect the body.

The Sorbonne University in Paris has confirmed the work of Dr. Tomatis for founding a whole new discipline called Audio-Psycho-Phonology (APP). The research fills hundreds of journals and books and provides detailed accounts of how sound therapy can alleviate symptoms of deafness, epilepsy, hyperactivity and autism. Moreover, it can boost alertness, thinking and memory.

The Soviet discovery called Kirlian photography uses an electronic imaging process instead of light to process film after exposure to humans and plants. Biophysicists discovered that all living organisms have a brilliantly colored, light-filled energy pattern that emanates from and surrounds them. What's more, this pattern can be easily photographed! Before and after pictures were taken with subjects listening to baroque music (Bach's Brandenburg Concertos). The differences are startling. The "after" photos of the biofield, done using Kirlian photography, show a more aligned, organized, fluted and harmonized pattern of energy emanating from the listener. Music can indeed affect the body.

How else can music affect your listeners?   Pat Joudry wrote an interesting book called *Sound Therapy* . In it, she says, the brain and ear can become increasingly revitalized through the proper use of music and harmonic stimulation. Certain sound patters allow the brain to fully recharge, relax and energize is less time than the usual six to eight hour sleep. Users of her *Supersleep* programs find that they need two to three less hours of sleep per night. The treatment consists of classical music (especially Mozart) with a suppression of the lower frequency bands at 2000hz and below, the use of headsets, dominant use of right ear and special bursts of music in low-high sequences.

Example: You may have found that many types of music lead to enhanced states optimal for learning. Your students may enjoy background or foreground music when used sparingly and appropriately.

Implications: Many educators have found that although the original music suggested by Bulgarian learning pioneer Dr. Georgi Lozanov works well, other selections also work. Many have successfully used Reggae,

Latino, pop, jazz, New Age, big band, waltz, rap, rock, soul and other types for learning. The key is to become informed and closely monitor the effects. For example, researchers found that string music gave better results than other music. Why? Some think it has to do with the specific frequencies emitted by those instruments help recharge the brain better than others.

Action Steps: Use music in your learning situations. Since each different type of music can elicit a different type of psycho-physiological state, use a variety. When your learners arrive, you may want to play music that creates a state of anticipation or excitement (grand movie themes, upbeat classical). For storytelling, use music that has built-in peaks and valleys and engages fantasy and emotion (classical or romantic). For background, you may want to use low volume Baroque.

If you haven't been using it, start small, then work your way into it. Begin with one selection, one of your personal favorites from maybe Handel's Water Music, Bach's Brandenburg Concertos or Vivaldi's Four Seasons. Pick the right time (like the five minutes before starting a class) and begin to experiment. Over time, you'll be able to work with dozens of selections on a second's notice (and still have time to do other things).

Use music carefully and purposefully for best effect. Too much can create saturation to the listener, and it loses its effectiveness. As a general rule, include music in 30% or less of the total learning time, unless the class requires it by nature of its content (a music class). The artful use of music can educate, heal, inspire, boost learning and build confidence.

Best Bet Resources: *Sound Therapy for the Walkman* by Pat Joudry, Get resources from Superlearning Inc. 450 Seventh Ave. New York, NY 10123. Also Ostrander Associates, 4325 Steeles Ave. West, Suite 410, Downsville, Ontario, Canada M3N 1V7. (212) 279-8450. Tapes and books available. *Introduction to the Musical Brain,* by Don Campbell. Order from Institute for Music, Health and Education (303) 443-8484. Or, for a FREE bulletin called, "Thrilling Selections to Motivate Your Audience", see page 353.

Endorphins Triggered by Favorite Music

Research Summary: Scartelli reports that two ways to reduce learner tension are biofeedback and listening to calming music. When he combined the two in his research, however, he got the best results. There's an enormous difference in the types of music that can be played, but ultimately the listener's heartbeat is the best judge.

Pharmacologist Avram Goldstein researched at Stanford with medical and music students. He had them listen to their favorite types of music and gave them shots of either saline (a placebo) or the endorphin-blocker naloxone. In this double-blind study, he discovered that a third of the listeners (those that got the blocker) reported less intense feelings than they usually got from their music.

Example: You are listening to the radio. Maybe you're feeling so-so or a bit blah. Suddenly, on the radio, one of your all-time favorite songs is played. Maybe it is one you recall from a special time as a teenager or college student. Or maybe it's a song that brings back special memories of a first love. Whatever the associations, you immediately feel better. Once again, music has worked its charms.

Implications: In learning contexts, music may be under-used. Music can be used as a mood enhancer to get learners in a better state of readiness for learning. With a world of possibilities for creating positive triggers and releasing endorphins in learners, it would be a shame to miss out.

Action Steps: Get music which gives positive, upbeat messages. Make sure that it's in a major key. Use show business themes or music from the most popular epic motion pictures. Use local music that has a particular appeal just to your learners. Experiment a bit. Ask your learners what music they like to use when they want to get into a great mood.

Best Bet Resource: *100 Ways to Use Music and Your Voice in Teaching,* by Don Campbell

Music Impacts Learner's Brain & Body

Research Summary: Top music and brain expert Clynes explains how dramatically music can affect learners. The older, more traditional viewpoint was that music affected the non-dominant hemisphere. For example, a right-handed person is more likely to be left-hemisphere dominant. And that leads to using more of the right side of the brain for music. But Clynes says the following:

1) Both sides of the brain are involved in processing music.
2) The harmonic structure, interval quality, timbre, and the spatial, temporal, long-term patterns are recognized by our non-dominant hemisphere (in most of us, the right hemisphere). The short-term signatures, like rapidly varying volume, rapid and accurate pitch trajectory, pacing and words, are recognized by the dominant hemisphere (in most of us, the left).
3) Over the last hundred years, music has changed. Clynes says that the trend is toward "...a gradual shift of the 'focal point' of musical processing from the minor hemisphere, in, say, baroque or classical music, to the dominant hemisphere of today's avant garde music." In other words, today's music engages more of the brain.
4) The pulse of the body (heart rate) tends to synchronize with the beat of the music. The faster the music, the faster the pulse. In Clynes' words, "[A]n aspect of the transformation of sound pulse to motor pulse displays a tendency to follow the dynamic character of the sound pulse...."

Webb says that the effects of music on the mind and body are best summarized in these eight areas:

* the effects on muscular energy of tones and scales
* an increase in molecular energy
* the influence of rhythm on the heartbeat
* changes in metabolism, which affect physical energy
* a reduction of pain and stress and sped up healing in recovering surgery patients
* relief from fatigue and low energy
* the release of emotions, feelings and character
* the stimulation of creativity, sensitivity and thinking

Interestingly enough, a non-musician's and a musician's brains react differently to music. Dr. John Mazziotti measured blood flow and brain activity through brain scans while different learners listened to music. The

215

right hemisphere "lit up" when music was played to a musical novice, but the musician's left side of the brain was more active when listening to the music. There was also more activity in the limbic system.

Presumably, this occurred because the processing for this kind of listener is much more analytical, even to the point of processing nonconsciously the tones, tempo and rhythm. At the Montreal Neurological Institute, Justine Sergent confirmed, once again, that the whole brain is involved in the processing of music.

Example: Music affects all of us; its reputation as a universal language is well deserved. In a research study by Clynes, 40 Central Australian Aborigines of the Warlbiri Tribe scored high on recognition of musical sounds of joy, love, reverence, grief, anger, sex and hate. Their scores were equal to university students at the University of New South Wales, MIT, and the University of California at Berkeley.

Implications: Music can be used among many cultures. Use a diversity of music to reach the minds of your learners.

Action Steps: Experiment to find appropriate avenues for using music in learning. Use it for introductions, to set the mood, as an energizer, for background, and for celebrations and closures.

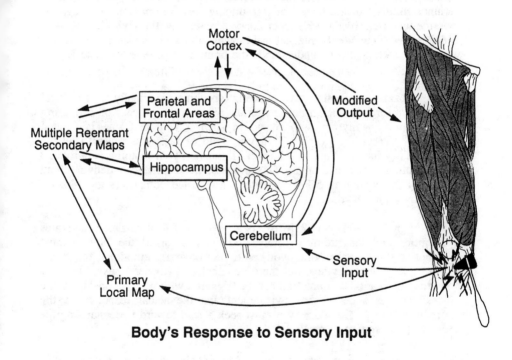

Body's Response to Sensory Input

Which Music is Best for Learning?

Research Summary: Is one type of music better for learning than another? The research says that it depends on the individual and what effect you are trying to get. Clynes and Walker say that, to be safe, there is a greater consistency in the body's pulse response to classical music than to rock music. In other words, you will get more predictable, safer and more consistent responses. This doesn't mean that contemporary music cannot work; just that much of it elicits less predictable responses.

Lozanov says that it depends on what you're trying to do with the music. His research says that classical (circa 1750-1825) and romantic (circa 1820-1900) are better for introducing new information. He suggests Baroque (circa 1600-1750) as a passive review at the end of a session. Others (Webb & Webb) suggest that dozens of types of music can work for learning, as long as one understands the brain and the effects music has on it.

Lozanov suggests active concerts (speaking theatrically with musical interplay) for introducing new material. This is the process of delivering information in rhythm with music in such a way that one is "sound surfing." When the music is dynamic, loud or fast, you pause to let the music carry itself. When it is slower or pausing, your material is delivered with enthusiasm and drama. This process, he claims, can deliver about 60% of the content in 5% of the time. Suggested composers are Mozart, Beethoven and Hayden.

How does this work? Music is a powerful signal carrier; it activates emotions and long term memory and fully engages the brain's most receptive states. From some, you can expect powerful emotional reactions; from others, less obvious, but there nonetheless. Roederer says, "In other words, motivation and emotion can be triggered with no relationship to the instantaneous state of the environment and the actual response of the organism to it." He adds, "We must seek a lead toward understanding the emotional response to music...."

Examples: You may have learned the alphabet with a song or know of an advertiser's jingle that stays in your mind. Music alongside content is very powerful.

Implications: There may be many other ways that we could use music to carry messages into the minds of receptive learners.

Action steps: Music can be used many ways. One is to use learner-generated songs. Have your students select five songs that they already know well (Jingle bells, birthday songs, simple and traditional folk songs, etc.). Then have them replace key words in the old lyrics with new words to be learned for the song. Sing the song several times. The new lyrics will be more easily transferred into the minds of the learners.

When you want to use music for dramatic introductions of content, use show music, movie themes or any other dramatic music. To deliver key content, classical or romantic music is best. For closed-eye review, Baroque is optimal. Many other forms of expression also work, from world music, to folk, jazz, country, gospel, traditionals, marches, pop and New Age. Experiment; keep using what's working, and change what's not.

Best Bet Resources: Send for booklet called, *"How to Use Music in Teaching & Training"*   available by catalog from Turning Point Publishing, see page 351.

Summary of Action Steps

1. Students who mumble, speak in monotones and are doing poorly may be candidates for a hearing test.

2. If you're not using music in your teaching, it may be a good time to start. If you are already, it may be time to expand or enhance your collection. Since each different type of music can elicit a different type of psycho-physiological state, use a variety.

When your learners arrive, you may want to play music that creates a state of anticipation or excitement (grand movie themes, upbeat classical). For storytelling, use music that has built-in peaks and valleys and engages fantasy and emotion (classical or romantic). For background, you may want to use low volume baroque.

3. Use music purposefully for best effect. Too much can create saturation to the listener, and it loses its effectiveness. As a general rule, include music in 30% or less of the total learning time, unless the class requires it by nature of its content (a music class).

4. Get music which gives positive, upbeat messages. Make sure that it's in a major key. Use show business themes or music from the most popular epic motion pictures. Use local music that has a particular appeal just to your learners. Experiment a bit. Ask your learners what music they like to use when they want to get into a great mood.

5. Have your students select five songs that they already know well (Jingle bells, birthday songs, simple and traditional folk songs, etc.). Then have them replace key words in the old lyrics with new words to be learned for the song. Sing the song several times. The new lyrics will be more easily transferred into the minds of the learners.

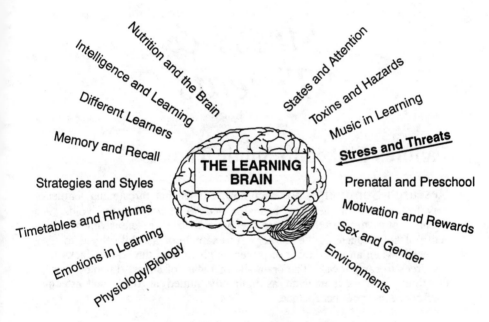

The Learning Brain

- Nutrition and the Brain
- Intelligence and Learning
- Different Learners
- Memory and Recall
- Strategies and Styles
- Timetables and Rhythms
- Emotions in Learning
- Physiology/Biology
- States and Attention
- Toxins and Hazards
- Music in Learning
- **Stress and Threats**
- Prenatal and Preschool
- Motivation and Rewards
- Sex and Gender
- Environments

Chapter Twelve

CHAPTER TWELVE

Stress &
Threats

Failures Linked to Subtle Threats

Research Summary: Research now tells us that threatening learners may foster more of the same behavior that we are trying to avoid. A threat is any stimulus that causes the brain to trigger defensiveness or a sense of helplessness in the learner. An example of a subtle threat to the learner is when an assignment or project is given, and the learner lacks the resources to carry it out. The brain sits in a state of stress. In some cases, the threat may be perceived as indirectly aimed at one's self-esteem, confidence and peer acceptance.

According to Jaques and Leonard, threats adversely affect one's ability to plan for the long-term and to stay engaged at a task for a long period of time. These abilities are critical for learners: some evidence links success with the ability to postpone immediate gratification and go for the long term. Caine says that threats, even if occurring indirectly through rewards, may hinder our abilities to tolerate ambiguity and to delay gratification, and that it may be "among the most important and devastating of all consequences."

Example: A learner is told that if he solves a problem (or has good behavior, perfect attendance, etc.) he will get a sticker, token, food or other reward. With every reward, there is an implied lack of reward (punishment) for a contra-behavior. Spielberger states that learner dependence on "flocking behaviors" (social conformity) and reliance on extrinsic rewards (bribes, stickers, etc.) actually increases with threat.

Another example can be seen with a learner who is constantly disciplined because of his inability to stay engaged in a task or inability to delay gratification. The discipline may actually create a "state of threat" which perpetuates the problem.

The most common threat in a classroom is when a teacher threatens to withhold teaching and attention until a student changes behavior ("I'll just wait until you're quiet and all ready to learn.").

Implications: We may need to redefine what we consider to be threats in a learning environment. We may need to utilize alternative forms of motivation. Any system of learning which uses heavy authority, position, laws, threats, rules, punishments and rewards will, over the long run, perpetuate the very behaviors it is trying to eliminate. The techniques may work initially, but soon the learner behavior will become rote, minimized and stereotyped.

Teenagers who feel picked on and threatened by adults are least likely to change behavior because the part of their brain that deals with "perceptual mapping" and complex behavior change is unable to be engaged. Both adults and teenagers stay in peer groups for identity and safety. So-called "low achievers" who are constantly threatened, disciplined and bribed with rewards may be unable to work for delayed gratification. The part of their brain they need to use, the frontal lobes, are less likely to be engaged under a system where others have control and they feel pressured to perform like a rat in a cage.

This may explain many of the common behaviors of gangs, so-called "low-achievers" and the drifting learners who seem unmotivated. The more they are threatened, the more the behaviors they'll have which demonstrate a lack of higher-order thinking skills and short-term thinking.

Action Steps: Identify substandard learner behaviors. Identify areas of threats, both implied and explicit. As much as possible, remove threats from the learning environment and introduce alternative forms of motivation, such as novelty, curiosity, positive social bonding and relevant content. Avoid reliance on extrinsic rewards.

Stress Affects Different Memory Levels

Research Summary: Christianson reviewed the literature on eyewitness memory and its relationship to stress. The classical view is that under stress, the learner's memory is impaired because of a decrease in available processing capacity. Presumably this occurs because of the brain's "minimizing," which Hart and Nadel have indicated prevents best functioning of the neocortex. But Christianson says that there are striking differences in memory levels. They are dependent on the:

1. Type of event
2. Time of day of the test
3. Type of detail needed
4. Information learned (and other factors)

Various stresses, event uniqueness and personality factors have a huge influence on what is recalled. He also says that emotional events receive some sort of preferential processing, which may explain their selectiveness and degree of imprinting.

Example: You may remember very little about an event that occurred two hours ago and every detail of something that happened a year ago. The difference in your memory of these events is related to the different stress conditions associated with them.

Implications: Learners need low stress at work and low stress in the learning context. Low stress is different from no stress - that's bad for learning. Low stress means slight anxiety, a very fine edge of concern, anticipation and curiosity. Without these conditions, the learner may be judged as being a "low achiever" because of too much or too little stress.

Action Steps: Reduce stress, increase support and encouragement. Make the testing or other assessment times less stressful by encouraging partner work, allowing stretch breaks, giving immediate successes followed by engaging complex projects and giving verbal encouragement.

Threats "Minimize" Best Thinking

Research Summary: The work of Hart, Lozanov, Nadel, and Leonard has confirmed that the brain operates differently when any type of threat is perceived. Under threat, the brain uses less of the "higher order" thinking skills of the neocortex and resorts to using more of the fastest and most survival-oriented part of the brain, the "reptilian" brain stem.

Threats can be any stimulus that causes the brain to trigger a sense of fear, mistrust, anxiety or general helplessness in the learner. Threats can be defined as physical (harm from teachers, parents or other learners), intellectual (learner feels helpless, stressed for time, overmatched without needed resources or skills, challenged or mocked on the basis of expressed ideas) or emotional (embarrassed, humiliated, made fun of, disciplined publicly or made an example of through isolation or a "lesson" taught). The groundbreaking work of O'Keefe and Nadel has revealed that under any type of perceived threat, the brain:

* loses its ability to take in subtle clues from the environment
* reverts to the familiar "tried and true" behaviors
* loses some of it's ability to index, store and access
* becomes more automatic and limited
* loses some of its ability to perceive relationships and patterns
* is less able to do the "higher order" thinking skills
* loses some memory capacity
* tends to over-react to stimuli - in an almost "phobic" way

Example: You're taking an important exam: the pressure is on, and you are having trouble thinking of an answer. But the moment you turn the test in and walk outside, the pressure's over and voila! The answer pops into your head. But now it's too late.

Similarly, the teacher suddenly calls a student for an answer. The student may or may not know the answer, but in the "moment of truth," while everyone else is watching and waiting, he forgets what he knows. The teacher then calls on another student (another "victim" of the minimizing).

Implications: Many learners may actually be much better thinkers, use more complex problem-solving skills, be more intelligent and less troublesome than previously thought IF the threats are removed from their environment.

Action Steps:
Threats have to be removed from the learning environment. If you have a reward system, you automatically have threat, too. The presence of rewards makes their withdrawal a threat.

Make the learning environment a safe, relaxed environment. Eliminate reward systems which either are controlled by an outside agency (you, the institution, etc.) or provide material rewards with market value (food, coupons, discounts, etc.).

Avoid calling on learners unless they volunteer. Eliminate discipline policies which work by threat, score keeping or embarrassment. Never threaten a student by saying you'll send them to a higher authority, kick them out or call their parents. Give more time for classwork. Reduce the threat of grades by providing more frequent feedback. Make the assessments more genuine and meaningful by making them less stressful and less threatening.

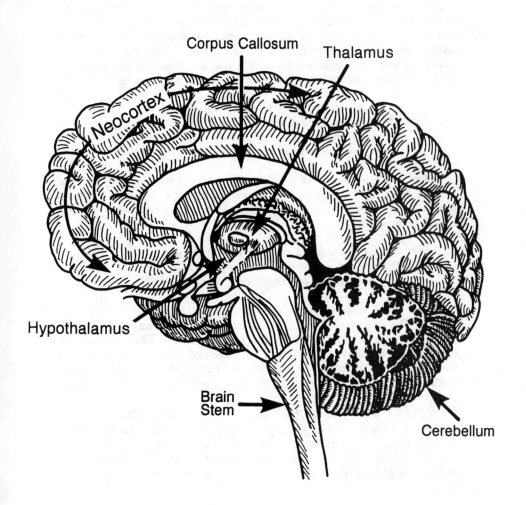

Corpus Callosum

Thalamus

Neocortex

Hypothalamus

Brain
Stem

Cerebellum

Different Stresses Produce Different Results

Research Summary: Researchers O'Keefe and Nadel, Jacobs and Nadel, and Dientsbier discovered that the body has "good stress" and "bad stress". The positive forms of stress occur when we feel challenged and want to "rise to the occasion". In those cases, the body releases adrenaline and noradrenaline, which actually heighten our perceptions, increase motivation and even enhance physical strength. The circumstances for positive stress are particular. Positive stress occurs when we feel we have:

* perceived a solution to a problem
* have the ability to resolve a problem
* have some control over a situation
* get sufficient rest between challenges

The negative form of stress ("distress") occurs when we feel stressed by some kind of threat, such as embarrassment, loss of prestige, being pressed for time or having lack of choice. It also occurs when we feel helpless because we:

* don't perceive a solution to a problem
* lack the resources to solve a problem
* have little or no control over a situation

The body responds to negative stress by releasing the hormone cortisol. The area of the brain most affected is the hippocampus, which is very sensitive (reacting negatively) to this hormone. That weakens the brain's locale memory and indexing systems, and may narrow perceptual "mapping". The hippocampus is also the center of the body's immune system, so the release of cortisol weakens the body's ability to fight disease.

Example: Some people lead highly busy, tightly scheduled lives, working 10-12 hours a day, six days a week, and they are healthy, stress-free and happy. Others have routine, predictable jobs, working 30-40 hours a week, and they feel tired, stressed and unhappy. The differences in their feeling of well-being come from the two different kinds of stresses at work.

Implications: It's possible that some learners who are under-performing are simply under distress. It was either created by others or themselves, but they may not have the resources to recognize or change the stress level. They may not even know they are living under this stress if it's been with them all their lives. The stresses may be originating in the learner's home or work life or in the classroom or training room.

228

Action Steps: Insure that learners have the following conditions met: 1) they perceive a solution is possible; 2) they have the resources to solve it; 3) they have control over the situation; 4) they have sufficient time to do the learning; 5) they have the knowledge and skills to recognize and manage their own stress levels. Utilize exercise, hydration and "purposeful play" (learning games) to keep the learning stress low. It may also be up to the instructional leader to do relaxation training.

Learner Anxiety Impairs Visual Acuity

Research Summary: In what ways does the brain respond to stress? Could test anxiety and high pressure teaching cause eyes to underperform? Yes, says researcher and optometrist Dr. Ray Gottleib. His work at the Eye Gym and the results of another Connecticut study have prompted him to speak out. He says, "A major cause of nearsightedness and other visual problems is the tension generated by current methods of education."

In one study, nearsightedness was reduced by 50% when teachers used stress reducing techniques at exam time and the teaching was more multi-sensory. The body's physical response to stress and threat can vary from constricted breathing, increased heartbeat, excessive blinking, and poor posture to diminished thinking capacity. Gottleib's work and the Connecticut study are the first to show actual changes in eyesight.

Example: Watch a learner under moderate to high stress and you'll see constant blinking and fidgeting behavior.

Implications: We are just beginning to comprehend and appreciate all of the deleterious effects of stress on the body and brain.

Action Steps: Keep stress low and threats out of the learning environment.

Best Bet Resource: Contact: Gottleib, 1433 Crenshaw Blvd. Los Angeles, CA 90019, (213) 936-5230.

Stress & Violence Can Devastate Brain

Research Summary: Dr. Christopher Coe, a University of Wisconsin psychologist, has done extensive research on the effects of prenatal stress, poor parenting, infant stress and traumatic childhood events. Researcher Kotulak reports that Coe's work shows consistent and dramatic effects indicating how the brain is devastated.

In an over stressed child, excess adrenaline and cortisol are released. This overproduction cannot be processed by the system efficiently so that it can eventually return to a normal unstressed state. Instead, the excess hormones can mutate the learner's genes, switching them on and off at the wrong times. This causes the brain to build abnormal brain-cell networks.

In this groundbreaking research, Coe says that certain kinds of negative stimulation causing bad experiences can organize the brain's trillions of cells into diseased networks. The damage to the learner, the evidence indicates, is that he is more likely to develop learning disorders, aggression, language failures, depression and immunity problems. The damage may also lead to asthma, epilepsy, hypertension and diabetes. Coe says, "Bad parenting may stamp an individual for a lifetime, not only in terms of their behavior and emotions, but literally their predisposition for disease."

Others agree. Neuroscientist Bruce McEwen of Rockefeller University says, "This means that the environment... has a major role in shaping our individuality by shaping the expression of genes." Then he describes the implications: "People need to be aware that the brain is so... vulnerable, if something happens early in life it can have permanent consequences for how a kid develops and learns." Baylor College neurologist Pierson has discovered that bad developmental experiences can cause deadly seizures 100% of the time in laboratory animals.

Former University of Chicago researcher and current Baylor neuropsychiatrist, Bruce Perry, says, "Developmental experiences determine the capability of the brain to do things. If you don't change those developmental experiences, you're not going to change the hardware of the brain and we'll end up building more prisons."

University of California, San Francisco neuroscientist Michael Merzenich adds, "We can now see how a learning disability could arise from a child's bad experiences." He further adds, "We can see how the brain can become unstable and why that instability can result in a variety of neurological [problems]." What is scary is that all of these problems keep increasing because the forces that create the stress and trauma keep increasing, too. In other words, more stress and violence in our society means more learning problems and a lower standard of living, more crime, health problems and costs for everyone.

Example: The Chicago public schools have long been criticized for their problems. But a study of more than 1,000 students from poor Chicago neighborhoods found that 74% had personally witnessed a violent crime. Half of them were themselves a victim of a violent crime. These students live their lives in a constant state of violence and stress. The chances are high that the students' brains (and genes) have been affected. Which means that their genes will be passed on to their children, perpetuating the problem.

Implications: One in five children in America is raised in poverty. Sociologists have long equated poverty with higher levels of stress and violence. In the last 25 years there has been a dramatic increase in the rates of depression, violence and drug abuse. In another study, one child in five under age 18 was reported to have a learning, emotional or behavioral disorder. Just a coincidence? Unlikely.

Action Steps: The solution is twofold: First, give students a sense of self-worth, a feeling of importance and uniqueness. Second, teach them that they are not helpless. Help the learner to discover what areas of life can be controlled so that the "victim" mentality is never cultivated. Teach learners how to influence more of their lives. Help your own learners to develop the skills, strategies and motivation to take greater control of their lives.

Summary of Action Steps

1. Identify substandard learner behaviors. Identify areas of threats, both implied and explicit. Avoid reliance on extrinsic rewards. As much as possible, remove threats from the learning environment and introduce alternative forms of motivation, such as novelty, curiosity, positive social bonding and relevant content.

2. Make the learning environment a safe, relaxed environment. Avoid calling on learners unless they volunteer. Eliminate discipline policies which work by threat, score keeping or embarrassment. Give more time for classwork. Reduce the threat of grades by providing more frequent feedback. Make the assessments genuine and meaningful.

3. Insure that learners have the following conditions met: 1) they perceive a solution is possible; 2) they have the resources to solve it; 3) they have control over the situation; 4) they have sufficient time to do the learning; 5) they have the knowledge and skills to recognize and manage their own stress levels. You may need to do relaxation training as well.

4. Increase support and encouragement. Make the testing or other assessment times less stressful by encouraging partner work, allowing stretch breaks, giving immediate successes followed by engaging complex projects and giving verbal encouragement.

5. Give students a sense of self-worth, a feeling of importance and uniqueness. Teach them that they are not helpless. Help the learner to discover what areas of life can be controlled so that the "victim" mentality is never cultivated.

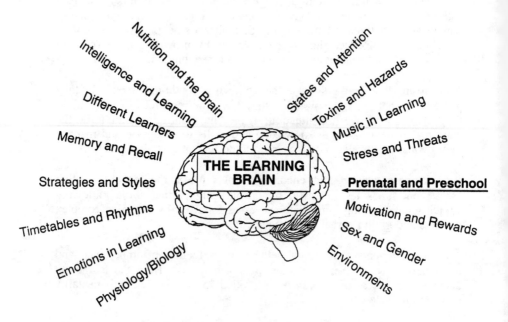

Nutrition and the Brain
Intelligence and Learning
Different Learners
Memory and Recall
Strategies and Styles
Timetables and Rhythms
Emotions in Learning
Physiology/Biology

States and Attention
Toxins and Hazards
Music in Learning
Stress and Threats
Prenatal and Preschool
Motivation and Rewards
Sex and Gender
Environments

THE LEARNING
BRAIN

Chapter Thirteen

CHAPTER THIRTEEN

Prenatal &
Preschool

Cell Growth Explosive in Young Brains

Research Summary: University of Chicago neurobiologist Peter Huttenlocher discovered critical information about brain growth. His research showed just how fast the early brain grows. A 28 week old fetal brain tissue sample showed 124 million brain connections. A newborn brain tissue sample had 253 million connections, and an eight month old infant had 572 million.

But the growth of the number of connections, Huttenlocher soon learned, slowed down by the end of the first year and stabilized at about 354 million per tissue sample. He says, "It was strange.... The number of connections kept going up and up and then they started to go down." His research proved that the fetal brain over-produces cells and that unless they find a connection or a "job" to do in the body, they die off. After birth, there is major "die-off" of cells unless they are used and that half can disappear by puberty. He says that under stimulation and lack of interaction with the outside world causes the cell death. The future number of brain cells could vary by as much as 25% depending on the quality and quantity of enrichment offered to the learner.

Example: Huttenlocher says the brain has spurts of growth so fast that it would be like trying to count raindrops in a heavy, driving thunderstorm. Obviously, the total number of connections available in the entire brain at the early stages of development is nearly incalculable.

Implications: It is extremely important to provide stimulation and the best of care for the newborn. The brain is ripe for many new learning experiences.

Action Steps: Provide education to pregnant women and mothers of newborns about the brain, their child, and the potential for growth and learning.

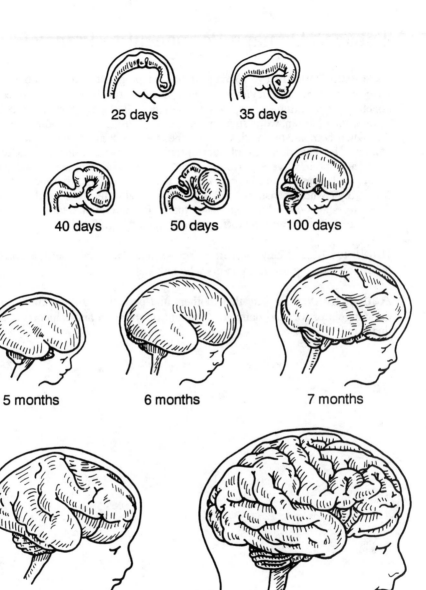

25 days

35 days

40 days

50 days

100 days

5 months

6 months

7 months

8 months

9 months

Tobacco Damage Permanent to Prenatals

Research Summary: Many studies on pregnant women who smoke have been done and reviewed. Fox et al. says that the evidence is conclusive: smoking causes lifelong damage. If the mother continued to smoke, the children were smaller and less intelligent. The good news is that when comparison studies were done, the children of women who quit smoking for the duration of their pregnancies were taller and heavier. And their brain's were different, too: these children performed at a "statistically significant higher level" on the General Cognitive Index of the McCarthy (which measures thinking skills). Naturally, to keep the studies accurate, statistical adjustment was made for environmental, social and personality factors, and the differences were still significant.

Implications: Many learners in school may have had damage done to their brains by unknowing parents who smoked.

Action Steps: Be sure that mothers and potential mothers know about the dangers of tobacco damage. Provide information and support to help them quit.

Prenatal Protein May Boost Learning

Research Summary: Rush, Stein & Susser report that when high-protein supplements were given to pregnant mothers, their newborn children began demonstrating superior learning behaviors even as early as the first 12 months of age. These mothers were divided into three groups, each given daily supplements in different combinations, as follows: 1) low doses of mineral and vitamin supplements; 2) high doses of vitamin and mineral supplements; and 3) mineral, vitamin, and protein supplements. The mothers receiving the protein supplements bore children who were more attentive in tests, and demonstrated rapid adaptation to repeated events.

Example: The babies of the women who took protein supplements explored their environments more, were more aware of changes and had played for longer periods of time.

Implications: Early persistence, attentiveness and alertness are strongly influenced by maternal diet.

Action Steps: Provide information about the importance of prenatal nutrition, including the positive role of protein in the diet.

Stressful Pregnancies Spawn Disorders

Research Summary: Judy Lauter, language disorder specialist at the University of Oklahoma Health Center, and Dr. Paula Tallal, co-director of the Center for Molecular and Behavioral Neuroscience at Rutgers University, confirm that a low-stress pregnancy is critical. Otherwise, there's a higher likelihood that learner problems may develop, reports Kotulak.

Schneider has also verified this phenomenon. His studies on primate infants showed that stress significantly impaired the performance of the infant on a standardized battery of neuromotor tests. Language problems are also associated with stressful pregnancies because of a developmental quirk: the male sex hormone testosterone exerts a profound effect on the fetus during the first six weeks following conception; during this amazing prenatal formative time, a stress-induced, late-developing left hemisphere means language problems.

Example: The frequency and impact of these effects continues to rise. You may have noticed that there are more learners diagnosed with language disorders--one of the stressful pregnancy effects. One of many correlations is that stress levels in society have never been higher.

Implications: Stress is more than annoying. It is more than a killer. It just may be helping to create a whole generation of impaired learners.

Action Steps: Educate expectant mothers about the importance of keeping stress low whenever possible. Keep stress low in your own learning environments.

Permanent Effects of Prenatal Malnutrition

Research Summary: A synthesis of research on prenatal nutrition by Morgane et al. explains clearly why some students have learning difficulties. Morgane says that nutrition is the single greatest influence on the fetus and protein deficiencies are the most destructive. The effects are widespread: there are distorted proportions of neurons and glia, poor formation of neuronal circuits and alterations of normal patterns of axonal and dendritic pruning.

Malnutrition also results in deviations in normal age-related sequences of brain maturation and formations of neurotransmitter systems. The most critical deficit is in the creation of functional neuronal isolation from the environment. This single effect impairs attentional and interactive relationships with the outside world. As a result, learning disabilities are highly likely.

Example: In areas where adequate nutrition is lacking, there's a high correlation to learning disorders, slower learners, illiteracy and learning disabilities. Third world countries and low income rural and urban areas all have the same learning problems.

Implications: Through early prevention, we may be able to prevent many problems that occur in learners later on in life.

Action Steps: Focus on improving the nutrition as much as the learning and education of children who are malnourished. Provide newsletters and bulletins about nutrition for expectant mothers and other parents with school children. Make sure pregnant mothers get adequate protein. This promotion of nutrition can best be encouraged in a cross-disciplinary manner, incorporating behavioral, sociological, educational and culturally sensitive approaches.

Infants Born With Pre-Learned Languages

Research Summary: Research by psychologist Kuhl at the University of Washington in Seattle, and reported by Grunwald and Goldberg, has proven that even infants six months old can recognize sounds and make language distinctions of up to 150 sounds in human speech. Kuhl thinks that this verifies that babies, even those from four months old and up, are "universal linguists," able to lip read and connect vowel sounds with lip movements.

University of San Diego psychologist Thal confirms this. She says that although we don't know exactly how many words babies understand, we know from simple listen-response games and testing that they understand a lot. In fact, her studies indicate that the ratio of "known words" to "spoken words" (comprehension to expression) may be as high as 100 to one.

Example: You may be talking to an infant as you put him to bed. The baby cannot talk back to you, but may understand fairly well what you are saying.

Implications: Parents may want to be much more careful about how they speak around their infants. By talking "down" too much (using overly simple infant wording instead of normal adult talk), you may simply be delaying their development.

Also, if you'd like your child to learn a foreign language, the best way is to expose them to it briefly during the pre-school years. All they need is to learn about ten to fifteen phrases in a conversational context, and the brain will have the patterns, rhythms and tonality for the future, more thorough learning of that language.

Action Steps: Be a role model of good language skills for your infant. Avoid profanity. Avoid "baby talk". Be patient and use a great deal of body language to help your infant learn.

Best Bet Resource: *What Infants Know* by Mehler and Dupoux

Early Stimulation Critical to Development

Research Summary: Research by neurobiologists Shatz at UC Berkeley and Jacobs at UCLA, and quoted by Kotulak, proves that early stimulation is more critical than earlier thought. These scientists now say that most brain functions of memory, learning, attention, stress response and emotion are molded in early development when the brain is most malleable.

Their research verifies that the fetal brain is a very different entity from the infant brain which, in turn, is very different from the adolescent brain; and the adolescent brain is very different from the adult brain. Shatz says, "That takes people by surprise.... [T]hey always think the brain just gets bigger." There is a specific receptivity to certain functions that will dramatically influence later life. If that receptivity is not accessed, learning capacity is diminished.

Harvard child specialist, Dr. Felton Earls, agrees: "A kind of irreversibility sets in.... There is this shaping process that goes on early, and then at the end of this process, be that age 2, 3, or 4, you have essentially designed a brain...." That is not to say that you can't learn as much or as fast. But the structure of your learning is defined early.

What is amazing is that now scientists know that everyday events, as well as traumatic ones, physically re-shape the brain. In fact, almost anything can alter the structure as well as the content of the brain. "The new thing is that the brain is very dynamic," said Dr. Robert Post, the chief of biological psychiatry at the National Institute of Mental Health. He adds, "At any point in this process you have all the potentials for either good or bad stimulation to get in there and set the microstructure of the brain."

Example: Children whose parents talk to them frequently and gently develop better language skills than those whose parents don't. Lack of visual stimulation in the first weeks after birth will permanently impair vision development. Early exposure to violence and stress increases impulsiveness and likelihood for hypertension. Infants who get enriched sensory stimulation with plenty of touching and handling become more mentally alert and physically stronger.

Implications: Give children the best possible early years and they'll be more likely to be a contributing member of society. Head start and other positive pre-school programs may be essential for bringing up healthy children.

Neurobiologist Pierson says, "If you fail to learn the proper fundamentals at an early age, then you are in big trouble. You can't suddenly learn to learn when you haven't first laid down the basic brain wiring.... That's why early education is so important." Dr. Goodwin at the National Institute of Mental Health says, "We are underinvested in our children.... We spend seven times more per capita on the elderly than we do on our children. Now that we have better concepts of the plasticity of the brain, it's obvious that we are wasting a tremendous resource." Neurobiologist Huttenlocher says, "If you want to significantly influence a child's ability to think and acquire knowledge, the early childhood years are very critical."

We now know how critical are the pre-school and free lunch programs. Every bit of help we give infants and pre-schoolers will return the investment many-fold. Not only that, but because of the brain's special receptivity at an early age, the absolute best time to reach them is those first few years.

Action Steps: Support preschool and early childhood schooling and adequate nutrition. Let parents know what they can do to positively influence their children. Hold a parent workshop or print up a newsletter. Get referral sources for better parenting classes.

Best Bet Resources: *Your Child's Growing Mind,* by Healy. *Awakening Your Child's Natural Genius,* by Armstrong.

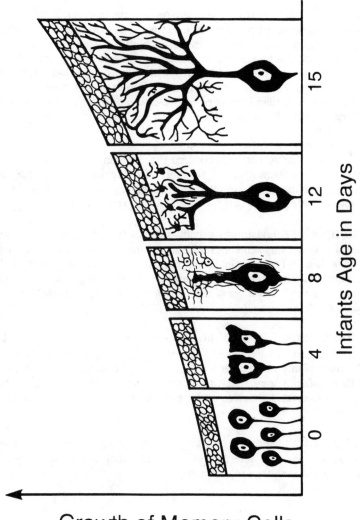

Growth of Memory Cells

Infants Age in Days

Talking to Babies Builds Better Brains

Research Summary: Kotulak reports on research done by Janellen Huttenlocher of the University of Chicago. She's done landmark studies on how the brain utilizes its enormous capacity to learn, even as an infant. Studies show that babies whose mothers talked to them, regardless of the vocabulary level, grew better brains with more connections, and increased their vocabulary sooner. At 20 months, babies of talkative mothers knew 131 more words than infants of untalkative mothers, and by two years, the difference was 295 words. She says that the babies listen, even though they can't understand.

While the research discovered the importance of talking, there was something else interesting. The study also highlighted the importance of pointing out things to infants. By linking up the words and the objects, actions or persons, the babies' vocabularies grew even faster.

Example: Television as a baby-sitter is no substitute for mother. The inert TV blurts out sentences without the real-world context needed in the infant's life. The slower-paced question and answer style of "Mister Roger's Neighborhood" is far superior to the fast-paced cartoon-styled "Sesame Street", but a book read (interactively) by a parent or sibling is the best.

Implications: Today's high-speed, microwave lifestyle could have serious effects for tomorrow's learners. The busy single working parents who have plenty to do after a long, hard day of work (with no time to read to their infants) may find that both are getting short-changed. Frequent day care users and absentee parents risk language development lags in their children.

Action Steps: Educate working parents about the dangers of absentee parenting. Provide alternatives to insure that the children are getting attention and language interactions.

Infant Brain Ready for Pattern Recognition

Research Summary: Do infants recognize more complex facial patterns or only simple and basic objects? Researcher Grunwald reports on studies conducted by Carnegie Mellon Institute's Mark Johnson. He did experiments with infants as young as ten minutes past birth. Infants in that study demonstrated a marked preference for human faces over random drawings or blank ovals. Johnson believes that infants are all pre-programmed to recognize the human face because it "aids our survival by helping us recognize our meal ticket."

Example: An infants sees the familiar face of his mother and smiles, makes a gesture, kicks or makes a sound.

Implications: This is news to traditional child development pioneers who believed that babies are born with a "blank slate" brain. Current research is validating the theory that we are genetically programmed to learn much of what we need to know for daily survival.

Action Steps: Treat newborns and infants with great respect. They already have a lot going for them, beginning at birth.

Best Bet Resource: *What Infants Know* by Mehler and Dupoux

Memory Develops Surprisingly Early

Research Summary: Grunwald and Goldberg report that even infants can recall elaborate details about past events. In research by Rovee-Collier at Rutgers University, infants can remember four-step sequences after only five tries and recall them months later. Psychologist Clifton, working with Meyers at the University of Massachusetts, has proved that even at six months old, infants can recall things two years later. Meyers says, "[W]e didn't think that infants could represent in their memories the events that were going on around them, but put them back in a similar situation, as we did, and you make the memory accessible."

The work on infants by Hayne, Boller, and Rovee-Collier shows an early and lasting ability of infants to recall information when it is embedded in place cues. Boller says, "We conclude that each individual training episode is encoded in terms of the context in which it occurs. The memory of a given episode, however, is recorded in terms of the most recent context in which it is active. This mechanism permits memories that are highly context-specific to be updated and subsequently retrieved in new and potentially appropriate settings."

Example: Infants remember who introduced them to certain toys, where something happened and how to play with a toy that hasn't been used for six months.

Implications: Many events--both good and bad--that we think go unnoticed by infants are in fact being stored in their memory and will be recalled in the future.

Action Steps: Avoid underestimating an infant's ability to remember what is happening around him or to him. There is more ability inside his brain than he is usually able to communicate to you.

Amazing Brain Pre-Programmed in Math

Research Summary: Researchers have devised fascinating experiments to determine what pre-language infants know and don't know. Karen Wynn, a psychologist at the University of Arizona, reported that infants as young as five months old can do basic addition and subtraction. In experiments with infants, she documented that infants look longer at things that are novel or unexpected to them. She used dolls and puppets and enacted simple addition and subtraction, grouping them and making them appear and disappear.

Using a video, she recorded the reaction of the infants, which ranged from expressions of acceptance ("I know that") to expressions of surprise, indicated by looks of "You tricked me" or "Hold it, that's not right." This is a pre-language indicator of what they know or don't know. In her testing, infants proved that they can predict the outcome of simple addition and subtraction with solid objects. Because this ability appears in infants before any instruction, Wynn believes that the babies' basic numerical understanding is "an innate mechanism, somehow built into the biological structure."

Strauss, at the University of Pittsburgh, agrees: "Five-month olds are clearly thinking about quantities and applying numerical concepts to their world." Levine et al. add, "These results suggest that children's earliest ability to add and subtract is based on experiences combining and separating sets of objects . . . and that this ability precedes the development of conventional verbal methods of calculating."

Example: You hide objects under a blanket and an infant waits in suspense. Once the blanket is removed, the expression on the infant's face tells you whether your actions were a surprise or anticipated.

Implications: This research reminds us that we may not be born with a "blank slate". Rather, we may be already programmed to learn certain things.

Action Steps: Support early childhood programs that allow children, when ready, to start learning challenging subjects.

Best Bet Resource: Glen Doman's Better Baby Institute in Philadelphia or *What Infants Know* by Mehler and Dupoux

Baby's Brain "Pre-Wired" to Learn Physics

Research Summary: In studies by Vygotsky, children consistently were able to formulate scientific concepts far ahead of the more expected thinking and development stages. In another more recent article, Grunwald and Goldberg report that Cornell University psychologist Elizabeth Spelke has discovered that even four month-old babies know the basics of physics.

Using video cameras to record infant reactions, Spelke has discovered that infants respond differently based on whether they predict or expect a certain reaction or demonstration to occur. She sets up her infants in front of a puppet stage and re-creates various expected and unexpected actions: rolling a ball, bouncing a ball, suspending the ball, moving around or through objects. Some of the ball movements are ordinary and predictable and others are impossible in the world of everyday physics. The reactions that infants have can tell the researcher whether the baby thinks the outcome is "right" (infant agrees; it was anticipated) or "wrong" (infant shows look of surprise or disbelief).

Example: Mothers or fathers often enjoy playing the game "peek-a-boo". It deals with surprise and expectancy. But it also proves what babies predict and what they are genuinely surprised by.

Implications: From a developmental point of view, we may have vastly underestimated the minds of infants and been slowing their development. Our lowered expectations can cause slower development.

Action Steps: Support early learning programs. Provide a wide range of novelty and challenges for infants. Give infants many ways and chances to enjoy learning and prove abilities.

Personality Predictable at 10 Months

Research Summary: University of Wisconsin professor Dr. Richard Davidson has been using brain imaging devices to read left-right hemispheric patterns in infants. Kotulak reports that his research shows particular patterns that predispose a child to become a good learner or a poor one. In fact, Davidson can even predict whether a child will cry or not when separated from his mother. These traits have to do with how the 10-month old infant's brain reacts to fear, novelty or stress. The children who cry have less left hemispheric activity than those who don't.

Children who are hesitant to explore and are more fearful also have less left hemispheric activity. These children are often more prone to depression and learning disorders. As they grow, they are more likely to blame themselves for failures and get depressed. Those who are more left-hemisphere dominant, on the other hand, tend to look for factors that they can control and adapt to new learning situations by correcting previous mistakes. Davidson says that, unless specific counter-measures are taken, "[t]hese individual differences are stable trait-like attributes. They show up early in life and are consistent over time."

The brain not only gives personality hints early in life, it is also very malleable, too. One could be diagnosed as having a strong pattern which would make a future learning disorder likely; one could also do therapy early enough so that the problem is solved before the child even comes to school. A top researcher has just released studies showing that learning disorders, anxiety, depression, sleep disorders and emotional problems can be predicted very early in life.

The good news is that because of the prediction qualities of the current brain imaging technologies, early detection and intervention is possible. Once these "at-risk" infants are identified, new positive learning experiences can be offered which will help re-wire the brain into a less fearful one, more capable of learning. Davidson thinks that by training young children in how to think and learn from mistakes, we can reduce many problems later on in life.

Example: Mother leaves the room and her infant starts crying. Mother doesn't know why.

Implications: Right and left hemispheric brain development may have many more implications than earlier thought.

Action Steps: One strategy suggested is to encourage more left-hemisphere processes from infants. These include talking more, counting games, problem-solving and puzzles. Give infants more physical activity and have them spend less time in a car seat, walker or other restraining device. Encourage more cross lateral activities like walking, crawling and play.

Infant Nutrition Boosts Intelligence

Research Summary: In a study on food supplements given to children during the first year of their lives, there appeared a significant difference in later IQ scores compared to the scores of those who did not receive the supplements, says Connors. The children who took the enriched supplements (iron-fortified foods, high protein breakfasts and vitamin enriched fruit juice) far outpaced their siblings on intelligence measures.

Example: The supplements worked: The gain was a 17 point IQ advantage on verbal and 13 point gain on nonverbal.

Implications: Good nutrition in the early years can make a real difference in intelligence levels later on.

Action Steps: Make education about proper nutrition available to parents. Encourage appropriate dietary or nutritional supplements. A breakfast with eggs, juice and multi-vitamin and mineral supplements is excellent. Let parents and children know about the long-term effects.

Learning Disorders Predictable at One Year

Research Summary: Grunwald and Goldberg report that Nathan Fox at the University of Maryland has found that troubled infants have a predictable brain wave pattern which foretells later emotional and learning problems. Fox has the infants wear an EEG (electrocephlagram) bonnet which measures specific brain wave responses to toys and games. He found that inhibited babies have a different pattern than the emotionally healthy ones.

Dr. Mary Rothbart of the University of Washington says that parents need to have a soothing, reassuring relationship with their babies, so that they never feel abandoned. Dr. Stanley Greenspan of Bethesda, Md., says that we can now treat the common "garden-variety" of disorders that infants have in just a few sessions. (It's the parents who get the treatment.)

Example: How can you tell if the baby is a likely candidate for learning disorders? Here's one of many ways. An infant is separated from his mother for thirty seconds in a supermarket. Does the baby get puzzled and start to look for his mother? Or, does the baby panic, start screaming and cry? The infant who reacts with terror is more likely to have learning problems later on. Why? The baby has been brought up to feel insecure far too easily.

Implications: We are raising, through thoughtless or ignorant parenting, countless children who may develop learning problems.

Action Steps: What babies need the most are often what parents are least able to give them: time and touching. Encourage parents to find or make the time to do both. Also make sure parents know about all of the books, workshops, counseling or tapes, and any other resource available.

Start Foreign Language Learning Early

Research Summary: Kotulak reports that UCLA neurologist Harry Chugani can show conclusive biological and chronological receptivities towards learning languages. He used PET (positron emission tomography) to measure brain activity at all ages. He found that the brain spurt from ages 4-10 was so explosive that the brain literally craves any and all new experiences. The neurons desperately await any stimulation, experience or learning that will justify their existence and create a new learned structure.

How we go about learning languages is a perfect example. Words heard by an infant send electrochemical signals to specific parts of the brain where they activate learning in meaning, sentence construction and intonation. Millions of cells with heightened receptivity and sensitivity are mobilized to learn virtually any language. Without this activation, the brain is cheated. By age ten, many of the cells most receptive to learning languages are starting to dying off.

Of course, new languages can be learned after age 10 - but with much effort and usually with an accent. Chugani says, "Who's the idiot that decided that children should learn foreign languages in high school? We're not paying attention to biological principles.... [T]he time to learn these is in preschool or elementary school.... There should be more emphasis on earlier education for all key areas - language, music, math and problem-solving."

Education expert Dr. Nico Spinelli agrees. "A better plan ... would be for children to learn to pronounce perfectly fifty or so words of, say, German, French, Japanese and Spanish. Later on, one or more of these languages could be learned more easily and with no accent, because the brain would have been primed for it."

Example: A native Japanese learning English at age 13 will have a Japanese accent. He will have difficulty pronouncing the English "R" sound. But a Japanese child born and raised in America speaks perfect English, with no difficulty pronouncing the "R".

Implications: A great deal of optimal language instruction opportunity is missed when schools start foreign languages at age 13 or 14.

Action Steps: Make foreign language learning mandatory for all first, second and third graders. Expose them to at least three languages. Plant the seeds. As long as they have learned the intonation, rhythm and 100-200 key phrases, the language basics will be available for life. Even if the language is not studied until later years.

Summary of Action Steps

1. Provide education to pregnant women and mothers of newborns about the brain, their child, and the potential for growth and learning.

2. Be sure that mothers and potential mothers know about the dangers of tobacco damage. Provide information and support to help them quit.

3. Provide information about the importance of prenatal nutrition, including the positive role of protein in the diet.

4. Educate expectant mothers about the importance of keeping stress low.

5. Focus on improving the nutrition as much as the learning and education of children who are malnourished. Provide newsletters and bulletins about nutrition for expectant mothers and other parents with school children. Make sure pregnant mothers get adequate protein. This promotion of nutrition can best be encouraged in a cross-disciplinary manner, incorporating behavioral, sociological, educational and culturally sensitive approaches.

6. Be a role model of good language skills for your infant. Avoid profanity. Avoid "baby talk". Be patient and use a great deal of body language to help learning.

7. Educate working moms about the dangers of absentee parenting. Provide alternatives to insure that the children are getting attention and language interactions.

8. Do not underestimate an infant's ability to remember what is happening around him or to him. There is more inside his brain than he is able to communicate to you.

9. Encourage more left-hemisphere processes from infants. These include talking more, counting games, problem-solving and puzzles. Give infants more physical activity and have them spend less time in a car seat, walker or other restraining device. Encourage more cross lateral activities like walking, crawling and play.

10. Make foreign language learning mandatory for all first, second and third graders. Expose them to at least three languages. Plant the seeds. It will pay off dramatically in the later years.

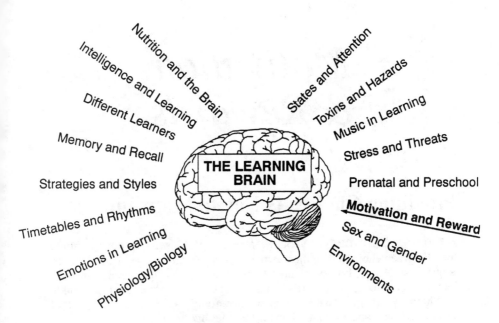

Nutrition and the Brain

Intelligence and Learning

Different Learners

Memory and Recall

Strategies and Styles

Timetables and Rhythms

Emotions in Learning

Physiology/Biology

THE LEARNING BRAIN

States and Attention

Toxins and Hazards

Music in Learning

Stress and Threats

Prenatal and Preschool

Motivation and Reward

Sex and Gender

Environments

Chapter Fourteen

CHAPTER FOURTEEN

Motivation & Rewards

Providing Choices is Key to Motivation

Research Summary: Should learners be told what to do, or should they be given choice? The answer partly depends on the age of the learner. Regardless of age, however, most learners are given little choice in their learning situations, which are organized, routed, facilitated and structured for them by others. That's not good, according to the research teams of Deci and Ryan, and Deci, Vallerand, Pelletier and Ryan.

When students are given control over the content and process of their learning, motivation goes up, say Mager and McCann. But to motivate learners, it is important to allow them to make choices "about personally relevant aspects of a learning activity." Students need to be able to align self-determination goals with instructional goals.

In addition, learners who tend to focus more on fun and friendships may be able to be engaged when there are ample opportunities for self-determination and peer interaction, says Wentzel. These provide ways to meet personal goals and, to some, degree, instructional goals. In other words, the more ways the goals can serve the learner's own agendas, the better.

Example: A student is willing to work on a team project because there's another person on the project that he likes and would like to get to know better.

Implications: There are ways to tap into learning, excitement and participation levels for many learners who appear to be unmotivated.

Action Steps: Help learners to become more aware of their own personal, academic, health, social, athletic and career goals. Design instructional experiences that allow for more ways for learners to meet their own goals. They need ways to show off, meet new people, be an expert in something, grow, get in shape or become well-respected.

"Flow State" is Compelling for Learning

Research Summary: Noted University of Chicago psychologist Mihaly Csikszentmihalyi explains that optimal learning requires a state of consciousness known as "flow". This uninterrupted state in which one "loses oneself" in the performance is well known as a timeless, pleasure-producing absorption in the experience. Children, teenagers and athletes often get into this state more easily than adults.

But in new research, Csikszentmihalyi says that adults can get into this "magical state" everyday. The formula is simple, he says. When "[C]hallenges are greater than your skills, that's anxiety. When your skills exceed the challenges, that's boredom." But match up the challenge and skill levels, and whamo! Jackpot! You get the perfect learning state, or "flow".

Example: Studies done on task difficulty at the National Institute of Mental Health in Maryland showed greater brain activity when the tasks increased in complexity and difficulty. Even when the learners were unsuccessful on very challenging experiments, the brain continued to be actively engaged. You play much better in a game of tennis than your partner. You get bored and want to quit. But then Jim Courier or Steffi Graff invites you to play and you experience anxiety.

Implications: Much of what passes for instruction is not the "flow" experience. It is didactic lecturing that lacks joyfulness and abandonment to the flow of learning.

Action Steps: Start a task simply and upgrade the challenge to the point where it provides challenge without anxiety. You'll know you're at that stage when you lose track of time and automatically screen out distractions.

Rewards Destroy Learner Creativity

Research Summary: A study by Brandeis University researcher Teresa Amabile found that, in many areas, reward systems lower the quality of the work produced. She conducted more than two dozen studies over nearly 20 years with the same results: in the long run, rewards don't work. Among artists, creativity (as judged by their peers) dropped when they already had signed a contract to sell the work upon completion. The fact that they knew for sure that they were going to be paid for the work lessened their fullest expression.

Example: In reading, learners were offered rewards for getting the reading done and for remembering key bits of information. The results were devastating: learners not only had worse memory for the "key" information, but also the recollection of "incidental" information dropped to almost nothing.

Implications: The example above perfectly demonstrates the disadvantage of rewards. In terms of reading enjoyment, the incidental and peripheral information is often equally or more important than the key information. It is also considered essential to creativity and understanding because of the contextual base it provides.

Action Steps: Reduce or eliminate the use of rewards.

Best Bet Resources: *Punished by Rewards* by Alfie Kohn, *Growing up Creative*, by Teresa Amabile. *Seven Kinds of Smart*, by Thomas Armstrong.

Optimal Motivation Conditions Discovered

Research Summary: Drawing from the combined work of Singer, Glasser, Hart, Wlodlowski, Murphy and Donovan, we can outline what the brain needs for optimal motivation:

1) Meaning derived from perceived needs and relevant content.
2) Positive social bonding.
3) Low stress and high challenge "states." Some call these states of "relaxed alertness" adjustable, flexible goals.
4) Control over our learning.
5) Distinctive, thematic "real-world" immersion environments.
6) A risk-free, playful and safe learning climate.
7) Hope.

Example: Optimal motivation conditions would be present for learners working on a team, with members they like (and feel safe to dialog with), choosing how to solve a problem (that they originally chose), with a moderate, but not constricting, time deadline in an interesting environment.

Implications: Rarely are the most motivating conditions for learning met in either a school or business context. This may explain why so many have been labeled as "underachievers" or "low" students.

Action Steps: Do your best to implement as many of the optimal motivating conditions possible as much of the time possible. Avoid labeling any learner as a "low" or unmotivated student until he has had the consistent experience of optimal conditions and a chance to prove himself.

Best Bet Resource: *45 Student Motivational Strategies,* available by catalog from Turning Point Publishing, see page 351.

Reward Systems Perpetuate Low Achievers

Research Summary: The above headline can be inferred from the work of many researchers. The work of O'Keefe and Nadel was important because it demonstrated that in stressful situations, rat behavior becomes rigid and stereotyped with repeated, predictable responses, "completely eliminating the participation of the locale system." The locale system is the part of the brain that may be responsible for certain types of memory and spatial mapping. We know from research that the use of rewards increases learner stress.

Spielberger's work is profound because it links up the physiological states of anxiety, negative stress and threat with thinking and human performance. He says that anxiety:

1) reduces the ability to solve complex problems;
2) reduces learner responsiveness to the environment;
3) increases stereotyped, low-risk behavior;
4) increases learner attentiveness to and reliance upon external systems of rewards and punishments.

Deci says that there is evidence linking extrinsic motivation with work involving noncreative tasks, rewards and punishments, memorized skills and repetitive tasks. In order to get learners to be creative and have greater subject interest, higher self-esteem and the ability to be reflective, there must be intrinsic motivation. Reward systems prevent this.

Make no mistake about it: *Learners who are experiencing stress and anxiety in their environment will prefer external motivation,* meaning a system of rewards for a preferred behavior. Paradoxically, the worse the learner environment is for motivation, the more the learner seeks rewards. The rewards are initially welcomed by the learner, where predictability and certainty are the trade-offs for lowered anxiety. Stressed, anxious learners *are* more likely to look to others for safe, predictable role modeling, to listen to others for goals and to increase their own stereotyped, lower-order thinking.

This creates a "Catch-22." Rewards, at a low level, work. The teacher continues their usage. The learner now is a victim of the "glass ceiling" principle: he learns to perform to the lowest level needed to get the reward. Caine says, "In effect, they prefer external forms of motivation and lose sight of internal motivation."

Example: The learner who has been on a reward system seems to like it and want more. He complains when it is dropped and his performance goes down. The teacher uses this as evidence to say, "I know I shouldn't bribe him, but the system works!"

Implications: The problem is that the system does work - too well. But then again, holding a gun to someone's head works, too! It will get them to do all kinds of things, but it's not good for the learner's brain (among other things). Rewards lead to learners who become preoccupied with "playing the game" and not really doing quality learning. Why? The ability to alter perceptual maps, to do higher-order thinking and to create complex thematic relationships with the subject is not available to the brain when it experiences the anxiety of a reward system.

The more you use a reward system, the more you evoke the "two-headed dichotomous dragon". That means: 1) the psychological anxiety of performance increases and 2) every reward carries with it an implied certainty of success or failure - but which one? The learner then wants to reduce the uncertainty, so he picks tasks that have a high degree of predictability (often boring, repetitive skills). The learner also is more likely to pick goals set by others instead of himself (even the goals he does pick are often the basic, overworked, media-reinforced, cliché types).

Action Steps: Replace rewards with positive alternatives. These include peer support, positive rituals, self-assessment, acknowledgments, love of learning role modeled, enthusiasm, increased feedback, more options for creativity and student control over the work.

Best Bet Resources: *Punished by Rewards,* by Kohn or *Eager to Learn,* by Wlodlowski

Multiple Social Contexts Boost Motivation

Research Summary: In research by Wentzel, it was found that optimal learning does not necessarily require massive motivation. Often, when students who would not ordinarily be engaged focus on their own self-determination, learning becomes the positive by-product. Ford says that multiple social contexts provide greater opportunities for learner goal attainment and satisfaction. In fact, the argument is made that the learner's brain is in a better state for learning when traditional "learning" is disguised. In other words, in areas where the learning is a "by-product" of the activity, the learner may excel the most.

Example: Multiple contexts may include a learner who also does peer teaching, one who works with other grade levels, performs in a church, does community service, works at a part-time job, serves on committees, is in clubs, plays on various teams.

Implications: We may be underestimating many learners based on single class experiences when, outside that context, they're totally different.

Action Steps: Employ many different settings. Use partner work and teamwork, so that the learner feels accountable to the partner or group.

Best Bet Resources: *Whatever Happened to Teamwork?*   by Alice Cornyn-Selby.

Overdoing Learner Praise Can Backfire

Research Summary: Researcher Kohn says that we may want to be cautious in how praise is used. Children can become negatively dependent on it just as they can on any other external reward. This dependency can lead to lower self confidence, loss of the joy of learning and decreased self-esteem. The praise can also be interpreted as being manipulative. Brophy also suggests that the use of praise can easily backfire. This occurs for two reasons: the learner interprets the praise as 1) "You're controlling my behavior, and I resent it" or 2) "My current capabilities must be sub-par and in real need of improvement."

Case Western Reserve University researcher Roy Baumeister's experiments verified that heavy praise given to a learner can backfire. While intermittent praise can be positive, praise from authority figures can increase "pressure to perform" and result in performance anxiety. Subjects who were given praise right before a skills test consistently performed worse than those who did not receive praise. Students heavily praised became more tentative in their answers and gave up on their own ideas more quickly than those who were not.

Example: A teacher continually praises students for doing homework or for sitting quietly in class. Soon, the learner discovers that it is the praise that he seeks, not the behavior that the teacher is attempting to reinforce.

Implications: The most striking and permanent interpretation of a positive judgment is that it's still a judgment.

Action Steps: Reduce praise from you and increase peer feedback and support. That's much more motivating to the learner Encourage rather than praise. Say, "You're on the right track", or "Let's give it a great effort." Give praise that is not contingent on performance. Encourage the learner to take risks. Provide affirmation, not back-slapping. When the task is completed, ask the learner what his or her assessment of the task is. That way the learner begins to develop a sense of quality about the learning or task instead of pressure to perform just to get it over with. Teach learners how to give supportive feedback to their peers.

Best Bet Resource: *Punished By Rewards*, by Kohn

Learner Conflicts With Reward Systems

Research Summary: Some, like Kohn, might say that most all rewards are bad. But Ford argues that it depends on whether the reward creates a conflict with the learner's existing goals. The three most likely times this occurs are:

1. *If the learner feels manipulated by the reward:*
   "You just want me to give up my guitar lessons." (Deci & Ryan)
2. *The reward interferes with the real reason the learner started:*
   "Now that I'm getting rewarded for getting good grades, I care only about what's on the test, not real learning."
3. *The reward devalues the task and the learner feels bribed:*
   "This class must be pretty bad if they're giving us a bribe just for attending it."

These three categories cover most situations where the reward system might be used; it seems that there are few other situations where the need would arise.

Example: A school is having problems with attendance. The administration decides to reward those who come every day. Now, each student gets a reward for having a 100% attendance month. Students immediately feel bribed for coming to school. They think, "This must be really bad for them to have to bribe us." But they still do the rewarded behavior. "We'll play the game", they say. But now school is about "working the system" instead of learning.

The best way to discover whether learners have been impacted by rewards is to listen to the classic comment, "Will this be on the test?" If they ask that, it means that they have had the joy of learning conditioned out of them, they perceive learning as work and only want to do it to get some extrinsic reward.

Implications: Many rewards are doing more harm than good, encouraging results other than those originally intended.

Action Steps: Stop using reward systems. It makes more sense to make school or work a worthwhile place to be than to try to bribe people to attend.

Best Bet Resource: *Punished by Rewards,* by Kohn.

Rewarded Behaviors Often Short-Lived

Research Summary: In research by Alan Kazden following a decade of post-reward analysis, the conclusions are clear: when the goodies stop, the behavior stops, too. Kazden, who once was a proponent of rewards, set up a token economy system in a health care institution. At first, he was excited about the behavior changes. In his first publication, *The Rich Reward of Rewards*, he talked about how much patient behavior had changed. And that's what people remembered the most. But ten years later, in *The Token Economy: A Decade Later*, he changes his mind. Kazden says, "[R]emoval of token reinforcement results in decrements in desirable responses and a return to baseline or near-baseline levels of performance."

Every learner has his or her own bias which they bring to a particular context. The biases constitute personal beliefs, hopes, expectations, fears, values and emotions. These are what hold a behavior in place. In fact, Hart says, "To change the behavior, the biases must be changed, not the behavior directly." The rewards are designed to change the behavior, not the biases. Hence, any reward-driven activity is likely to fail in the long run.

Example: Teachers often offer rewards for attendance, homework or discipline. Pizza Hut had a program designed to reward students for reading by offering pizzas. The follow-up may show that the ones who read the most were the ones who were reading already. They just decided to play the game. Many of the readers who were not ordinarily reading before the promotion may not now be readers. Long-term follow up will tell.

Implications: Many learners could become very intrinsically motivated if given a chance. But as long as a reward system is in place, they'll play the game and undermine their own progress in the long-term.

Action Steps: Reduce or eliminate all rewards. Use the alternatives of celebrations, increased variety and quantity of feedback.

Rewards Can Kill Intrinsic Motivation

Research Summary: In Amabile's work, the relationship between motivation and rewards is explored. In profound, far-reaching research on the creative process, she says, "extrinsic motivation inhibits intrinsic motivation." The ability to be creative is strongly linked to intrinsic motivation, since it gives the brain "freedom of intellectual expression," which fuels even more thinking and motivation.

A reward system prevents the establishment of intrinsic motivation because there's rarely an incentive to be creative-only to do the asked for behavior. Creativity is rarely part of any reward system-in fact the two are usually at far ends of the scale. You get either intrinsically motivated creative thinking or extrinsically motivated repetitive, rote, predictable behaviors.

Caine and Caine say it best: *"[A] system of rewards and punishments can be selectively demotivating in the long term, especially when others have control over the system."* (Sound like a school or business?) Their contention is that the existence of any behavior-oriented threats and anxiety, coupled with a lack of learner input and control, will "downshift" learner thinking, causing learners to prefer repeated, predictable responses to lower anxiety, and making teachers think the reward system is working. This makes it harder to initiate changes within the system, since any changes in the system will create "threat and anxiety" to both students and teachers, meaning we will get more of the same.

Example: In kindergarten, a learner gets a smiley sticker for good work. By third grade, it's cookies or candies. By fifth grade, the reward is a pizza for a class that behaves well. By eighth grade a student is being bribed by his parents. Is it any wonder that by the time a student reaches eleventh grade, and the teacher wants him to do a research paper, the student response is, "What do I get?" Or he may simply ask, "What for?"

Implications: Learners who have been bribed for either good work or good behavior find that soon the last reward wasn't good enough. A bigger and better one is wanted. Soon, all intrinsic motivation has been killed off and the learner is labeled as "unmotivated." Like a rat in a cage pushing a food bar, the learner's behavior becomes just good enough to get the reward.

Action Steps: If you are using any kind of reward system, let it run its course and end it as soon as you reasonably can. If you stop it abruptly, you may get a rebellion. Remember, the research says that learners who have been on a reward system will become conditioned to prefer it over free choice. The learners will need a "de-tox" or "rehabilitation" time to get off the "reward drug".

Author's Note:

Be sure you understand exactly what is and is not a reward. A reward is defined as a compensation or consequence which is both:
  1) predictable and *2) has market value.*

If it's only predictable, but has no market value (e.g., a smile, a hug, a compliment, a certificate, an awards assembly, public approval, etc.), then it is simply an acknowledgment, not a reward. If it has market value, but no predictability (a spontaneous party, pizza, cookies, gift certificates, small gifts, trips, tickets, etc.), then it is a celebration, not a reward. If you offer something that has both of those qualities, you are, in fact, bribing the learner. You have a reward system, regardless of what you try to call it. At the earliest possible convenience, end the system and replace rewards with alternatives. Suggestions for alternatives are listed below.

a) **Acknowledgments,** both verbal and non-verbal. These alone can replace rewards. Certificates, praise and hugs are all acknowledgments.

b) **Boost the quantity & quality of feedback:** learners need consistent feedback, every single class session, even if it's simply a group choral recall, partner feedback, or team feedback. In the absence of feedback, learners want rewards--after all, it's just another form of feedback.

c) **Celebrations,** small or large, spontaneous displays marking periodic success. These could be a pizza party, or a day trip or just a toast of apple cider.

d) **Demonstrate and role model the joy of learning.** Every time you can, share your own excitement and enthusiasm over something you learned. That will give your learners the important message that learning, in and of itself, is valuable and rewarding.

e) **Enhance relationships.** Sharing more of yourself, learning and caring more about the learners you work with, is critical. Often the single most important reason that learners like a subject has to do with the relationship they have with you, the instructional leader. Social scientists call this "positive social bonding". The bonding can be from a learner to his or her teammate, colleague or partner. It also occurs in the teacher-learner relationship. The goal is to have a strong, positive relationship, but also one of respect. Keep some professional distance, but be genuinely interested in your students.

f) High need/high relevance. When the content of the material is perceived as being needed by the learner, motivation goes up. Or, if it's personally meaningful, the intrinsic rewards are highly likely to happen on their own. Extrinsic, gimmicky rewards are almost ludicrous compared to something personally motivating.

g) Choice & creativity. Constant control and manipulation of the learner creates resentment and disempowerment. Offer ways that the learner can make choices about how the learning is done. Input, suggestion boxes, student teaching and teamwork can all contribute to a more motivated learner.

h) Role model the love and joy of learning to the learners.

i) Optimal environment, consisting of four parts:

    1) Characterized by "states" of high challenge and low stress.

    2) Physically safe.

    3) Low-risk, meaning emotionally safe to make mistakes.

    4) Provides hope. This last criterion may, in fact, be the most powerful motivator. It's why people play the lottery, why some work 60 hours a week, why some kids practice basketball late into the night.

Replacing rewards with alternatives gets a bit tricky in two cases. First, in schools, the entire system of marking and grading is a reward and punishment system. The rewards are good grades which leads to teacher approval, scholarships and university entry. How can an instructional leader work properly (without bribes and rewards) within a system that is so thoroughly entrenched? Use the six options outlined above. Learners will be able to make the distinctions after some time and will prefer your way of learning. Be patient.

Secondly, getting a certificate may be just an acknowledgment when you give it, but its role may become complicated. What if the learner takes it home and the parent rewards him with money? Then it becomes a reward in spite of your best intentions. The solution is to try to make parents aware of the destructive effects of rewards at an open house night or by letter. Naturally, schools have to be careful of this "step ladder" effect, where accumulated acknowledgments (certificates, etc.) can lead to a reward.

The primary point to be made here is that you don't have to bribe learners to learn. The human brain loves to learn! Simply follow the "rules" for brain-compatible learning and learners will re-kindle their thirst and hunger to learn.

How to Replace Rewards in Learning

Research Summary: There are three considerations when removing rewards, says Kohn. First, (1) students should be consulted about the change. Teachers who make unilateral decisions about classroom operations are ignoring student input and reinforcing a sense of student powerlessness. Teachers, at the earliest years appropriate, should engage the students in an active, unguided discussion about the real cost of rewards and ask the students to talk, too.

Second, (2) removing the rewards does not assure the teacher that genuine, authentic, intrinsic learning will take place. That is achieved through a complex set of orchestrated, interactive, empowered learner choices. It's based on perceived needs, values, belief systems, emotions and goals. Unless those needs are addressed, the removal of a reward system will only address a small part of the problem you want solved.

Third, (3) the larger context of reward dependence must be addressed. The role of testing, grades, scholarships and working for rewards must be brought into significant discussion. Learners must choose to learn something for their own reasons, and that's more likely when teachers openly talk about it.

Example: Students who ask "Is this going to be on the test?" are really saying to you, "I've had the love of learning bribed out of me by unknowing teachers. So, do I really have to do this? Otherwise, I don't want to learn it for its own sake."

Implications: It is a systemic process to get rid of reward systems. It takes time, careful attention and cooperative planning.

Action Steps: Do it right. Make sure that all who are involved in and affected by the decisions are a part of the process.

Controlling Learners Can Be Demotivating

Research Summary: Often, instructional leaders want to change learner behavior for conformity or expediency. But research by Ford makes an important distinction: one-time short-term vs. multiple long-term strategies. He says, "Highly controlling motivational strategies such as real or implied threats, strong punishments, compelling rewards and forced competition are sometimes effective... however, they are likely to produce negative developmental consequences if they are repeated across many different behavioral episodes."

In other words, by consistently using controlling means on your learners, you'll undermine their overall success. In fact, Ford says, "there is a compelling literature on the motivational consequences of controlling experiences that indicates people lose interest in activities when they feel coerced or manipulated to engage in those activities, even when the motivational strategies used were intended to be positive and motivating". Additional research by Deci, Lepper, Deci and Ryan, Ryan and Stiller, and Kohn confirms this.

Example: School starts off being fun and motivating with high initial interest. By later years, that enthusiasm has been replaced with resentment, complacency and avoidance. Controlling strategies, lack of creativity and choice, and parental pressure have killed intrinsic motivation for another year.

Implications: We may have much more to do with the behaviors of our learners than we previously thought.

Action Steps: Hold a staff meeting. Get everyone aligned on this issue. Develop a policy that everyone can buy into. Eliminate rewards; replace them with the alternatives of choice, creativity, enthusiasm, multi-context learning and celebration.

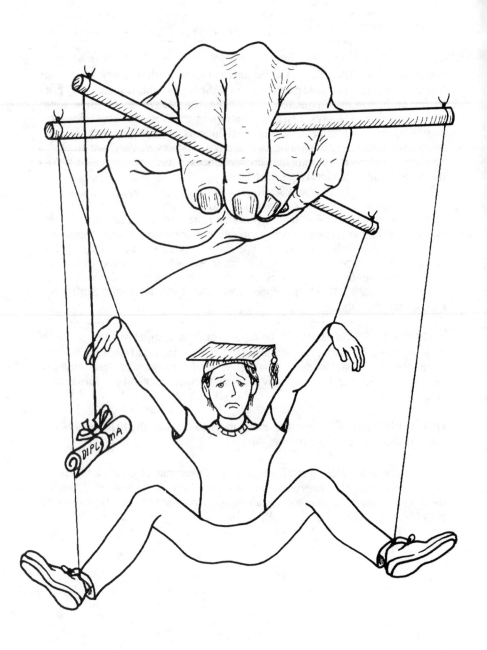

Is There *Ever* a Time & Place for Rewards?

Research Summary: If rewards are counterproductive in so many areas, is there a time and place for them at all? Yes, says Kohn. "If your objective is to get people to [temporarily] obey an order, show up on time and do what they're told," rewards can work, he says. But, he adds emphatically, rewards are simply changing the specific, "in the moment" behavior and not the "person". However, if your objective is to achieve any of the following, rewards simply don't work:

* *long-term quality performance*
* *becoming self-directed learners*
* *developing values of caring, respect and friendliness*
* *creativity and higher-order thinking skills*
* *honesty, integrity and self-confidence*
* *inner drive and intrinsic motivation*

Is there ever a time and place for rewards? Yes; here's an example. It's the end of class and you have six heavy boxes to move to a storage closet. You don't feel like moving them. A couple of strong students are getting ready to leave. You ask them to help out. They grumble and say something about having to get home to clean the garage. You offer to buy each of them a Coke or Pepsi if they'll help. They change their mind and help out. No damage done; everybody's happy.

Example: Fourth graders were asked what kind of reward they'd like for doing a simple classroom task. Later, when it was time to do the task, they performed more poorly on the task than the group that was not offered a reward.

Implications: The reward had come to symbolize the teacher trying to get them to use or like the activity. As a consequence, the students perceived that the task was intrinsically undesirable. A fundamental concept is: If the learner is doing the task to get the reward, it will be understood, on some level, that the task is inherently undesirable.

Action Steps: Forget the use of rewards. Any that you are using now, phase out slowly. Use other strategies such as increased feedback, peer support, creativity and love of learning.

Best Bet Resource: *Punished by Rewards,* by Kohn

Schools Structure Can Demotivate Learners

Research Summary: The unmotivated learner is a myth. To arrive at school, a training session, or classroom requires some sort of motivation. Once the learner is in the seat, either they are bringing a positive motivating attitude with them, or the instructional leader needs to elicit one. The fact is that the demotivated learner's negative behaviors and beliefs are either triggered by or reinforced by an artificial, unresponsive school environment. Identifying, classifying, grouping, labeling, evaluating, comparing, and assessing these demotivated learners has done little to solve the problem.

In fact, much attention lately has been focused on "at-risk" learners and their behaviors. But Kagan says that "factors within classrooms and schools transform students at risk into a discrete subculture that is incompatible with academic success." These students are consistently demoralized by what Ford calls negative "social comparisons with 'smarter' peers, lack of school-initiated peer support for achievement, and an emphasis on avoiding failure or avoiding 'hassles' rather than on learning.... " When these students move to a more responsive environment, their behaviors change, say Edmonds and Kagan. This is further proof than in spite of all the educational restructuring and reform, there is one single change that would do more to motivate learners than any other: make school more like real life. Researcher Bishop makes the distinction very well:

> "Young people are not lazy. In their jobs after school and on the football field, they work very hard. In these environments they are part of a team where individual efforts are visible and appreciated by teammates. Competition and rivalry are not absent, but they are offset by shared goals, shared successes and external measures of achievement...On the sports field, there is no greater sin than giving up, even when the score is hopelessly one-sided. On the job, tasks not done by one worker will generally have to be completed by another... "

Example: A student seems unmotivated all week long. But on Saturday, he has his guitar lessons. He practices for hours without any bribe or external motivation.

Implications: Schools and businesses can change all they want, but until they make the true distinctions between what motivates learners in "real life" and what is going on in their own environments, it's all going to get the same result: good, curious, motivated people who are demotivated, and then branded as lazy.

Action Steps: The research shows that this approach will work:

1) Reorganize tasks and activities so that all of the routines involve some kind of team and partner work.
2) Elicit genuine short-term academic goals from all students and align school goals with students' own lives and social and personal goals.
3) Provide an environment which is responsive to student goals.
4) Infuse student learning with emotion, energy and enthusiasm.
5) Utilize student values, such as autonomy, peer approval and responsibility, to provide maintenance structures for school systems.
6) Create a new model of teacher-to-teacher support so that every teacher knows every other teacher's best ideas.
7) Establish a "bottom-up" administrative approach wherein students experience that their beliefs, goals, and values are consistently integrated into school design.

Summary of Action Steps

1. Start a task simply and upgrade the challenge to the point where it provides challenge without anxiety.

2. Reduce praise from you and increase peer feedback and support. Encourage rather than praise. Say, "You're on the right track", or "Let's give it a great effort." Give praise that is not contingent on performance. When the task is completed, ask the learner what his or her assessment of the task is. That way the learner begins to develop a sense of quality about the learning or task instead of pressure to perform just to get it over with.

3. Employ many different settings. Use partner work and teamwork, so that the learner feels accountable to the partner or group.

4. Do your best to implement as many of the optimal motivating conditions possible as much of the time possible. Avoid labeling any learner as a "low" or unmotivated student until he has had the consistent experience of optimal conditions and a chance to prove himself.

5. If you are using any kind of reward system, let it run its course and end it as soon as you reasonably can. Replace rewards with positive alternatives. These include peer support, rituals, self-assessment, acknowledgments, love of learning, enthusiasm, increased feedback, more options for creativity and student control over the work. Make sure that all who are involved in and affected by the removal of rewards systems are a part of the process.

6. Create a motivating learner environment using the following guidelines:
    1) Reorganize tasks and activities so that all of the routines involve some kind of team and partner work.
    2) Elicit genuine short-term academic goals from all students and align school goals with students' own lives and social and personal goals.
    3) Provide an environment which is responsive to student goals.
    4) Infuse student learning with emotion, energy and enthusiasm.
    5) Utilize student values, such as autonomy, peer approval and responsibility, to provide maintenance structures for school systems.
    6) Create a new model of teacher-to-teacher support so that every teacher knows every other teacher's best ideas.

7) Establish a "bottom-up" administrative approach wherein students experience that their beliefs, goals, and values are consistently integrated into school design.

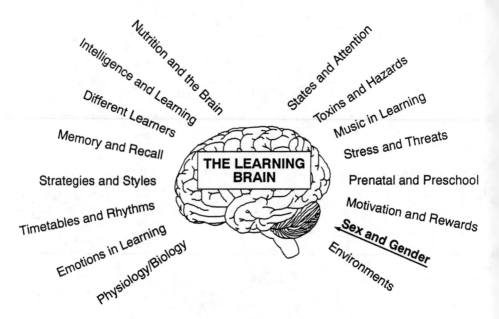

Nutrition and the Brain

Intelligence and Learning

Different Learners

Memory and Recall

Strategies and Styles

Timetables and Rhythms

Emotions in Learning

Physiology/Biology

States and Attention

Toxins and Hazards

Music in Learning

Stress and Threats

Prenatal and Preschool

Motivation and Rewards

Sex and Gender

Environments

THE LEARNING BRAIN

Chapter Fifteen

CHAPTER FIFTEEN

Sex & Gender

Gender Inequities Need Complex Solutions

Research Summary: There are pervasive demotivating influences on females in academics and subsequent career pursuits in technology, mathematics, science and computer-related fields. The most common solutions are often one-dimensional (such as single-sex schools). But Miura says this problem requires more complex and integrated solutions. Gender inequities are expressed in the following ways:

1. Personal goals. Until females have clear objectives that include technology, disadvantages will be dismissed as "peripheral."
2. Emotional arousal. There's a need to eliminate all variations of "technophobia" and any other related fears, concerns, etc.
3. Capability beliefs. Questions arise such as "Can I?" or "Is it hard?" These represent issues of self-confidence and skill assessment.
4. Context beliefs. There are a host of issues that surface when females enter technological fields. These include peer disapproval and "responsive environment" issues.

The research on gender inequities shows that progress is being made. But the rate of progress could be greatly enhanced by a more comprehensive program. Ford concludes by adding that "interventions designed to address just one aspect of this problem would probably yield disappointing results." Encouraging girls (who otherwise wouldn't) to take up a math, science or computer class is a great idea. But unless you address the issue of peer pressure, increase the capability beliefs, support the context beliefs and jumpstart the emotions, there's little chance for success.

Example: Many girls are encouraged to take higher level math. But girls don't stay in the math programs for long. Something causes them to leave. There's a 13-to-1 ratio of males to females in higher level math classes.

Implications: To get more females into technological fields, we must address the less obvious underlying problems. Beliefs, emotions, and goals all need to be aligned.

Action Steps: Interview girls. Find out what interests them, what would encourage them to pursue studies and maintain interest in technology programs.

Best Bet Resource: For a FREE bulletin, "How To Really Understand The Opposite Sex" available by catalog from Turning Point Publishing, see page 351.

Male-Female Brains Develop Differently

Research Summary: Healy, Epstein, and other scientists and developmental specialists have found that in the early years, brain growth rates may vary from as little as a few months to as many as five years. And there are definite differences in how the male and female brains develop. Therefore, assessing and grouping children chronologically is as ridiculous as it would be to group teachers or business persons chronologically by age in their jobs.

Whitleson says that boys show a much earlier specialization of the right brain than girls do. In a study of 200 right-handed children, the boys outperformed the girls on spatial tasks. But linguistically, the girls show earlier dominance than the boys. Boys often have trouble, because of right brain specialization, in learning to read early in life. Since reading is both spatial and linguistic, it makes sense that boys learn to read later than girls.

The brain not only grows differently, it decays differently. We now know that the right brain of females has longer plasticity than that of males. This means it stays open to growth and change for more years in girls than in boys. Wree reports that the degeneration of nerve cells in the male brain precedes that of females by 20 years. Although the rate of loss by females is greater than that of males, it is still not enough to overtake them. The researchers say that their estimates of cell loss are conservative.

Example: There may be a reason why adolescent boys are more physical than adolescent girls. That part of the brain is much more developed in males at that time in their life. For females, the part of the brain used for interpersonal skills is more developed and plays an integral role in teenage girl culture.

Implications: The differences between males and females are so prevalent that same-sex teaching methods might need to be reconsidered. On the average, developmentally, girls read earlier than boys. If we actually accounted for differing brains, we'd suddenly find that 15-25% of all boys who are now considered "developmentally slow" would immediately be reclassified as normal. Many male-female behaviors make much more sense when considered in the context of brain development.

Action Steps: Eliminate groupings by age or grade. They tend to cause feelings of inadequacy. Learners are being measured against those with developmental advantages instead of by effort. Keep students in age clusters, such as ages 2-4, 5-7, 8-10, 11-13, 14-17.

Hormones Bias Learner's Sexuality

Research Summary: Geneticist Anne Moir and D. Jessel summarized over 65 studies on the brain and sexuality. They say that evidence is conclusive that hormones are the key to whether the brain develops as a more male (lateralized) or female (equalized) brain. At conception, an XX chromosome pairing means the girl template is created and an XY means a boy. But in the six weeks following conception, the final determination of the sexuality is determined by the amount of the male hormone testosterone present in the womb.

If a girl template (XX) fetus is not exposed to significant amounts of testosterone in the womb, the result will be a female by appearance and a female brain type. If the XX is exposed to a small amount of the male hormone, the result will be a female body with a male brain type. Exposure to significant amounts of testosterone results in a male body with a male brain, even though the chromosomes are XX.

The reverse is also true. An XY embryo (male template) can either become a male, gay male or female, depending on the amount of testosterone present in the uterus. In fact, in experiments on rats, researchers were able to change the sex of the rat (and alter brain-type) through hormonal injections at the critical time in development.

Research by Hofman and Swaab shows that so far there are no differences discovered in the hypothalamus of heterosexual males and homosexual males. He says that this "contradicts the view that male homosexuals have a female hypothalamus." Other biological differences and inferences, such as neocortex similarities, were not ruled out, however.

Research by Whitleson and others has proven that women have a comparatively larger, thicker and heavier corpus callosum, the connecting nerve fibers between the left and right hemisphere. The differences are caused by prenatal sexual hormones which affect the embryo. In homosexuals, the lower levels of testosterone make for less aggressive behavior and greater multi-tasking. In addition, male homosexuals are more like females than other males in their brain-dominance pattern. This pattern affects behavior, thinking and even the processing of our five senses. One example is that the visual fixation pattern is opposite: whereas heterosexuals are left-field dominant, homosexuals are equally sensitive on either side.

But research by Friedman and Downey says that the only research model complete at this time is a biopsychosocial model. Their review of all research on the differences between males and females has led them to conclude that "human sexual orientation is . . . complex and diverse."

Example: Often, gays seem to have greater behavioral similarities to females than to heterosexual males. Career choices often favor high interpersonal or nurturing skills. Lesbians seem to have greater behavioral similarities to males than other females. Career choices are often in fields that are physical, authoritarian or technologically oriented.

Implications: There may be very little choice going on when it comes to choosing one's own sexuality. Prenatal hormones may have already determined this.

Action Steps: Educate yourself and others around you. Remain open-minded about this topic as there is much more research to be done.

Best Bet Resource: *BrainSex*, by Moir & Jessel; *Brain-Mind Bulletin*, 12: 11G, August 1987, (213) 223-2500 (for research on heterosexuals and homosexuals).

Male & Female Brain Structurally Different

Research Summary: After years of persuasive research by Kimura and dozens of other eminent neuroscientists, including Butler, Levy, McGlone, Nyborg and Whitleson, the conclusions are profound: The male and female brain not only act differently, they are structurally different. And these verifiable physical differences may explain vastly different processing methodologies by male and female brains.

Barrett says that the male brain, on the average, weighs 49 ounces and the female brain, 44 ounces. There is still some dispute over the scope and magnitude of other differences. LaCoste at Yale and Holloway at Columbia reported corpus callosum differences. Some studies confirmed this; others did not. Allen and Gorski also found conflicting data. Denenberg at the University of Connecticut has stated that the differences are still unclear.

Diamond at Berkeley, Stewart of Concordia in Montreal, Kolb of the University of Lethbridge in Alberta, Canada, and LaCoste all reported clear-cut male-female brain differences. Kimura says, "Taken altogether, the evidence suggests that men's and women's brains are organized along different lines from very early in life." Variances within the same sex do exist, but certainly not to the same extent as those found between the opposite sex.

The list below of sexually determined differences makes a strong statement. It seems that hormonal influences are the primary difference-maker. And while every single brain will not have equal amounts of sexually differentiated characteristics, the generalizations still hold. Not all women are five foot five and not all men are five foot nine. But on the average, men are taller than women. The range of the differences listed below is more like a continuum. In the same spirit of averages, neuroscientists have found many physical differences. Examples of sexually determined differences include:

* length of the nerve cell connectors
* nucleus volume in hypothalamus
* pathways that the neurotransmitters follow
* density of nerve cell strands
* shape of the nucleus in the hypothalamus
* thickness of left and right side of the cortex control centers
* the number of vasopressin neurons in hypothalamus
* thickness and weight of the corpus callosum

    * location of control centers for language, emotions & spatial
       skills

Implications: We may want to consider whether we have gone overboard in trying to make education "gender-bias free". Equal education does not mean that everything should be done the same; it means that it should provide equal opportunity. There are real, physical differences.

Action Steps: Change some expectations about behavior and learning. Be holistic and ecological, using a "systems" approach to insure greater success. Girls and boys have very different brains. Educate others about the differences.

Best Bet Resource: *BrainSex,* by Moir & Jessel.

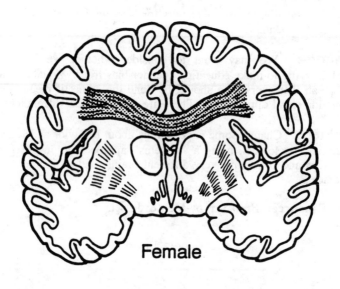

Female

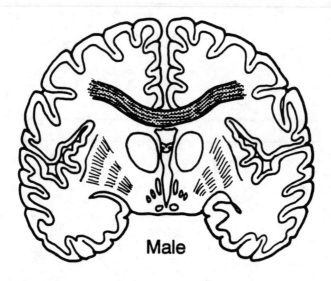

Male

Shaded area (corpus callosum) is generally thicker and
carries more "traffic" (information) between hemispheres
in females than it does in males. (example is exaggerated).

Females & Males Process Input Differently

Research Summary: Researchers Garai and Scheinfield, McGee, McGuiness, and Bracha say that the female brain is very different from the male brain with regard to sensory perception. Literally hundreds of studies have been done to eliminate cultural biases from experiments so that researchers can really tell what are the true differences, not what has been socially programmed in.

One hundred years ago, it was assumed that all sensory differences were genetic. In 1970, it was commonly assumed that the differences were cultural. Now we know that both are true. While there are proven functional differences between males and females, there are also still biases which affect infants' early brains, which, in turn, change to respond to the bias. Nature or nurture? It's both! Here is a summary of some differences between males and females:

Hearing: The female ear is better able to pick up nuances of voice, music and other sounds. In addition, females retain better hearing longer throughout life. Females have superior hearing, and at 85 decibels, they perceive the volume twice as loud as males. Females have greater vocal clarity and are one-sixth as likely as a male to be a monotone. They learn to speak earlier and learn languages more quickly. Three-quarters of university students majoring in foreign languages are female. Women excel at verbal memory and process language faster and more accurately. Infant girls are more comforted by singing and speech than males. In contrast to this summary of research, however, Klutky says females showed no significant auditory advantage in his own studies.

Vision: Males have better distance vision and depth perception than females. Women excel at peripheral vision. Males see better in brighter light; female eyesight is superior at night. Females are more sensitive to the red end of the spectrum; excel at visual memory, facial clues and context; have a better ability to recognize faces and remember names. In repeated studies, women can store more random and irrelevant visual information than men.

Touch: Females have a more diffused and sensitive sense of touch. They react faster and more acutely to pain, yet can withstand pain over a longer duration than males. Males react more to extremes of temperature. Females have greater sensitivity in fingers and hands. They are superior in performing new motor combinations, and in fine motor dexterity.

291

<u>Activity:</u>   Male infants play more with objects, more often, than females. Females are more responsive to playmates. The directional choice, called "circling behavior," is opposite for men and women. In other words, when right-handed males walk over to a table to pick up an object, they are more likely to return by turning to their right. Right-handed females are more likely to return by circling around to their left.

<u>Smell and Taste:</u>   Women have a stronger sense of smell and are much more responsive to aromas, odors and subtle changes in smell. They are more sensitive to bitter flavors and prefer sweet flavors. A "significant advantage" in olfaction memory was found by Klutky. Differences in the brain also relate to the effects of contaminants. By using neuroradiological imaging to assess brain shrinkage, Harper and Kril found that women are "more susceptible to the damaging effects of alcohol than males."

Example: Women often report having experiences that men don't understand, such as intuition, food preferences or social interaction clues.

Implications: Males and females truly live in a different world created by the processing of very different sensory information.

Action Steps: Become informed. Know the differences between culturally reinforced stereotypes and real physical differences. Keep expectations high and avoid stereotyping.

Males & Females Differ in Problem-Solving

Research Summary: Kimura says that males and females have very different ways of approaching and solving problems. She has been a pioneer for decades on the anatomical and functional differences between the sexes. Here is a summary of the research on differences in problem-solving, broken down by gender. In general, females do better than men in the following areas:

1) Mathematical calculation
2) Precision, fine-motor coordination
3) Ideational fluency
4) Finding, matching or locating missing objects
5) Use of landmarks to recall locations in context, maps

The problem-solving tasks that favor men are:

1) Target-directed motor skills (archery, football, baseball, cricket, darts, etc.)
2) Spatial: mentally rotating objects
3) Disembedding tests (locating objects, patterns from within another)
4) Mathematical reasoning, word problems
5) Use of spatial cues of distance, direction in route-finding

So, are these differences environmental or genetic? There is considerable research going on to determine this. So far, the consensus is that the answer indicates both factors playing a role.

Example: There are many activities in which females excel over males: assembly, needlework, precision crafting, micro-production, communication, sewing, nursing, pharmacy and many of the arts. Think of the ones in which males excel: gross motor skills like sports, mechanics, construction and sculpture.

Implications: Many problems may not be problems at all. They may simply be an expression of the "natural" way in which one sex or another really operates.

Action Steps: Open up discussions with your colleagues about the research and its implications.

Are Female Brains Built for Multi-Tasking?

Research Summary: One of the foremost researchers on hemisphericity, Dr. Jerre Levy of the University of Chicago, says the stronger corpus callosum link in the female brain may explain "women's intuition" as well as "male superiority" in mechanics, accounting, engineering and math. Men and women have long suspected that there are genetic physical differences in the actual brain, and both are correct. The female brain has a larger and thicker corpus callosum, which is the bridge carrying communication traffic between the left and right hemisphere. The female brain may "talk to itself" better than the male brain. This may help in integrating and interpreting all of the subtle details and nuances of a situation.

Example: A woman comes home from work. Her husband is watching a "big game" on the television. She goes into the kitchen and begins putting dishes away and talking on the phone to her girlfriend. Her daughter comes into the kitchen so she stops and helps her unpack her lunch box. In the middle of all this, she asks her husband, "What do you want for dinner?" Her husband, who is focused on watching television, says, "I'm busy, can you wait till the commercial to talk?" While many strong feminists dismiss this example as sexist, the reality is that this type of interaction actually occurs every single day, millions of times around the world.

Implications: Many speculate that this example shows why women excel in multi-tasking. It may also explain why the more "compartmentalized" male brain is better at tasks where precision, focus and prolonged concentration is required with a limited number of details.

I often ask audiences of women if the above scenario actually happens. Typically, I get a roaring, enthusiastic agreement from 80-90%. Yet, there is some debate over whether the above behavior is a result of a different brain or culturally conditioned behaviors. Because there are so many other variables affecting the subjects, one must be careful to avoid generalizing a physical difference into a behavioral change. Right now, our best guess is that it's a matter of both nature and nurture. But if research confirms more of these discoveries, we may be able to explain many gender-related behaviors.

Action Steps: Dialoguing with your colleagues is still the best starting point. It's important to get everyone involved in the decisions.

Optimal Monthly Learning Cycles

Research Summary: Is there a best time for women to learn? Researchers Kimura, Kopera, Messant, Rossi, and the teams of Kimura and Hampson and Meleges and Hamburg think so. In addition, Elizabeth Hampson of the University of Western Ontario proved that women's learning and task performance levels changed throughout the menstrual cycle, varying with the levels of estrogen.

According to the research on hormonal influences on the brain, a woman's 28-day menstrual cycle may explain why some learning succeeds and some doesn't. During the first 14-day half of the menstrual cycle, estrogen alone is present. Estrogen specifically promotes more active brain cells, increases sensory awareness and increases brain alertness. The brain, flooded with this hormone, experiences feelings of pleasure, sexual arousal, well being, enthusiasm and self-esteem. Researchers say that this may be the optimal time for female learning.

During the second half of the cycle, progesterone is present with the estrogen. Progesterone induces a profound reduction in cerebral blood flow, oxygen and glucose consumption, and produces sluggish, unmotivated behavior. It is also responsible for a sense of calm and acceptance. But in the five final days before menstruation, both levels drop. In this state, there is little estrogen to promote well-being and little progesterone to calm the moods.

As a result, females often experience mood swings, aggression and depression. Learning is negatively affected by depression, lower self-confidence and irritability. Females who do not experience such fluctuations may have more of a "male brain", meaning that there is more hemispheric laterality and higher levels of testosterone.

Interestingly, these variations are matched in men. Spatial ability is higher when testosterone is lower. So is musical ability. Margaret Henderson, a research physiologist and endocrinologist, says that men appear to have a temperature cycle that is synchronous with the menstrual cycle of their cohabiting partner. Researchers have already verified that temperature changes are known to affect sexuality, attention, immunity and learning.

Example: One week your learning seems like "high performance" and the next week it seems like you've gone "brain dead."

Implications: Sometimes the difference may be due to hormones. How long should we all be pretending that boys and girls are identical? In spite of all the awareness about stereotyping, boys and girls still do things at their own respective paces. As they grow up, their timetables remain different.

Action Steps: Awareness, awareness, awareness. There is a fine line between stereotyping and being honest about differences. Strive to find that middle ground.

Summary of Action Steps

1. Interview girls. Find out what interests them, what would encourage them to pursue studies and maintain interest in technology programs.

2. Educate yourself and others around you about the predetermining hormonal factors in one's sexual orientation. Remain open-minded.

3. Eliminate groupings by age or grade. They tend to cause feelings of inadequacy. Learners are being measured against those with developmental advantages instead of by effort. Keep students in age clusters, such as ages 2-4, 5-7, 8-10, 11-13, 14-17.

4. Become informed about the differences between the male and female brain. Educate others. Engage in discussions with colleagues regarding the implications of the research. Know the differences between culturally reinforced stereotypes and real physical differences. Avoid stereotyping. Change some expectations about behavior and learning.

5. Monitor your own lows and highs. Do it over a period of months. Discover which of the research discoveries match up with your own learning experiences.

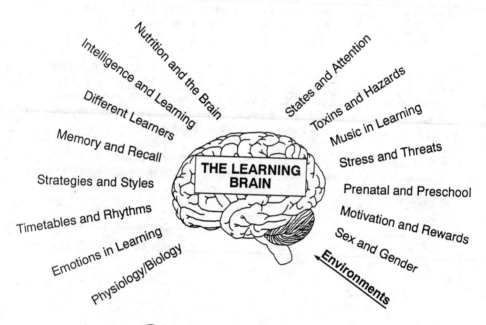

Nutrition and the Brain

Intelligence and Learning

Different Learners

Memory and Recall

Strategies and Styles

Timetables and Rhythms

Emotions in Learning

Physiology/Biology

States and Attention

Toxins and Hazards

Music in Learning

Stress and Threats

Prenatal and Preschool

Motivation and Rewards

Sex and Gender

Environments

THE LEARNING BRAIN

Chapter Sixteen

CHAPTER SIXTEEN

Environments

Enriched Environments Build Better Brains

Research Summary: In groundbreaking research by UC Berkeley pioneer Dr. Marion Diamond and University of Illinois researcher William Greenough with Anderson, an amazing plasticity to the brain was discovered. Many types of rat groups were studied in various conditions. They divided the experiment into three groups: control groups, those in impoverished environments and those in enriched environments.

Time and time again, for over 30 years of varied experiments, the rats in enriched environments grew better brains. Greenough found that he could increase the number of connections in animal brains by 25% by exposing them to an enriched environment. Dr. Diamond summarizes the data:

> "[W]ith increasing amounts of environmental enrichment, we see brains that are larger and heavier, with increased dendritic branching. That means those nerve cells can communicate better with each other. With the enriched environment we also get more support cells because the nerve cells are getting bigger. Not only that, but the junction between the cells--the synapse--also increases its dimensions. These are highly significant effects of differential experience."

But does this research translate to humans? The research of UCLA neuroscientist Bob Jacobs confirms that enrichment does happen, says Kotulak. He found that in autopsy studies on graduate students, there were up to 40% more connections than with high school dropouts. Yet education alone was not enough. Frequent new learning experiences and challenges were critical to brain growth. The brain of graduate students who were "coasting" through school had fewer connections than those who challenged themselves daily.

Challenges must engender learning, not just exercise. The work of Greenough and Black confirmed this. They used complex environments to grow better brains. When Black isolated other factors, such as aging and stress, from complex environments, he affirmed that it was the motor learning, not simply the activity, that caused the brain growth.

The most astonishing research may have come from Wallace et al. They discovered that in just four days, there are significant "structural modifications" in the dendritic fields of cortical neurons. The measurements were made in the visual cortex and were done on dendritic length and total number of branches. Sirevaag and Greenough found that brain enrichment happens in stages, from surface level to depth growth.

The research draws three important conclusions:
1) rats in enriched environments actually grow heavier brains, with more dendritic connections that communicate better, increased synapses, greater thickness in sensory areas, increases in enzymes and more glial cells (the ones that assist in growth and signal transmission).
2) the enriched environments needed to be varied and changed often to maintain the differences in rat intelligence. This meant larger cages, other rats, more toys and frequent challenges.
3) Rats of any age could increase their intelligence if they were provided challenging and frequent new learning experiences.

Horn says, "[E]vidence demonstrates that the central nervous system is plastic... [and the knowledge that] synaptic plasticity is indeed involved in learning and memory is relatively recent."

Examples: In working with children, Craig Ramey at the University of Alabama found that the results were similar to those found with rats. Ramey's intervention program worked with children of low IQ parents who were divided into two groups. The children who were exposed to the enriched environment had significantly higher IQs than the control group. They were, in fact, 20 points higher. And the stronger results lasted; when the children were retested after 10 years, the effects of early intervention had endured.

Implications: We suffer from a "poverty of time" where fathers are working more hours, mothers are working more hours and children are left to themselves. Most parents don't take the time to create interesting or creative home learning environments. Television is never a substitute for quality interaction with people or the outside world.

The implications cut across all age groups. It may be that putting the elderly in a rest home where stimulation is restricted is the absolute worst thing for their brains (and life). What they need is frequent new learning experiences, a sensory-rich environment and challenges.

Action Steps: Be more purposeful about your learning environment. Reduce television watching time. Create a more multi-sensory environment. Add posters, aromas, music and more engaging and relevant activities. Increase social interaction. Use different rooms and, if possible, larger rooms, too. Change the environment often to create novelty and challenge.

Encourage children to explore and create new things. Give them quality, trusted adult time for learning and practicing critical skills like categorizing, counting, labeling, language, cause and effect, and thinking. Give plenty of positive feedback and fun celebrations with each accomplishment. Provide a rich use of several languages in a variety of contexts. Reduce all forms of severe negative experiences and disapproval.

Best Bet Resource: *Enriching Heredity,* by Marion Diamond.

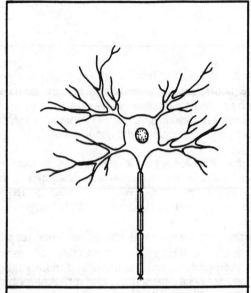

**Impoverished Environment:
Isolation, Boredom and Inactivity**

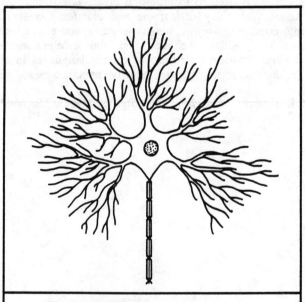

**Enriched Environment:
Challenge, Activity and Novelty**

Brain Prefers Real World Environment

Research Summary: Do brains "grow" better in the real world than in artificial learning environments? Yes, according to top neural plasticity researcher, Dr. Marion Diamond. The UC Berkeley researcher says that she found new data when she experimented with groups of rats. The rats who "grew" the best brains (even better than the rats in an enriched environment of toys, lights and other rats) were those let loose out into the wild, then recaptured and measured.

Norman Frederiksen has documented the differences between "real-life" activity and "artificial" activity in many schools. He says that learners suffer from consistent intrinsic under motivation. Yet for the more real-world tasks, there is greater intrinsic motivation. In fact, Jaques says that it is the long-term projects and only the realistic, real-world projects that tap into the learner's best talents and abilities.

Implications: We may be able to enhance brain growth and learning by altering the types of experiences offered. Speculation is that the most important influences for brain growth are interactive learning with novelty, unlimited choice, challenge and learner-derived meaning from frequent new experiences.

Example: Have you ever noticed that when learners share their home, travel or neighborhood experiences there is personal connectedness and real meaning to it? They talk with motivation, passion and meaning about the real-world experiences they have had, much more so than from the "book learning" they get.

Action Steps: Use field trips, varied work environments, home environments, the park, on-the-job training, the zoo, a convention, a rally, a vacation or anything rich and varied that would naturally occur in life. Reduce "contrived" learning and encourage your learners to go out into the real world for as much learning as possible.

Best Bet Resource: *Playful Perception,* by Leff.

Peripheral Surroundings Influence Learning

Research Summary: Researchers Lozanov, Nadel, and Rosenfield have verified that the brain learns from both the traditional, focused kind of attention and from surrounding peripherals. They discovered that colors, decoration, sounds, smells and other stimuli are processed by the brain at a more subtle, nonconscious level. Yet they do influence the learner.

Example: Rosenfield quotes a study done by Lozanov which used visual suggestion by color-coding key items. Five hundred subjects showed much greater recall than subjects who did not get the color-coded material. Time had positive effect: consciously learned material went from 80% to 50%; the peripherals went from 85% to 91%. Even when the audience knows it's being used, the method works: scores from 600 people were 93% and 96%

Quiet background Baroque music is being played. The learners may not notice it, but the music can quietly evoke positive states of relaxation. Inspiring or relaxing posters or quotations on the walls of the room can also subliminally create a relaxing effect.

Implications: A passive approach to surroundings on the part of the instructional leader can actually detract from the learning, making it less enriching than if an effort was made to enhance the visuals and/or audios.

Action Steps: A purposeful plan should be made for positively influencing the learner in ways aside from the traditional lesson. In the learning environment, assess what influences you have right now. Are they positive? What's the reaction of the learner to your environment? Could it be better?

Also, the use of music can be quite powerful. Make the room a happy, pleasant place to be in. Colors affect learner moods, too. Peripherals in the form of positive posters, learner work and symbols of expression, change, growth or beauty can be powerful. Make sure the furniture is arranged in a way so that learners can see each other, which usually provides the most interesting visual enhancement of all.

Best Learner Environment Discovered

Research Summary: Ford researched optimal motivating environments and found that four factors were critical to what he calls "context beliefs". These are the functional elements that are "in vitro", meaning embedded within the learner's situation. According to Ford, all of them must be present to create an optimal environment:

1) The environment must be consistent with an individual's personal goals. This means that the learning environment must be a place in which the learner can reach his or her own personal goals.
2) The environment must be congruent with the learner's bio-social and cognitive styles. This means that if abstract learning is taking place in a crowded, competitive room with fluorescent lighting, it will be a problem for a concrete learner who needs space and works cooperatively.
3) The environment must offer the learner the resources needed. In addition to materials, advice, tools, transportation and supplies, another key resource is time and affordability.
4) The environment must provide a supportive and positive emotional climate. Naturally, trust, warmth, safety and peer acceptance are critical.

Example: As a child, you found yourself naturally and effortlessly engaged in learning. Why? So many of the qualities that were motivating were naturally a part of the environment.

Implications: Many students whom you thought of as being unmotivated may be very motivated, if you provide the right conditions.

Action Steps: Make a big poster featuring the four conditions of the optimal learning environment. Post it in the back of the room you work in the most often. Let it be your guide for how to motivate learners.

Best Bet Resource: *Optimal Learning Environments,* available by catalog from Turning Point Publishing, see page 351.

Lighting Changes Impact Learning

Research Summary: In the *Brain-Mind Bulletin* (April 1988), an article about Dr. Wayne London's experiments caught worldwide attention. London, a Vermont psychiatrist, switched the lighting in three elementary school classrooms half way through the school year. He was curious about whether the type of lighting mattered to the students. During the December Holiday break, he changed the current fluorescent lighting to Vitalite full spectrum lighting. Although the experiment was not a double blind one, no one expected any particular result.

The results, however, were amazing. London found that the students who were in the classrooms with full-spectrum lighting missed only 65% as many school days as those in the other classrooms. London was not surprised. He said, "Ordinary fluorescent light has been shown to raise the cortisol level in the blood, a change likely to suppress the immune system."

Harmon studied 160,000 school-age children and found that by the time that they graduated from elementary school over one-half of them had developed problems related to their learning environment, and specifically, related to lighting. Changes were made in the children's environment and a six month follow-up was done. The results were remarkable:

Visual problems decreased 65%   Chronic infections decreased 43%
Postural problems decreased 25%   Chronic fatigue decreased 55%

What about bright versus dim lights? Many students relax, focus and actually perform better in low-light situations, says Krimsky, Dunn and Dunn, et al. Brighter lights, especially fluorescent, seemed to create restless, fidgety learners. Low-level lights seemed to have a calming effect, especially at the younger ages.

Example: Have you gotten any complaints about lighting? It may not be just an irritable learner. Lighting can affect the brain and learning. Some students seem to prefer certain seats simply because of the lighting.

Implications: Many learners may be underperforming simply because the lighting is difficult on their eyes.

Action Steps: Give your learners some choice in where they sit. More natural, brighter lighting is better.

Best Bet Resource: *Office Biology* by Edith Weiner and Arnold Brown

Is Learning Boosted By Negative Air?

Research Summary: Maguire says that if you are feeling groggy, lethargic, sleepy or depressed, it may be the electrical charge in the air. In areas of higher population, the atmosphere's healthy balance of positive to negative ions is disrupted. Human activity, it seems, destroys negative ions. And they affect the oxygen that we breathe and the mind. It seems that when it comes to air, the more negatively charged it is, the better. Smoke, dust, smog, pollutants, electrical emissions, heating systems, coolers and traffic are all culprits. The air becomes more highly electrified (too many positive ions) and humans react. Somewhere between 20-40% of the population is strongly affected.

Examples: When you stand in front of a waterfall, or step outdoors just after a rain, or stand atop a mountain or just get out of a shower, you often feel fresher, inspired and energized.

Implications: Many lethargic or underperforming learners may simply be very highly susceptible to the ionization changes in the air.

Action Steps: You may want to purchase an environmental ionizer. Be sure to get one powerful enough for the size of room you're using.

Noisy Environment Best for Some Learners

Research summary: Price says that many learners understand and recall better when music is being played. The percentage of learners who fall into this type of category varies dramatically. Among musicians, you would get a different response than from more visual learners. Learner preference for some low-level background music (such as Baroque, in a major key) will run from a low of 20% to a high of 75-80%. Variables include the cultural background of the learner, the learning styles, the circumstances, the way the music is used, the volume, the type of music and carrier of the music. Best results have come from experimenting.

Some learners perform better in a noisy, busy environment; others need total silence. In one study, (Carbo, Dunn and Dunn), one-fifth (20%) of learners preferred a noisy environment to a quiet one. On the other hand, some students need so much silence that only earplugs can filter out enough noise for their tastes. McCarthy says that even the amount of neatness and clutter in the learning environment varies by student.

Example: You play some music while students are working and learning. A student comes up to you and asks to have the music turned off. It bothers him, but the other 80-95% prefer to keep it on.

Implications: We may be accidentally driving our learners crazy by stressing uniformity in the environment. We may want to have either separate environments or to rotate the type used. Many of our learners are underperforming because the environment does not suit their own, best learning style.

Action Steps: Add variety to the learning environments you create. Over a span of two weeks, vary your lighting, use music, provide silence, provide earplugs and encourage cooperative learning as well as individual learning.

Memory for Colors Stronger Than Verbal

Research Summary: An interesting study was done by researchers Backman, et al. and Allen on the relative value of using verbal cues versus color cues in learning and memory. Backman and his researchers found that when memory for verbs and memory for colors were tested, learners recalled color better. And when objects were tested against color, once again, color memory was stronger. Even an intention to remember did not affect the outcome of the experiment.

Should you paint your environment? Maguire says that different colors affect your moods and learning. Calming colors are light blue and light green. Red is an engaging and emotive color best for restaurants. For optimal learning, choose yellow, beige or off-white. Those colors seem to stimulate positive feelings.

Weiner says darker colors lower stress and increase feelings of peacefulness. Brighter colors such as red, orange and yellow spark energy and creativity. They can also increase aggressive and nervous behavior. The most neutral color? A textured, light gray.

Example: You walk into a room and immediately feel comfortable. In another room, you feel happy and inspired, and in yet another, you feel "heavy" and depressed enough to want to leave. The colors may be responsible. When asked to identify a person, we say "the white guy" or "the girl with the orange jacket". We remember colors first, content next.

Implications: We may be vastly underutilizing the potential of color in learning.

Action Steps: Use colored handouts, color your overhead transparencies, use colorful posters and encourage the use of color in mind maps.

Best Bet Resource: *Visual Perception* by Vicki Bruce & Patrick Green

Visual Learning Importance Revealed

Research Summary: Over 90% of all information that comes to our brain is visual. The retina accounts for 40% of all nerve fibers connected to the brain. Our eyes can register 36,000 visual messages per hour.

Researchers Treisman and Gormican discovered the primary aspects of vision,what the brain is designed to see soonest and easiest. She identified the building blocks, the essentials to how our eyes actually compose meaning from our visual field. These essential elements are contrast, tilt, curvature, line ends, color and size, and are perceived before the learner actually understands what was seen. This provides a framework for the ways we can best attract and keep learner's attention.

Our brain responds fastest to wavelengths of color, lightness and darkness, motion, form, and depth. We blink every 2-10 seconds, either as a nonconscious habit to keep the eye moist or clean, or as a signal from our brain that we have just understood or received a "bite" of information. By observing blink rates, you'll be able to get clues about how the learner is accepting the new information.

Treisman also discovered that the brain is wired to identify objects more quickly when they differ from the rest of the objects in basic features. These differences are analyzed in parallel by the brain so that while the learner may be observing location, the brain may also be processing changes from one object to another.

Example: There are many ways to access the brain's inherently fast response to color, shape and size. For example, in labeling stored boxes, it makes sense to color code them by types of content instead of labeling them with words only.

Implications: In education and training, we may have been underutilizing some of our brain's visual system's best qualities.

Action Steps: Utilize more visuals, more motion in the visuals and more changes in location in visuals to get and keep attention.

Heat Stress Impairs Human Performance

Research Summary: In U.S. Defense Department studies, Taylor and Orlansky report that heat stress dramatically lowers scores in both intellectual and physical tasks. In combat tests where special protective clothing was worn, Taylor found that high temperatures were responsible for decreases in performance requiring accuracy, speed, dexterity and physical acuity. While many types of obstacles and barriers are known to reduce or impair learning, heat stress is one of the most preventable.

Ornstein speculates that it was evolutionarily beneficial for humans to become upright and begin walking. He says that development helped to keep the brain cooler, since the air temperature is a bit cooler at two meters off the ground than it is at just one meter. A "rise of only 1-3 degrees centigrade in brain temperature above normal is enough to disturb brain functions," says Ornstein. In fact, anthropologist Dean Falk says that as brain size has increased over the last two million years, one of the most important adaptations was the cooling mechanisms. Our very survival is vested in keeping the brain at the right temperature.

Choice may be the most important variable in the temperature of the learner's environment. There is a wide variety of perceptions, say Dunn and Dunn, in what constitutes a warm or cool room. The optimal is NOT always 68-72 degrees Fahrenheit for all learners, says Murrain. There are differences among ages, peers, and genders which can change with seasons, moods, and other miscellaneous factors. Having said that, it is a great baseline or standard temperature to start off a learning environment.

Example: A room that's cool for you may be hot for the learner. They complain, and you're perplexed. Some researchers (Della Valle, Hodges, Shea, Kroon) have found that the environment (seating choices, comfort levels, lighting) and learning styles (global, sequential, concrete, abstract, etc.) are a significant factor in determining the success of students.

Implications: We may be creating learning environments that are too rigid. They may lack options for learners to sit where it's cooler or warmer, which might help their learning.

Action Steps: Provide choice. Be more responsive to the temperature. It's better to be too cool than too warm. But it is best to be neither of these.

311

Aromas Discovered to Stimulate Learning

Research Summary: There's a strong link between the olfactory glands and the autonomic nervous system. Olfaction (the neuroscience of smell) drives the human basics such as anxiety, fear, hunger, depression and sexuality.

In experiments on neonatal rats, Sullivan, et al. found that conditioned odor stimulation and tactile stimulation "are addictive in their effects on learning". The positive learning effects came from a peppermint odor injected into various norepinephrine receptor blockers, a procedure which allowed researchers to rule out other causes for the change.

Dr. Alan Hirsch, a Chicago neurologist, has found that certain floral odors increase the ability to learn, create and think. Working with recovering patients, he used thinking and creative puzzles with control groups and with those exposed to a flowery scent. Those with the scent consistently solved the puzzles 30% faster.

Dr. Lewis Thomas, President Emeritus of the Sloan-Kettering Cancer Center in Ohio, says, "The act of smelling something, anything, is remarkably like the act of thinking.... [Y]ou can feel the mind going to work...." McCarthy says that some scents are effective in re-triggering specific optimal learning states. Lavabre agrees that specific aromas are highly influential and consistent in triggering specific bodily reactions.

Harry Walter, Chairman of International Flavors and Fragrances, has been researching the psychobiology of aromas. He says, "Brain inputs from smell and taste receptors are known to affect vital brain functions,reproductive behavior, learning, memory and emotional states." Smells can regulate stress and alter our flight or fight response.

The olfactory regions are also rich receptors for endorphins, signaling the body's response to feelings of pleasure and well-being. The human brain's ability to detect changes in the environment are well documented. "People can distinguish odors with tiny variations in the chemical structures of the odor molecule."

Example: The smell of fresh baked bread is in a classroom or training room. You walk into it and immediately feel positive, happy, almost like at a special home meal.

Implications: Smell is an entire sense that we have been underutilizing in learning. Attention to the influence of aromas could be a very powerful strategy to reach many types of learners.

Action Steps: Start simple. Get one aroma and test it out. Not every day, but once a week. Gauge the reaction. If it's positive, try a new aroma. For mental alertness, try using peppermint, basil, lemon, cinnamon and rosemary. For calming and relaxation, use lavender, chamomile, orange and rose.

Best Bet Resources: *Aromatherapy Workbook,* by Marcel Lavabre. Contact person: International Flavors and Fragrances, 521 West 57th, NY, NY 10019, (212) 765-5500.

Can Plants Boost Human Learning?

Research Summary: Scientists at the National Space and Aeronautics Administration have discovered that the use of plants makes for a better scientific, learning and thinking environment for astronauts. Could their same research apply to learners indoors? Dr. Wolverton, who headed the Environmental Research Laboratory, says that certain plants have improved life for the astronauts and his own personal life at home. He says that they remove pollutants from the air, increase the negative ionization and charge it with oxygen. In fact, according to the Federal Clean Air Council, studies proved that plants raised the oxygen levels and increased productivity by 10%.

Example: A single plant can often affect 100 square feet of space. Yet, learners in a sterile, stark classroom or hotel room are often much more unresponsive than those in en environment filled with plants.

Implication: We have underestimated the impact of walls, wood, concrete and glass. We also have been unaware of all the positive benefits of certain plants.

Action Steps: The best plants for optimal pollutant reduction, oxygen and enhancing indoor learning environments are: ficus benjamina, philodendrons, dracena deremensis, peace lilies, bamboo palms, yellow chrysanthemums, and gerbera daisies.

Seating & Posture Affect Learner Success

Research Summary: Two researchers, Shea and Hodges, did studies to determine the effects of "formal" (hard-backed chairs facing the front of the room) and "informal" (seated on pillows, lounge chairs, floor, according to student choice) seating in the classroom. Shea found that students who preferred "informal" seating arrangements performed "significantly" better on language (English) comprehension tests. Another group scored much higher in mathematics when they taught and tested in the seating of their choice.

Dunn and Dunn say that at least 20% of learners are significantly affected, positively or negatively, based just on the type of seating options. To be at their best, they need to have choice. Some students need the floor, a couch or beanbag furniture to be at their best in learning.

Does location matter? Can you position your learners for maximum learning success? Wlodlowski says that circles, U shapes and V shapes are best. When given a choice, good spellers tend to sit on the right side of the classroom. This may be related to handedness (hemispheric dominance), or left-brain-right field of vision, or the fact that visual creativity is dominant on the upper left side of the eye pattern range.

Some researchers (Della Valle, Hodges, Shea, Kroon) have found that the environment (seating choices, comfort levels, lighting) and learning styles (global, sequential, concrete, abstract, etc.) are a significant factor in determining the success of students.

Example: You go to a seminar and sit on the left hand side of the room. You change the seating at the break and sit on the right hand side. You'll discover that it's almost a different seminar just by switching seats.

Implications: We may accidentally reduce motivation and learning by keeping a traditional seating pattern.

Action Steps: Change seating patterns often. Provide choice and make it easy to change types of seating arrangements.

THE S.A.D. EFFECT:

⬚ Minimal

⬚ Moderate

■ Heavy

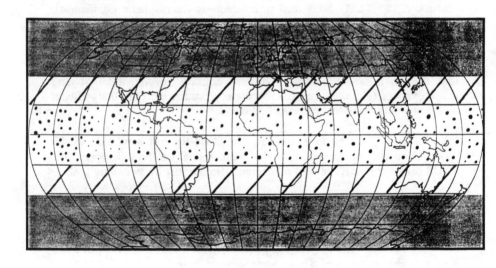

Sunlight Affects Learners' Minds

Research Summary: Can sunlight affect our learning? Definitely, says Orlock. The length and brightness of daylight affects our body's melatonin and hormone levels and influences the release of neurotransmitters. A portion of the hypothalamus (located in the midbrain area), which scientists call the SCN, gets direct information from the eyes and sets our bodies' clocks. This affects our alertness, responsiveness and moods. Each of these, in turn, affects our learning.

A lack of exposure to sunlight during the winter months creates a specific condition which was identified and labeled as Seasonal Affective Disorder (SAD) in 1987 by the American Psychiatric Association, which officially recognized this as a biomedical problem.

Orlock says that residents closer to the equator face less than a two percent chance of being affected by SAD, but those farthest from the equator face up to a 25% chance. It could be that *the best time* for learning is when the hours of the day are longest: from June to August in the Northern Hemisphere and December to February in the Southern Hemisphere. For most schools, these are when the least number of days and hours of learning are scheduled.

Researchers have found that a small amount of artificial or sunlight therapy can alleviate the symptoms if the dosage of light is strong enough. Phototherapists measure light in lux units. Typical outdoor light measures between 10,000-80,000 lux units. Successful light therapy requires a whopping 2,500 lux to be effective. To put that in perspective, a typical indoor light has 500-700 lux, and 1,500 lux only works partially. Treatment sessions can last from 30 minutes to four hours a day.

Carbohydrate cravings may be triggered by SAD and premenstrual syndrome (PMS), says Wurtman. She says that the brain neurotransmitter serotonin may be involved in regulating eating habits and diet successes or failures. She also adds that eating a high carbohydrate dinner may alleviate some of the PMS symptoms.

Example: A woman who was suffering from SAD got light therapy treatments of an hour a day for six weeks. Her anxiety and depression ended. Research shows that 85% of SAD learners respond positively to similar light therapy.

Implications: We may be able to improve learning by simply improving the lighting during those darker winter months.

Action Steps: Explore your options for improving the lighting in your environment during periods of low sunlight. Ask others if they have witnessed the SAD symptoms or if their students have experienced them.

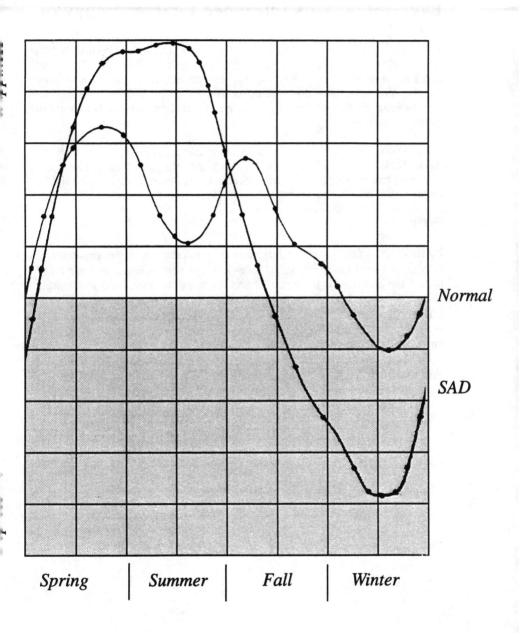

Normal

SAD

Spring | Summer | Fall | Winter

319

Dress Standards Influence Learner Behavior

Research Summary: We know from the Pygmalion experiments that teacher expectations of the learner's ability affects his learning. But what about the reverse? Do student expectations about teachers affect how they learn? Yes, according to clothing consultant John Malloy. He set up experiments to discover whether student perceptions of teacher clothing impacted their learning.

Malloy summarized the conclusive results: "[T]he clothing worn by the teachers substantially affected the work and attitudes of the pupils." He says that teachers who were better dressed had fewer discipline problems, better work habits and learned more. He added that at different socio-economic levels, learners responded differently to the various types of clothing.

Example: You go to a conference or workshop and the presenter is very casual or sloppily dressed. There's a different reaction in your mind than if the presenter is professional and businesslike, with good grooming.

Implications: Your clothing conveys powerful messages about yourself, the organization you work with, and what you think of the job and your customers (or students).

Action Steps: Dress professionally, but don't overkill. Look like you are a professional of status and pride. Half of your presentation is how you are as a person. The other half is your selection of clothes.

Environments Often Ignore Learning Brain

Research Summary: Most of the school reform/restructuring strategies that are suggested, mandated or implemented are doomed. Why? Based on recent brain research, they will only exacerbate the problem, not solve it. Research by Ryan et al., Paris, Ryan and Stiller, and Covington all suggest that educational leaders may want to reconsider these fatal paths:

* curriculum mandates (removes student choice & buy-in)
* high stakes testing (creates teaching to the test and causes student's brains to "minimize")
* rigid performance evaluations of teachers (causes teachers to perform according to the assessments; discourages creativity)
* strong controls on student behavior (creates resentment, apathy)
* bureaucratic, hierarchical, controlling and punitive systems and tactics (school can be made to feel more like a prison)

Example: A student drops out of school. He's not unmotivated; he just wanted a more responsive environment, which the world outside of school promises.

Implications: If we can make dramatic, positive alterations in the school's climate, policies, teacher methodologies and systems, we can keep the focus on learning and hook learners in for a lifetime.

Action Steps: Start up a list of suggestions centering around the brain-based learning research found in this book. Discuss ideas with others. Set up deadlines. Get support. Get others excited about them. Implement positive changes in your teaching methods and learning environment right away. You have little to lose and much to gain.

Summary of Action Steps

1. Be more purposeful about your learning environment. Reduce television watching time. Create a more multi-sensory environment. Add posters, aromas, music and more engaging and relevant activities. Increase social interaction. Use different rooms and, if possible, larger rooms, too. Change the environment often to create novelty and challenge.

2. Encourage children to explore and create new things. Give them quality, trusted adult time for learning and practicing critical skills like categorizing, counting, labeling, language, cause and effect, and thinking. Give plenty of positive feedback and fun celebrations with each accomplishment. Provide a rich use of several languages in a variety of contexts. Reduce all forms of severe negative experiences and disapproval.

3. Reduce "contrived" learning and encourage your learners to go out into the real world for as much learning as possible.

4. A purposeful plan should be made for positively influencing the learner in ways aside from the traditional lesson. The use of music can be quite powerful. Make the room a happy, pleasant place to be in. Colors affect learner moods, too. Peripherals in the form of positive posters, learner work and symbols of expression, change, growth or beauty can be powerful. Make sure the furniture is arranged in a way so that learners can see each other, which usually provides the most interesting visual enhancement of all.

5. Add variety to the learning environments you create. Give your learners some choice in where they sit. Change seating patterns often. Vary your lighting, use music, provide silence, provide earplugs and encourage cooperative learning as well as individual learning.

6. Utilize more visuals, more motion in the visuals and more changes in location in visuals to get and keep attention. Use colored handouts, color your overhead transparencies, use colorful posters and encourage the use of color in mind maps.

7. Be more responsive to the temperature. It's better to be too cool than too warm. But it is best to be neither of these.

8. Use plants in the learning environment for optimal pollutant reduction, oxygen and enhancing indoor learning environments. Some suggestions are: ficus benjamina, philodendrons, dracena deremensis, peace lilies, bamboo palms, yellow chrysanthemums, and gerbera daisies.

9. Explore your options for improving the lighting in your environment during periods of low sunlight.

10. Dress professionally, but don't overkill. Look like you are a professional of status and pride. Half of your presentation is how you are as a person. The other half is your selection of clothes.

Bibliography & Further Readings

Alkon, D. *Memory's Voice*. New York: Harper Collins, 1992.

Allen, C. K. "Encoding of Colors in Short-Term Memory." *Perceptual and Motor Skills* 71.1 (1990): 211-215.

Amabile, Teresa. *Growing Up Creative*. New York: Crown Publishing, 1989.

--- and C. Rovee-Collier. "Contextual Variation and Memory Retrieval at Six Months." *Child Development* Oct. 1991: 1155-66.

Ames, Carole. Children's Achievement Attributions and Self-Reinforcement: Effects of Self-Concept and Competitive 345-55.

---. "Competitive Versus Cooperative Reward Structures: The Influence of Individual and Group Performance Factors on Achievement Attributions and Affect." *American Educational Research Journal* 18 (1981): 273-87.

---. "Achievement Goals and the Classroom Motivational Climate." *Student Perceptions in the Classroom*. Ed. Dale Schunk and Judith Meece. Hillsdale, NJ: Erlbaum, 1992.

---. "Classrooms: Goals, Structures, and Student Motivation." *Journal of Educational Psychology* 84 (1992): 261-71.

---. "The Enhancement of Student Motivation" *Advances in Motivation and Achievement*. Eds. Maeher and Kleiber Vol. 5. Greenwich CT: JAI, 1987.: 123-148.

Anderson, R. C. and P. D. Pearson. "A Schema-Theoretic View of Basic Processes in Reading Comprehension." *Handbook of Reading Research*. Ed. Pearson. New York: Longman, 1984.

Armbruster, B. and T. Anderson. "The Effect of Mapping." *Center for the Study of Reading* 182735th ed. Urbana, Ill.: University of Illinois, 1980.

Armstrong, Blake. "Studying and Television." *Bottom Line Personal*. Rep. of research at University of Wisconsin. 12 June 1991: 9.

Asbjornsen A., K. Hugdahl, G. W. Hynd. "The Effects of Head and Eye Turns on the Right Ear Advantage in Dichotic Listening." *Brain and Language* 39.3 (1990): 447-58.

Backman L., L. G. Nilsson, and R. K. Nourp. "Attentional Demands and Recall of Verbal and Color Information in Action Events." *Scandinavian Journal of Psychology* 34.3 (1993): 246-254.

Bandler, R. *Learning Strategies: Acquisition and Conviction*. Videotape. NLP Comprehensive, Boulder, CO., 1988.

Bandura, A. *Social Foundations of Thought and Action: a social cognitive theory*. Englewood Cliffs: Prentice-Hall, 1986.

Barden, R. C., and M. E. Ford. *Optimal Performance in Golf*. Minneapolis: Optimal Performance Systems, 1990.

Barkley R. *Attention-Deficit Hyperactivity Disorder.* Lecture at conference, "The Many Faces of Intelligence." Washington, D.C., Sept. 1988.

Barrett, Susan. *It's All in Your Head.* Minneapolis: Free Spirit Publishing, 1992.

Baumeister, R. F. "Choking Under Pressure: Self-Consciousness and Paradoxical Effects of Incentives on Skillful Performance." *Journal of Personality and Social Psychology* 46 (1984): 610-20.

---. "Of humor, Music, Anger, Speed and Excuses: Reflections of an Editorial Team After One Year in Office." *Cardiovascular Research* 12 (1992): 1161-3.

---, T. F. Heatherton and D. M. Tice. "When Ego Threats Lead to Self-Regulation Failure: Negative Consequences of High Self-Esteem." *Journal of Personality and Social Psychology* 64.1 (1993): 141-56.

Becker, Robert. *Cross Currents.* Los Angeles: Jeremy Tarcher, Inc., 1986.

Benton, D., and G. Roberts. "Effect of Vitamin and Mineral Supplementation on Intelligence of a Sample of Schoolchildren." *The Lancet* (1988): 140-143.

Bergin, D. "Student Goals for Out-of-School-Learning Activities." *Journal of Adolescent Research* 4 (1989), 92-109.

Berliner, D. C. "The Half-Full Glass: A Review of Research on Teaching." *Using What We Know About Teaching.* Ed. P.L. Hosford. Alexandria, VA: Association for Supervision and Curriculum Development, 1984.

Biggee, Al. *Learning Theories for Teachers.* 4th ed. New York: Harper & Row, 1982.

Black J. E., et al. "Learning Causes Synaptogenesis, Whereas Motor Activity Causes Angiogenesis, in Cerebral Cortex of Adult Rats." Proc. of a conference of the National Academy of Sciences. 87.14 July, 1990: 5568-72.

---. "Effects of Complex Experience on Somatic Growth and Organ Development in Rats." *Developmental Psychobiology* 22.7 (1989): 727-52.

Blackman, et al. "Cognitive Styles and Learning Disabilities." *Journal of Learning Disabilities* n2 15 (1982): 106-115.

Block R. A., et al. "Unilateral Nostril Breathing Influences Lateralized Cognitive Performance." *Brain and Cognition* 9.2 (1989): 181-90.

Bloom, et al. *Brain, Mind and Behavior.* W. H. Freeman and Co.: 1988.

Boller, K. and C. Rovee-Collier. "Contextual Coding and Recoding of Infant's Memories." *Journal of Experimental Child Psychology* 53.1 (1992): 1-23.

Botella, J. and C. W. Eriksen. "Filtering Versus Parallel Processing in RSVP Tasks." *Perception and Psychophysics* 51.4 (1992): 334-43.

Bourre, J. M., et al. "Function of Polyunsaturated Fatty Acids in the Nervous System." 48.1 (1993): 5-15.

325

Bower, G. H. and T. Mann. "Improving Recall by Recoding Interfering Material at the Time of Retrieval." *Journal of Experimental Psychology* 18.6 (1992): 1310-20.

--- and D. G. Morrow. "Mental Models in Narrative Comprehension." *Science* 247.4938 (1990): 44-8.

Bracha, S., "Circling Behavior in Righthanders." *Brain Research* 411 (1987): 231-235.

Braun, C. M. "Estimation of Interhemispheric Dynamics from Simple Unimanual Reaction Time to Extrafoveal Stimuli." *Neuropsychological Review* 3.4 (1992): 321-65.

Breier, A. "Noise and Helplessness." *American Journal of Psychiatry* 144 (1988): 1419-25.

Brewer, C. and D. Campbell. *Rhythms of Learning.* Tucson: Zephyr Press, 1991.

Bricker, William, McLoughlin and Caven. "Exploration of Parental Teaching Style: Technical Note." *Perceptual & Motor Skills* n3 Pt. 2 55 (1982): 1174.

Brophy, J. "Teacher Praise: A Functional Analysis." Review of Educational Research 51 (1981): 5-32.

---. "Socializing Student's Motivation to Learn." *Advances in Motivation and Achievement.* Eds. Maeher and Kleiber. Vol.3. Greenwich, CT: JAI, 1987. 181-210.

Buckley, R. and C. Hawley. "Hyperkenesis and Dye Sensitivity." *Journal of Orthomolecular Psychiatry* 2 (1977): 129-137.

Burton, L. A.and J. Levy. "Sex Differences in the Lateralized Processing of Facial Emotion." *Brain and Cognition* 11.2 (1989): 210-28.

Buzan, Tony. *The Mind Map Book: Radiant Thinking.* London: BBC Books, 1993.

Caine, Renate Nummela and Geoffrey Caine. *Making Connections: Teaching and the Human Brain.* Addison-Wesley. Boston, MA, 1994

Campbell, D. *Introduction to The Musical Brain.* St. Louis: Magnamusic, 1983.

---. *100 Ways to Improve Your Teaching Using Your Voice & Music.* Tucson: Zephyr Press, 1992.

---, ed. *Music and Miracles.* Wheaton, IL: Quest Books,1992.

Carbo, M. "An Analysis of the Relationship Between the Modality Preferences of Kindegartners and the Selected Reading Treatments as they Affect the Learning of a Basic Sight-Word Vocabulary." Diss. St. John's University, 1980.

---, R. Dunn, R. and K. Dunn. *Teaching Students to Read Through their Individual Learning Styles.* Englewood Cliffs: Prentice-Hall, 1986.

Cardinali, R. "Computer Hazards: Real or Imaginary?" *Health Care for Women International* 12.3 (1991): 351-8.

Carpenter, G. and S. Grossberg. "Normal and Amnesic Learning, Recognition and Memory by a Model of Corticohippocampal Interactions." *Trends in Neuroscience* 16.4 (1993): 131-7.

Carper, Jean. *Food: Your Miracle Medicine.* New York: Harper Collins Publishers, 1993.

Carruthers, S. and A. Young. "Preference of Condition Concerning Time in Learning Environments of Rural versus Eighth Grade Students." *Learning Styles Network Newsletter* 1.2 (1980): 1.

Centerwall, B. S. "Television and Violence: The Scale of the Problem and Where to go From Here." *Journal of the American Medical Association* 267.22 (1992): 3059-63.

Chi, M. "Interactive Roles of Knowledge and Strategies in the Development of Organized Sorting and Recall." *Thinking and Learning Skills.* Eds. S. F. Chipman, J. W. Segal, and R. Glaser. Vol 2. Hillsdale, New Jersey: Lawerence Erlbaum & Assoc., 1985.

Christianson, S. "Emotional Stress and Eyewitness Memory: A Critical Review." *Psychological Bulletin* 112.2 (1992): 284-309.

Chugani, H. T. "Imaging Human Brain Development with Positron Emission Tomography." *Journal of Nuclear Medicine* 32.1 (1991): 23-6.

Clynes, Manfred, ed. *Music, Mind and Brain.* New York: Plenum Press, 1982.

---. "Neurobiologic Functions of Rhythm, Time, and Pulse in Music." *Music, Mind and Brain.* Ed. Manfred Clynes. New York: Plenum Press, 1982.

Cohen, E. G. "Treating Status Problems in the Cooperative Classroom." *Cooperative Learning: Research and Theory.* Ed. S. Sharan. New York: Praeger Press, 1990.

Connors, Keith. *Feeding the Brain.* New York: Plenum Press, 1989.

---. *Food Additives and Hyperactive Children.* New York: Plenum Press, 1980.

Cotton, M. M., and K. Evans. "A Review of the Uses of Irlen (tinted) Lenses." *Australian and New Zealand Journal of Ophthalmology* 18.3 (1990): 307-12.

Covington, M. V. "Motivation, Self-Worth, and the Myth of Instensification." Paper presented at annual meeting of the American Psychological Association, San Francisco, CA., 1991.

Coward, Andrew. *Pattern Thinking.* New York: Praeger Publishers, 1990.

Crick, Francis. *The Astonishing Hypothesis: The Scientific Search for the Soul.* New York: Charles Scribner and Sons, 1994.

Csikszentmihalyi, M. & Isabella *Flow: The Psychology of Optimal Experience.* New York: Harper & Row, 1990.

Czeisler, C. A. "Arousal Cycles Can Be Reset." *Science* 233 (1986): 667-71.

Dansereau, D. F. "Learning Strategy Research." *Thinking and Learning Skills.* Eds. S. F. Chipman, J. W. Segal, and R. Glaser. Vol 1. Hillsdale, New Jersey: Lawerence Erlbaum & Assoc., 1985.

Dartigues, Jean-Francois. "Use It or Lose It" *Omni* Feb. 1994: 34.

Davidson, R. J. "Anterior Cerebral Asymmetry and the Nature of Emotion." *Brain and Cognition* 20.1 (1992) : 125-51.

Dean, Ward and Morgenthaler, John. *Smart Drugs & Nutrients.* Health Freedom Publications, Menlo Park, CA 1993.

Dean, Ward, Morgenthaler, John and Fowkes, Steven. *Smart Drugs II,* Health Freedom Publications, Menlo Park, CA 1994.

DeBello, T. "A Critical Analysis of the Achievement and Attitude Effects of Administrative Assignments to Social Studies Writing Instruction Based on Identified, Eighth-Grade Students' Learning Style Preferences for Learning Alone, With Peers, or With Teachers." Diss. St. John's University, 1985.

DeBono, Edward. *Lateral Thinking.* New York: Harper & Row, 1970.

Decety, J., and D. H. Ingvar. "Brain Structures Participating in Mental Stimulation of Motor Behavior: A Neuropsychological Interpretation." *Acta Psychologica* 73.1 (1990): 113-34.

Deci, E. "Application of Research on the Effects of Rewards." *The Hidden Costs of Rewards: New Perspectives on the Psychology of Human Motivation.* Ed. Lepper and Greene. Hillsdale, New Jersey: Lawerence Erlbaum & Assoc., 1978.

---, et al. "Effects of Performance Standards on Teaching Styles: Behavior of Controlling Teachers." *Journal of Educational Psychology* 74 (1982): 852-59.

---. *The Psychology of Self-Determination.* Lexington, MA: DD Heath, 1980.

---. "The Well-Tempered Classroom." *Psychology Today.* March 1985: 52-53.

---. and R. M. Ryan. *Intrinsic Motivation and Self-Determination in Human Behavior.* New York: Plenum, 1985.

---, et al. "Autonomy and Competence as Motivational Factors in Students with Learning Disabilities and Emotional Handicaps." *Journal of Learning Disabilities* 25 (1992): 457-71.

---, et al. "Motivation and Education: The Self-Determination Perspective." *Educational Psychologist* 26 (1991): 325-46.

Della Valle, J. "An Experimental Investigation of the Relationship(s) Between Preference for Mobility and the Word Recognition Scores of Seventh Grade Students to Provide Supervisory and Administrative Guidelines for the Organization of Effective Instructional Environments." Diss. St. John's University, 1984.

---, et al. "The Effects of Matching and Mismatching Student's Mobility Preferences on Recognition and Memory Tasks." *Journal of Educational Research* 79.5 (1986): 267-72.

Dennison, Paul, and Gail Dennison. *Brain Gym.* Teacher's Ed. Ventura, CA: Edu-kinesthetics, 1988.

Diamond, Marian. *Enriching Heredity: The Impact of the Environment on the Brain.* New York: Free Press, 1988.

328

Dienstbier, R. "Periodic Adrenalin Arousal Boosts Health, Coping." *Brain-Mind Bulletin* 14.9A (1989).

Dixon, N. *Preconscious Processing.* New York: Wiley, 1981.

Doll, W. E. J. "Complexity in the Classroom." *Educational Leadership* 47.1 (1989): 65-70.

Domino, G. "Interactive Effects of Achievement Orientation and Teaching Style on Academic Achievement." *ACT Research Report* 39 (1970): 1-9.

Donkin, Scott. *Sitting On the Job.* Houghton-Mifflin, Boston, MA. 1986.

Douglass, C.B. "Making Biology Easier to Understand." *American Biology Teacher* 41.5 (1979): 277-99.

Dryden, Gordon and Jeannette Vos. *The Learning Revolution.* Rolling Hills, CA: Jalmar Press, 1994.

Dunn, R. and K. Dunn. *Teaching Students Through Their Individual Learning Styles: A Practical Approach.* Reston, VA.: Reston Publishing Co., 1978.

---. "Dispelling Outmoded Beliefs About Student Learning." *Educational Leadership* 44.6 (1987): 55-61.

Dunn, R., et al. "Light Up Their Lives: A Review of Research on the Effects of Lighting on Children's Achievement and Behavior." *The Reading Teacher* 38.9 (1985): 863-69.

Edelman, G. *Bright Air, Brilliant Fire.* New York: Basic Books, 1992.

Ehret, C. From Report by the National Argonne Laboratory, Lemont, IL, 1981.

Emery, Charles. "Exercise Keeps the Mind Young." *American Health*, Oct 1986.

Engel, A. K., et al."Temporal Coding in the Visual Cortex: New Vistas on Integration in the Nervous System." *Trends in Neurosciences* 15.6 (1992): 218-26.

Epstein, H. "Phrenoblysis: Special Brain and Mind Growth Periods." *Developmental Psychology* 7 (1974): 207-24.

Fabiani M., D. Karis, and E. Donchin. "Effects of Mnemonic Strategy Manipulation in a Von Restorff Paradigm." *Electroencephalography and Clinical Neurophysiology* 75.2 (1990) : 22-35.

Feingold, D. *Why Your Child is Hyperactive.* New York: Random House, 1985.

Feldman, R. G.and R. F. White. "Lead Neurotoxicity and Disorders in Learning." *Journal of Child Neurology* 7.4 (1992): 354-9.

Felix, Uschi. "The Contribution of Background Music to the Enhancement of Learning in Suggestopedia: A Critical Review of the Literature." *Journal of the Society for Accelerative Learning and Teaching* 18.3-4 (1993): 277-303.

Fiske, S. T., and S. E. Taylor. *Social Cognition.* Reading, MA: Addison-Wesley, 1984.

329

Fitch, R. H., C. P. Brown, and P. Tallal. "Left Hemishere Specialization for Auditory Temporal Processing in Rats." *Annals of the New York Academy of Sciences* 682 (1993): 346-7.

Ford, Martin. *Motivating Humans.* Newbury Park, CA: Sage Publications,1992.

Ford, R. N. *Motivation Through the Work Itself.* New York: American Management Association, 1969.

Fox, N. A. "If It's Not Left, It's Right. Electroencephalograph Asymmetry and the Development of Emotion." *American Psychologist* 46.8 (1991): 863-72.

---, M. Sexton, and J. R. Hebel. "Prenatal Exposure to Tobacco: Effects on Physical Growth at Age Three." *International Journal of Epidemiology* 19.1 (1990): 66-71.

Frederiksen, N. "Implications of Cognitive Theory for Instruction in Problem-Solving." *Review of Educational Research* 54 (1984): 363-407.

Freeley, M. E. "An Experimental Investigation of the Relationships Among Teacher's Individual Time Preferences, Inservice Workshop Schedules, and Instructional Techniques and the Subsequent Implementation of Learning Style Strategies in Participant's Classroom." Diss. St. John's University, 1984.

Friedman, R. C., and J. Downey. "Neurobiology and Sexual Orientation: Current Relationships." *Journal of Neuropsychiatry and Clinical Neurosciences* 5.2 (1993): 131-53.

Frijda, N. H. "The Laws of Emotion." *American Psychologist* 43 (1988): 349-58.

Fuchs, J. L., M. Montemayor, and W. T. Greenough. "Effect of Environmental Complexity on the Size of Superior Colliculus." *Behavioral and Neural Biology* 54.2 (1990): 198-203.

Gadow, K. D., and J. Sprafkin. "Field Experiments of Television Violence With Children: Evidence for an Environmental Hazard?" *Pediatrics* 83.3 (1989): 399-405.

Garai, J. E., and A. Scheinfield. "Sex Differences in Mental and Behavioral Traits." *Genetic Psychology Monographs* 77 (1968): 169-229.

Gardner, Howard. *Frames of Mind.* New York: Basic Books, 1985 .

Gazzaniga, M. *Nature's Mind.* New York: Basic Books, 1992.

Gelb, Michael. *Body Learning.* New York: Delilah Books, 1981.

---. *Present Yourself.* Rolling Hills, CA: Jalmar Press, 1988.

Glasser, William. *Stations of the Mind.* New York: Harper & Row, 1981.

---. *Control Theory.* New York: Harper Collins, 1985.

Gleik, J. *Making a New Science.* New York: Viking, 1987.

Goldman, J., et al. "Behavioral Effects of Sucrose on Preschool Children." *Journal of Abnormal Child Psychology* 14 (1986): 565-78.

Gouchie, C., and D. Kimura. "The Relationship Between Testosterone and Cognitive Ability Patterns." *Research Bulletin* 690 [University of Ontario, London, Canada] 1990.

Gratton, G., M. G. Coles, and E. Donchin. "Optimizing the Use of Information: Strategic Control of Activation of Responses." *Journal of Experimental Psychology* 121.4 (1992): 480-506.

Green, K.P., et al. "Integrating Speech Information Across Talkers, Gender and Sensory Modality: Female Faces and Male Voices in the McGurk Effect" *Perception and Psychophysics* 50.6 (1991): 524-36.

Greenough, W. T., and B. J. Anderson. "Cerebellar Synaptic Plasticity: Relation to Learning Versus Neural Activity." *Annals of the New York Academy of Science* 627 (1991): 231-47.

---, G. Withers, and B. Anderson. "Experience-Dependent Synaptogenesis as a Plausible Memory Mechanism." *Learning and Memory: The Behavioral and Biological Substrates.* Eds. I. Gormezano, I. and E. Wasserman. Hillsdale, NJ.: Erlbaum Associates, 1992. 209-29.

---, and B. Anderson. "Cerebellar Synaptic Plasticity." *Annals of the New York Academy of Sciences* 627 (1991): 231-47.

Grinder, Michael. *Righting the Educational Conveyor Belt.* Portland, OR: Metamorphous Press, 1989.

---. *ENVOY.* Michael Grinder & Associates. Seattle WA. 1994.

Grunwald, L., and J. Goldberg. "Babies Are Smarter Than You Think." *Life Magazine* July 1993: 45-60.

Hagan-Heimlich, J. E., and S. D. Pittelman. "Classroom Applications of the Semantic Mapping Procedure in Reading and Writing." *Program Report* 84.4 (1984).

Halpern, S. *Sound Health.* New York: Harper & Row, 1985.

Hampden-Turner, Charles. *Maps of the Mind.* New York: Macmillan Publishing, 1981.

Hampson, E. and D. Kimura. "Reciprocal Effects of Hormonal Fluctuations on Human Motor and Perceptual Spatial Skills." *Behavioral Neuroscience* 102.3 (1988): 456-9.

Harper, A. E., and J. C. Peters. "Protein Intake, Brain Amino Acid and Serontonin Concentration and Protein Self-Selection." *Journal of Nutrition* 119.5 (1989): 677-89.

Harper, C., and J. Kril. "Neuropathology of Alcoholism." *Alcohol and Alcoholism* 25.2-3 (1990): 207-16.

Hart, Leslie. *How the Brain Works: A New Understanding of Human Learning.* New York: Basic Books, 1975.

---. *Human Brain and Human Learning.* White Plains, New York: Longman Publishing, 1983.

Harter, S. "The Perceived Competence Scale for Children." *Child Development* 51 (1980): 218-35.

---. "A Developmental Perspective on Some Parameters of Self-Regulation in Children." *Self-Management and Behavior Change: From Theory to Practice.* Eds. P. Karoly and F. H. Kanfer. New York: Pergammon Press, 1982.

Hassler, M. "Testosterone and Musical Talent." *Experimental and Clinical Endicrinology* 98.2 (1991): 89-98.

Hayne, H., C. Rovee-Collier, and M. A. Borza. "Infant Memory for Place Information." *Memory and Cognition* 19.4 (1991): 378-86.

Healer, Janet. "Microwave Towers May Affect Brain." *Brain/Mind Bulletin* 2.14E (1977).

Healy, J. *Endangered Minds: Why Our Children Can't Think.* New York: Simon and Schuster, 1990.

---. *Your Child's Growing Mind.* New York: Doubleday, 1987.

---. "Why Kids Can't Think." *Bottom Line Personal* 13.8 (1993): 1-3.

Hermann, D.J. & Hanwood, J.R. 1980. "More evidence for the Existence of the Separate Semantic and Episodic Stores in Long-Term Memory" Journal of Experimental Psychology: Human Learning and Memory 6, 5: 467-478.

Herrmann, Ned. *The Creative Brain.* Lake Lure, N.C.: Brain Books, 1988.

Hirsch, A. "Floral Odor Increases Learning Ability." Presentation at annual conference of American Academy of Neurological & Orthopedic Surgery, 1993. Contact: Allan Hirsch, Smell & Taste Treatment Foundation, Chicago, IL.

Ho, Kevin. "The Dimensionality and Occupational Differentiation of the Hermann Brain Dominance Instrument." Department of Educational Psychology, Brigham Young University, March 1988.

Hobson, J. A. *Sleep.* New York: W.H. Freeman, 1989.

Hodges, H. "An Analysis of the Relationships Among Preferences for a Formal/Informal Design, One Element of Learning Style, Academic Achievement, and Attitudes of Seventh and Eighth Grade Students in Remedial Mathematics Classes in a New York City Alternative Junior High school." Diss. St.John's University, 1985.

Hofman M. A., and D. F. Swaab. "Sexual Dimorphism of the Human Brain." *Experimental and Clinical Endocrinology* 98.2 (1991): 161-70.

Hooper J., and D. Teresi. *The Three Pound Universe: The Brain, from Chemistry of the Mind to New Frontiers of the Soul.* New York: Dell Publishing, 1986.

Hopfield, J., D. Feinstein, and R. Palmer. "Unlearning Has a Stabilizing Effect in Collective Memories." *Nature.* July, 1983: 158-59.

Horn, G. "Learning, Memory and the Brain." *Indian Journal of Physiology and Pharmacology* 35.1 (1991): 3-9.

Horne J. "Sleep Loss and Divergent Thinking Ability." *Sleep* 11.6 (1989): 528-36.

---. "Human Slow Wave Sleep: A Review and Appraisal of Recent Findings, with Implications for Sleep Functions and Psychiatric Illness." *Experientia* Oct. 15, 1992: 941-54.

Horowitz, L., and J. M. Sarkin. "Video Display Terminal Operation: a Potential Risk in the Etiology and Maintenance of Tempromandidibular Disorders." *Cranio* 10.1 (1992): 43-50.

Houston, Jean. *The Possible Human: A Course in Enhancing Your Physical, Mantal and Creative Abilities.* Los Angeles, CA: Jeremy Tarcher, 1982.

Huttenlocher, P. R. "Morphometric Study of Human Cerebral Cortex Development." *Neuropsychologia* 28.6 (1990): 517-27.

Hynd, G. W. "Neurological Aspects of Dyslexia: Comment on the Balance Model." *Journal of Learning Disabilities* 25.2 (1992): 110-2, 123.

---, et al. "Attention-Deficit Disorder Without Hyperactivity: A Distinct Behavioral and Cognitive Syndrome." *Journal of Child Neurology* 6 (1991): S37-43.

---, et al. "Corpus Callosum Morphology in Attention Deficit-Hyperactivity Disorder: Morphometric Analysis of MRI." *Journal of Learning Disabilities* 24.3 (1991) : 141-6.

Introini-Collision, I. B., B. Miyazaki, and J. L. McGaugh. "Involvement of the Amygdala in the Memory-Enhancing Effects of Clenbuterol." *Psychopharmacology* 104.4 (1991): 541-4.

Isaacs, K. R., et al. "Exercise and the Brain: Angiogenesis in the Adult Rat Cerebellum After Vigorous Physical Activity and Motor Skill Learning." *Journal of Cerebral Blood Flow and Metabolism* 12.1 (1992): 110-9.

Jacobs, B. "Serotonin and Behavior: Emphasis on Motor Control." *Journal of Clinical Psychiatry* 52 (1991): Suppl. 17-23.

---, M. Schall, and A. B. Scheibel. "A Quantitative Dendritic Analysis of Wernicke's Area in Humans: Gender, Hemispheric and Environmental Factors." *Journal of Comparitive Neurology* 327.1 (1993): 97-111.

Jacobs, W. J., and L. Nadel. "Stress-Induced Recovery of Fears and Phobias." *Psychological Review* 92.4 (1985): 512-531.

James, Tad. *The Secret of Creating Your Future.* Honolulu, HI: Advanced NeuroDynamics, 1989.

---, Woodsmall, and Wyatt. *Timeline and the Basis of Personality.* Cupertino, CA: Meta Publications, 1988.

Jaques, E. "Development of Intellectual Capability." *Essays on Intellect.* Ed. F. R. Link. Alexandria, VA: Association for Curriculum and Development.

Jauchem, J. "Alleged Health Effects of Electromagnetic Fields: Misconceptions in the Scientific Literature." *Journal of Microwave Power and Electromagnetic Energy* 26.4 (1991): 189-95.

---, and J. H. Merritt. "The Epidemiology of Exposure to Electromagnetic Fields: An Overview of the Recent Literature." *Journal of Clinical Epidemiology* 44.9 (1991): 895-906.

---, and M. R. Frei. "Heart Rate and Blood Pressure Changes During Radiofrequency Irradiation and Environmental Heating." *Comparative Biochemistry and Physiology* 101.1 (1992): 1-9.

Jenkins, D. J., et al. "Nibbling Versus Gorging: Metabolic Advantages of Increased Meal Frequency." *New England Journal of Medicine* 321.14 (1989): 929-34.

Jernigan, T. L., and P. Tallal. "Late Childhood Changes in Brain Morphology Observable with MRI." *Developmental Medicine and Child Neurology* 32.5 (1990): 379-85.

Johnson, M. H., et al. "Newborns' Preferential Tracking of Face-Like Stimuli and its Subsequent Decline. *Cognition* 40.1-2 (1991): 1-19.

Kagan, D. M. "How Schools Alienate Students at Risk: A Model for Examining Proximal Classroom Variables." *Educational Psychologist* 25 (1990): 105-25.

Kandel, E. and R. Hawkins. "The Biological Basis of Learning and Individuality." *Scientific American* Sept. 1992: 79-86.

Kaplan, R. "Reader's Visual Fields Increase with Color Therapy." *Brain Mind Bulletin* 8. 14F (1983).

Karkowski, W., T. Marek, and C. Noworol. "Stimulating Work Found to Boost Pain Perception." *Work and Stress* 2 (1989): 133-37.

Kavet, R., and R. A. Tell. "VDT's: Field Levels, Epidemiology, and Laboratory Studies." *Health Physics* 61.1 (1991): 47-57.

Khachaturian, Zaven. "Mental Decline As We Grow Older." *Bottom Line Personal* 12.23 (1991): 9.

Khalsa, D., M. Ziegler, and B. Kennedy. "Body Sides Switch Dominance." *Life Sciences* 38 (1986): 1203-14.

Kim, I. K. and E. S. Spelke. "Infants' Sensitivity to Effects of Gravity on Visible Object Motion." *Journal of Experimental Psychology: Human Perception and Performance* 18.2 (1992): 385-93.

Kimura, D., "Male Brain, Female Brain: The Hidden Difference." *Psychology Today* Nov. 1985.

---. "How Different Are Male and Female Brains?" *Orbit* Oct. 1986.

---. "Are Men's and Women's Brains Really Different?" *Canadian Psychology* 28.2 (1987).

---. "Monthly Fluctuations in Sex Hormones Affect Women's Cognitive Skills." *Psychology Today* Nov. 1989: 63-66.

---, and E. Hampson. "Neural and Hormonal Mechanisms Mediating Sex Differences in Cognition." *Research Bulletin* 689 [Dept. of Psych. University of Ontario, London, Canada] April 1990.

---. "Sex Differences in the Brain." *Scientific American* Sept. 1992: 119-25.

King, Jeff. "Comparing Alpha Induction Differences Between Two Music Samples." Abstract from the Center for Research on Learning and Cognition, University of North Texas, 1991.

Klein and Armitage. "Brainwave Cycle Fluctuations." *Science* 204 (1979): 1326-28.

Kline, Peter. *Everyday Genius.* Arlington, VA: Great Ocean Publishers, 1990.

Klutky, N. "Sex Differences in Memory Performance for Odors, on Sequences and Colors." *Zeitscrift fur Experimentelle und Angewandte Psychologie* 37.3 (1990): 437-46.

Kopera, H. "Female Hormones and Brain Function." *Hormones and the Brain.* Eds. de Wied and Van Keep. Lancaster, England: MTP Press, 1980. 189-203.

Kotulak, Ronald. "Unraveling Hidden Mysteries of the Brain." *Chicago Tribune* 11-16 April 1993.

Krimsky, J. S. "A Comparitive Analysis of the Effects of Matching and Mismatching Fourth Grade Students With Their Learning Styles Preferences for the Environmental Element of Light and Their Subsequent Reading Speed and Accuracy Scores." Diss. St. John's University, 1982.

Kohn, Alfie. *No Contest: The Case Against Competition.* New York: Houghton-Mifflin, 1987.

---. *Punished by Rewards.* New York: Houghton Mifflin, 1993.

Kroon, D. "An Experimental Investigation of the Effects on Academic Achievement and the Resultant Administrative Implications of Instruction Congruent and Incongruent with Secondary Industrial Arts Student's Learning Style Perceptual Preferences." Diss. St. John's University, 1985.

Lakoff, G., and M. Johnson. *Metaphors We Live By.* Chicago: University of Chicago Press, 1980.

Lande, R. G. "The Video Violence Debate." *Hospital and Community Psychiatry* 44.4 (1993): 347-51.

Lavabre, Marcel. *Aromatherapy Workbook.* Rochester, VT: Healing Arts Press, 1990.

Lavond, D. G., J. J. Kim, and R. F. Thompson. "Mammalian Brain Substrates of Aversive Classical Conditioning." *Annual Review of Psychology* 44 (1993): 317-42.

LeDoux, J., and W. Hirst. "Attention." *Mind and Brain: Dialogues in Cognitive Neuroscience.* New York: Cambridge, 1986. 105-85.

Lepper, M. R. "Intrinsic and Extrinsic Motivation in Children: Detrimental Effects of Superfluous Social Controls. Ed. W.A. Collins. Aspects of the Development of Competence: The Minnesota Symposium on Child Psychology. Vol 14. Hillsdale, NJ: Lawerence Erlbaum, 1981. 155-214.

Levinson, HN. *A Solution to the Riddle Dyslexia.* Springer-Verlag, New York, 1980.

Levinson, H. "Why Johnny Can't Pay Attention." *Bottom Line Personal* 12.20 (1991): 11.

Levy, J. "Research Synthesis on Right and Left Hemispheres: We Think With Both Sides of the Brain." *Educational Leadership* 40.4 (1983): 66-71.

---. "Right Brain, Left Brain: Fact and Fiction." *Psychology Today* May 1985: 38.

Levine, S. C., N. C. Jordan, and J. Huttenlocher. "Development of Calculation Abilities in Young Children." *Journal of Experimental Child Psychology* 53.1 (1992): 72-103.

Lewicki, P., T. Hill, and M. Czyzewska. "Nonconscious Acquisition of Information." *American Psychologist* 47.6 (1992): 796-801.

Lieberman, H. R., J. J. Wurtman, and M. H. Teicher. "Circadian Rhythms in Healthy Young and Elderly Humans." *Neurobiology of Aging* 10.3 (1989): 259-65.

Lingerman, H. *The Healing Energies of Music.* Wheaton, IL: Theosophical Publishing House, 1983.

Livingstone, M., et al. "Physiological and Anatomical Evidence for a Magnocellular Defect in Developmental Dsylexia." *Proceedings of the National Academy of Science* 88 Sept. 1991: 9743-7947.

Locke, E. A. and G. P. Latham. "Work Motivation and Satisfaction: Light at the End of the Tunnel." *Psychological Science* 1 (1990): 240-46.

Lozanov, Georgi. *Suggestology and Outlines of Suggestopedy.* New York: Gordon & Breach, 1978.

---. "On Some Problems of the Anatomy, Physiology and Biochemistry of Cerebral Activities in the Global-Artistic Approach in Modern Suggestopedagogic Training." *The Journal of the Society for Accelerative Learning and Teaching* 16.2 (1991): 101-16.

Luiten, J., W. Ames, and G. Ackerson. "A Meta-Analysis of the Effects of Advance Organizers on Learning and Retention." *American Educational Research Journal* 17 (1980): 211-18.

MacLean, Paul. "A Mind of Three Minds: Educating the Triune Brain." *77th Yearbook of the National Society for the Study of Education.* Chicago: University of Chicago Press, 1978. 308-42.

---. *The Triune Brain in Education.* New York: Plenum Press, 1990.

MacMurren, H. "A Comparative Study of the Effects of Matching and Mismatching Sixth Grade Students With Their Learning Style Preferences for the Physical Element of Intake and Their Subsequent Reading Speed and Accuracy Scores." Diss. St. John's University, 1985.

Mager, R. F., and J. McCann. *Learner-Controlled Instruction.* Palo Alto, CA: Varian Press, 1963.

Maguire, J. *Care and Feeding of the Brain.* New York: Doubleday, 1990.

Malloy, John. *Dress for Success.* New York: Warner Books, 1975.

Malone, T., and M. Lepper. "Making Learning Fun: A Taxonomy of Intrinsic Motivations for Learning." *Aptitude, Learning and Instruction III: Cognitive and Affective Process Analyses.* Eds. Snow and Farr. Hillsdale, New Jersey: Lawerence Erlbaum, 1987. 223-53.

Mandler, G. "The Nature of Emotions." *States of Mind.* Ed. J. Miller. New York: Pantheon Books, 1983.

Mark, Vernon. *Brain Power.* Boston: Houghton-Mifflin, 1989.

Martin, R. C. "Short-Term Memory and Sentence Processing: Evidence from Neuropsychology." *Memory and Cognition* 21.2 (1993): 176-83.

McCarthy, B. "Using the 4MAT System to Bring Learning Styles to Schools." *Educational Leadership* 48.2 (1990): 31-37.

McCarthy, Michael. *Mastering the Information Age*. Los Angeles: Jeremy Tarcher, 1991.

McGaugh J.L. "Dissociating Learning and Performance: Drug and Hormone Enhancement of Memory Storage." *Brain Research Bulletin* 23.4-5 (1989): 339-45.

---, et al. "Involvement of the Amygdaloid Complex in Neuromodulatory Influences on Memory Storage." *Neuroscience and Biobehavioral Reviews* 14.4 (1990): 425-31.

McGee, M., "Human Spatial Abilities: Psychometric Studies and Environmental, Genetic, Hormonal and Neurological Influences." *Psychological Bulletin* 86.5 (1979): 889-918.

McGuiness, D. "Sex Differences in Organisation, Perception and Cognition." *Exploring Sex Differences*. Eds. B. Lloyd and J. Archer. London, England: Academic Press, 1976. 123-55.

---. *When Children Don't Learn*. New York: Basic Books, 1985.

McNamara, R. K., and R. W. Skelton. "The Neuropharmacological and Neurochemical Basis of Place Learning in the Morris Water Maze." *Brain Research Reviews* 18.1 (1993): 33-49.

Mehler, Jaques and Dupoux, Emmanuel. *What Infants Know*. Blackwell Publishers, Cambridge, MA. 1994.

Meese, J. L., A. Wigfield, and J. S. Eccles. "Predictors of Math Anxiety and its Influence on Young Adolescents' Course Enrollment Intentions and Performance in Mathematics." *Journal of Educational Psychology* 82 (1990): 60-70.

Meleges, F. T., and D. A. Hamburg. "Psychological Effects of Hormonal Changes in Women." *Human Sexuality in Four Perspectives*. Ed. F. A. Beach. Baltimore, Md.: Johns Hopkins Univ. Press, 1976. 269-95.

Messant, P. K. "Female Hormones and Behavior." *Exploring Sex Differences*. Eds. B. Lloyd and J. Archer, J. London, England: Academic Press, 1976. 183-211.

Michaud, E., and R. Wild. *Boost Your Brain Power*. Emmaus, PA: Rodale Press, 1991.

Milich, R., and W. E. Pelham. "The Effects of Sugar Ingestion on the Classroom and Playgroup Behavior." *Journal of Consulting & Clinical Psychology* 54 (1986): 1-5.

Mills, R. C. "Relationship Between School Motivational Climate, Teacher Attitudes, Student Mental Health, School Failure and Health Damaging Behavior." Paper at Annual Conference of the American Educational Research Association, Washington, D.C. April 1987.

Miura, I. T. "A Multivariate Study of School-Aged Children's Computer Interest and Use." Eds. M. E. Ford and D. H. Ford. *Humans As Self-Constructing Living Systems: Putting the Framework to Work*. Hillsdale, NJ: Lawerence Erlbaum, 1987. 177-97.

Miyamoto, R. T., et al. "Comparison of Sensory Aids in Deaf Children." *Annals of Otology, Rhinology and Laryngology* 142 Suppl. (1989): 2-7.

337

---. "Comparison of Speech Perception Abilities in Deaf Children With Hearing Aids or Cochlear Implants." *Otolaryngology and Head and Neck Surgery* 104.1 (1991): 42-6.

---. "Longitudinal Evaluation of Communication Skills of Children With Single or Multichannel Chochlear Implants." *American Journal of Otology* 13.3 (1992): 215-22.

Moir, Anne, and D. Jessel. *Brainsex.* New York: Dell, 1991.

Morgan, Brian, and Roberta Morgan. *Brainfood.* Los Angeles: Price, Stern, Sloan, 1987.

Morgan, M., and Granger. "Electric and Magnetic Fields from 60 Hertz Electric Power: What Do We Know About Possible Health Risks?" *Dept. of Engineering and Public Policy.* Pittsburg, PA: Carnegie Mellon University, 1989.

Morgane, P. J., et al. "Prenatal Malnutrition and Development of the Brain." *Neuroscience and Biobehavioral Reviews* 17.1 (1993): 91-128.

Murphy, M. and S. Donovan. *The Physical and Psychological Effects of Meditation.* San Rafael, CA: Esalen Institute, 1988.

Murrain, P.G. "Administrative Determinations Concerning Facilities Utilization and Instructional Grouping: An Analysis of the Relationship(s) Between Selected Thermal Environments and Preferences for Temperature, an Element of Learning Style." Diss. St. John's University, 1983.

Nadel, L. "Varieties of Spatial Cognition. Psychobiological Considerations." *Annals of the New York Academy of Sciences* 608 (1990): 613-26.

---, J. Wilmer, and E. M. Kurz. "Cognitive Maps and Environmental Context." *Context and Learning* . Eds. Balsam and Tomi. Hillsdale, New Jersey: Lawerence Erlbaum, 1984.

Nadler, J. V., et al. "Kindling, Prenatal Exposure to Ethanol and Postnatal Development Selectively Alter Responses to Hippocampal Pyramidal Cells to NMDA." *Advances in Experimental Medicine and Biology* 268 (1990): 407-17.

Nakamura, K. "A Theory of Cerebral Learning Regulated by the Reward System." *Biological Cybernetics* 68.6 (1993): 491-8.

Needleman, H. L., et al. "Deficits in Psychologic and Classroom Performance of Children with Elevated Dentine Lead Levels." *New England Journal of Medicine* 300 (1979): 689-695.

Nelig, A., J. L. Daval, and G. Debry. "Caffeine and the Central Nervous System: Mechanisms of Action, Biochemical, Metabolic and Poststimulant Effects." *Brain Research Reviews* 17.2 (1992): 139-70.

Neve, C. D., L. Hart, and Edgar Thomas. "Huge Learning Jumps Show Potency of Brain-Based Instruction." *Phi Delta Kappan* October 1986: 143-8.

Nisbett, R. E. and L. D. Ross. *Human Inference: Strategies and Shortcomings of Social Judgement.* Englewood Cliffs: Prentice-Hall, 1980.

338

Nummela, R., and T. Rosengren. "What's Happening in Student's Brain's May Redefine Teaching." *Educational Leadership* 43.8 (1986): 49-53.

---. "The Brain's Routes and Maps: Vital Connections in Learning." *NAASP Bulletin* 72: 83-86.

Oakhill, J. "Time of Day Affects Aspects of Memory." *Applied Cognitive Psychology* 2 (1988): 203-12.

Obler, L. K. and Fein, D. *The Exceptional Brain.* New York: Guilford, 1988.

O'Keefe, J., and L. Nadel. *The Hippocampus as a Cognitive Map.* Oxford: Clarendon Press, 1978.

Olds, James. "Mapping the Mind onto the Brain." *The Neurosciences: Paths of Discovery.* Eds. Frederic Worden, Judith Swazey, and George Adelman. Boston, MA: Birkhauser, 1992.

Olney, J. "The Toxic Effects of Glutamate and Related Compounds in the Retina and the Brain." *Retina* 2.4 (1982): 341-59.

Orlock, Carol. *Inner Time.* New York: Birch Lane Press, Carol Publishing, 1993.

Ornstein, R. *The Evolution of Consciousness.* New York: Simon & Schuster, 1991.

Ornstein, Robert and D. Sobel. *The Healing Brain and How It Keeps Us Healthy.* New York: Simon & Schuster, 1987.

---, and Richard Thompson. *The Amazing Brain.* Boston: Houghton-Mifflin, 1986.

Osberger, M. J., M. Maso, and L. K. Sam. "Speech Intelligibility with Cochlear Implants, Tactile Aids or Hearing Aids." *Journal of Speech and Hearing Research* 36.1 (1993): 186-203.

Ostrander, Sheila and Schroeder, Lynn. *Super-Memory.* Carroll & Graf Publishers, New York. 1991.

Paris, S. G., et al. "Developmental Perspective of Standardized Achievement Testing." *Educational Researcher* 20 (1991): 12-20.

Pelton, Ross. *Mind Food & Smart Pills.* Doubleday, New York. 1989.

Petty, R. E., and J. T. Cacioppo. "Motivational Factors in Consumer Response Advertisement." Eds. Green, Beatty, and Arkin. *Human Motivation: Physiological, Behavioral and Social Approaches.* Boston: Allyn & Bacon, 1984. 418-454.

Pfurtscheller, G. and A. Berghold. "Patterns of Cortical Activation During Planning of Voluntary Movement." *Electroencephalography and Clinical Neurophysiology.* 72 (1989): 250-58.

Pintrich, P. R., and T. Garcia. "Student Goal Orientation and Self-Regulation in the College Classroom." *Advances in Motivation and Achievement.* Eds. Maeher and Pintrich. Vol. 7 Greenwich, CT: JAI, 1991. 371-402.

Pizzo, J. "An Investigation of the Relationships Between Selected Acoustic Environments and Sound, an Element of Learning Style, as They Affect Sixth Grade Students' Reading Achievement and Attitudes." Diss. St. John's University, 1981.

Prasad, A. N., and C. Prasad. "Iron Deficiency; Non-Hematological Manefestations." *Progress in Food and Nutritional Science* 15.4 (1991): 255-83.

Price, G. "Which Learning Style Elements are Stable and Which End to Change?" *Learning Styles Network Newsletter* 4.2 (1980): 38-40.

Prigogine, I., and I. Stengers. *Order Out of Chaos*. New York: Bantam, 1984.

Prinz, R. J., W. A. Roberts, and E. Hantman. "Sugar Consumption and Hyperactive Behavior in Children." *Journal of Consulting and Clinical Psychology*. 48 (1980): 760-69.

Pulvirenti, L. "Neural Plasticity and Memory: Towards an Integrated View." *Functional Neurology* 7.6 (1992): 49-57.

Redfield, D. L. and E. W. Rousseau. "A Meta-Analysis of Experimental Research on Teacher Questioning Behavior." *Review of Educational Research*. 51.2 (1981): 237-45.

Restak, R. *The Brain*. New York: Warner Books, 1988.

---. *Receptors*. Manuscript, to be published, 1994.

Roederer, Juan. "Physical and Neuropsychological Foundations of Music." *Music, Mind and Brain*. Ed. Manfred Clynes. New York: Plenum Press, 1981.

Roland, P., et. al. "Functional Anatomy of Storage, Recall and Recognition of a Visual Pattern in Man." *Neuroreport: An International Journal for the Rapid Communication of Research in Neuroscience* 1.1 (1990): 53-6.

Rose, Colin. *Accelerated Learning*. New York: Dell Publishing, 1986.

Rose, F., M. Davey, and E. Attree. "How Does Environmental Enrichment Aid Performance Following Cortical Injury in the Rat?" *Neuroreport: An International Journal for the Rapid Communication of Research in Neuroscience* 4.2 (1993): 163-6.

Rosenfield, I. *The Invention of Memory*. New York: Basic Books, 1988.

Rosenfield, M., and B. Gilmartin. "Effect of Target Proximity on the Open-Loop Accomodative Response." *Optometry and Vision Science* 67.2 (1990): 74-9.

---, and K. J. Ciuffreda. "Effect of Surround Propinquity on the Open-Loop Accomodative Response." *Investigative Ophthalmology and Visual Science* 32.1 (1991): 142-7.

Rosenthal, R. and L. Jacobsen. *Pygmalion in the Classroom*. New York: Rinehart and Winston, 1968.

Rossi, A. S., and P. E. Rossi. "Body Time and Social Time: Mood Patterns by Cycle Phase and Day of the Week." *The Psychobiology of Sex Differences and Sex Roles*. Ed. J. E. Parsons. London, England: Hemisphere, 1980. 269-301.

---. "Hemisphereic Dominance Switches." 1986

Rovee-Collier, C., et al. "Infants' Eyewitness Testimony: Effects of Postevent Information on a Prior Memory Representation." *Memory and Cognition* 21.2 (1993): 267-79.

Rush, D., Z. Stein, and M. Susser. "Prenatal Nutritional Supplementation." *Pediatrics* 65 (1980): 683-97.

Ryan, R. M., J. P. Connell, and E. L. Deci. 1985. "A Motivational Analysis of Self-Determination and Self-Regulation in Education." *Research on Motivation in Education.* Eds. C. Ames and R. Ames. Vol.2. Orlando, FL: Academic Press. 13-51.

Ryan, R. M., and J. Stiller. "The Social Contexts of Internalization: Parent and Teacher Influences on Autonomy, Motivation, and Learning." *Advances in Motivation and Achievement.* Eds. M. L. Maeher and R. Pintrich. Vol. 7. Greenwich, CT: JAI, 1991. 115-49.

Santostefano, S. "Cognitive Controls, Metaphors and Contexts. An Approach to Cognition and Emotion." *Thought and Emotions: Developmental Perspectives.* Eds. D. J. Bearson and H. Zimilies. Hillsdale, NJ: Erlbaum, 1986.

Scartelli. *Journal of Music Therapy* 21 (1984): 67-78.

Schacter, D. L. "Understanding Implicit Memory." *American Psychologist* 47.4 (1992): 559-69.

Schatz, C. J. "Impulse Activity and the Patterning of Connections During CNS Development." *Neuron* 5.6 (1990): 745-56.

---. "The Developing Brain." *Scientific American* Sept. 1992: 60-7.

---. "Dividing Up the Neocortex." *Science* 9 Oct. 1992: 237-8.

Schneider, M. L., and C. L. Coe. "Repeated Social Stress During Pregnancy Impairs Neuromotor Development of Primate Infant." *Journal of Developmental and Behavioral Pediatrics* 14.2 (1993): 81-7.

Schneider, W. "Varieties of Working Memory As Seen in Biology and in Connectionist/Control Architectures." *Memory and Cognition* 21.2 (1993): 184-92.

Scholz, J. "Cultural Expressions Affecting Patient Care." *Dimensions in Oncology Nursing* 4.1 (1990): 16-26.

Schunk, D. H. "Goal Setting and Self-Efficacy During Self-Regulated Learning." *Educational Psychologist* 25.1 (1990): 71-86.

Segal, J., S. Chipman, and R. Glaser. *Thinking and Learning Skills.* Vol. I. Hillsdale, NJ: Erlbaum & Assoc., 1985.

Seligman, Martin. *Learned Optimism.* Pocket Books, 1992.

Senge, Peter. *The Fifth Discipline.* New York: Random House, 1992.

Shannahoff-Khalsa, David. "Rhythms and Reality: The Dynamics of The Mind." Psychology Today, Sept. 1984

Shea, T. C. "An Investigation of the Relationship Among Preferences for the Learning Style Element of Design, Selected Instructional Environments, and Reading Achievement of Ninth Grade Students to Improve Administrative Determinations Concerning Effective Educational Facilities." Diss. 1983.

Shields, P. J., and C. Rovee-Collier. "Long-Term Memory for Context Specific Category Information at Six Months." *Child Development* 63.2 (1992): 245-59.

Shipman, V. and F. Shipman. "Cognitive Styles: Some Conceptual, Methodological, and Applied Issues." Ed. E. W. Gordon. *Human Diversity and Pedagogy.* Westport, Conn: Mediax, 1983.

Silverman, K., and R. R. Griffiths. "Low-Dose Caffeine Discrimination and Self-Reported Mood Effects in Normal Volunteers." *Journal of the Experimental Analysis of Behavior* 57.1 (1992): 91-107.

Silverman, K., et. al. "Withdrawal Syndrome After the Double-Blind Cessation of Caffeine Consumption." *New England Journal of Medicine* 327.16 (1992): 1109-14.

Silverman, L. H. "A Comprehensive Report of Studies Using the Subliminal Psychodynamic Activation Method." *Psychological Research Bulletin* [Lund Univ.] 20.3: 22.

Silverstein, Alvin, and Virginia Silverstein. *The World of the Brain.* New York: Morrow Jr. Books, 1986.

Singer, J. "Ongoing Thought: The Normative Baseline for Alternative States of Consciousness." Ed. N. E. Zinberg. New York: Free Press, 1977.

Singer, W. "Synchronization of Cortical Activity and its Putative Role in Information Processing and Learning." *Annual Review of Physiology* 55 (1993): 349-74.

Sirevaag, A. M., and W. T. Greenough. "Plasticity of GFAP-Immunoreactive Astrocyte Size and Number in Visual Cortex of Rats Reared in Complex Environments." *Brain Research* 540.1-2 (1991): 273-8.

Smith, A. P., A. M. Kendrick, and Maben. "Effects of Caffeine on Performance and Mood in the Late Morning and After Lunch." *Neuropsychobiology* 26.4 (1992): 198-204.

Smith, B. D., R. A. Davidson, and R. L. Green. "Effects of Caffeine and Gender on Physiology and Performance: Further Tests on a Biobehavioral Model." *Physiology and Behavior* 54.3 (1993): 415-22.

Soloveichik, Simon. "Odd Way to Teach, But It Works." *Soviet Life Magazine* May 1979.

Sperry, R. "Hemisphere Disconnection and Unity in Conscious Awareness." *American Psychologist* 23 (1968): 723-33.

Squire, L. "Memory and the Hippocampus: A Synthesis from Findings with Rats, Monkeys and Humans." *Psychological Review* 99.2 (1992): 195-231.

Sternberg, Robert. *Beyond I.Q.: A Triarchical Theory of Human Intelligence.*

---, and J. Kolligan, Jr., eds. *Competence Considered.* New Haven, CT: Yale University Press, 1990.

Stone, C. L. "A Meta-Analysis of Advance Organizer Studies." *Journal of Experimental Education* 54 (1983): 194-9.

Strasburger, V. C. "Children, Adolescents and Television." *Pediatrics in Review* 13.4 (1992): 144-51.

Sullivan, R. M., J. L. McGaugh, and M. Leon. "Norepinphrine-Induced Plasticity and One-Trial Olfactory Learning in Neonatal Rats." *Brain Research* 60.2 (1991): 219-28.

342

Swabb, D. F., L. J. Gooren, and M. A. Hofman. "Gender and Sexual Orientation in Relation to Hypothalmic Structures." *Hormone Research* 38 [Suppl. 2] (1992): 51-61.

Swanson, James. 1980. Contact: Research Institute, HSC, Toronto, Ont, Canada. M5G 1X8

Spielberger, C. D., ed. *Anxiety: Current Trends in Theory and Research.* Vols. 1-2. New York: Academic Press, 1972.

Sylwester, R. and J. Cho. "What Brain Research Says About Paying Attention." *Educational Leadership* Jan., 1993: 71-5.

Tallal, P. "Hormonal Influences in Developmental Learning Disabilities." *Psychoneuroendocrinology* 16.1-3 (1991): 203-11.

---, R. Ross, and S. Curtiss. "Unexpected Sex-Ratios in Families of Language/Learning-Impaired Children." *Neuropsychologia* 27.7 (1989): 987-98.

---, S. Miller, and R. H. Fitch. "Neurobiological Basis for Speech: a Case for the Preeminence of Temporal Processing." *Annals of the New York Academy of Sciences* 682 (1993): 27-47.

Taylor, E. Subliminal Learning. 1988. Just Another Reality Publishing. Salt Lake, City, Utah.

Taylor, H. L., and J. Orlansky. "The Effects of Wearing Protective Chemical Warfare Combat Clothing on Human Performance." *Aviation Space and Environmental Medicine* 64.2 (1993): A1-41.

Thal, D. J., and S. Tobias. "Communicative Gestures in Children with Delayed Onset of Oral Expressive Vocabulary." *Journal of Speech and Hearing Research* 35.6 (1992): 1281-9.

---, and D. Morrison. "Language and Gesture in Late Talkers: A 1-Year Follow-Up." *Journal of Speech and Hearing Research* 34.3 (1991): 604-12.

Thayer, R. "Time of Day Affects Energy Levels." *Brain-Mind Bulletin* 12 (1986): 3D.

Tonge, B. J. "The Impact of Television on Children and Clinical Practice." *Australian and New Zealand Journal of Psychiatry,* 24.4 (1990): 552-60.

Torrance, P. and O. Ball. "Intensive Approach Alters Learning Styles in Gifted." *Journal of Creative Behavior* 12 (1978): 248-52.

Trautman, P. "An Investigation of the Relationship Between Selected Instructional Techniques and Identified Cognitive Style." Diss. St. John's University, 1979.

Treisman, A. and S. Gormican. "Feature Analysis in Early Vision: Evidence from Search Asymmetries." *Psychological Review* 95 (1988): 15-48.

Trevarthen, Colwyn. "Growth and Education of the Hemispheres." *Brain Circuits and Functions of the Mind: Essays in Honor of Roger W. Sperry.* Ed. Colwyn Trevarthen. New York: Cambridge University Press, 1990.

Tryphonas, H., and R. Trites. "Food Allergy in Children with Hyperactivity." *Annals of Allergy* 42 (1979): 22-7.

Turner, Judith. *Placebo Research Reviewed.* Journal of the American Medical Association, June 1994.

Uhl, F., et al. "Cerebral Correlates of Imagining Colors, Faces and a Map--Negative Cortical DC Potentials." *Neuropsychologia* 28.1 (1990): 81-93.

Unger, Georges. "Biochemistry of Intelligence." *Research Communications in Psychology, Psychiatry & Behavior* 1.5-6 (1976): 597-606.

Urban, M. J. "Auditory Subliminal Stimulation: A Re-examination." *Perceptual and Motor Skills* 74.2 (1992): 515-41.

U.S. Dept. of Education. *What Works.* Wash., DC, 1986.

Van Dyke, D. C., and A. A. Fox. "Fetal Drug Exposure and its Possible Implications for Learning in the Pre-School and School-Age Population." *Journal of Learning Disabilities* 23.3 (1990): 160-3.

Virostko, J. "An Analysis of the Relationships Among Academic Achievement in Mathematics and Reading, Assigned Instructional Schedules, and the Learning Style Time Preferences of Third, Fourth, Fifth and Sixth Grade Students." Diss. St. John's University, 1983.

Vos-Groenendal, Jeannete. "An Accelerated/Integrative Learning Model Program Evaluation: Based on Participant Perceptions of Student Attitudinal and Achievement Changes." Diss. [unpublished]. ERIC and NAU, Flagstaff, AZ., 1991.

Vygotsky, L. S. *Thought and Language.* Cambridge, MA: MIT Press, 1985.

Wallace, C. S., et al. "Increases in Dendritic Length in Occipital Cortex After 4 Days of Differential Housing in Weanling Rats." *Behavioral and Neural Biology* 58.1 (1992): 64-8.

Ward, C., and Jan Jaley. *Learning to Learn.* New Zealand: A & H Print Consultants, 1993.

Webb, D., and T. Webb. *Accelerated Learning with Music.* Norcross, GA: Accelerated Learning Systems, 1990.

Webster, J. S., et al. "A Scoring Method that is Sensitive to Right-Hemispheric Dysfunction." *Journal of Clinical and Experimental Neuropsychology* 14.2 (1992): 222-38.

Weil, M. O., and J. Murphy. "Instructional Processes." *Encyclopedia of Educational Research.* Ed. H. E. Mitzel. New York: The Free Press, 1982. 892-3.

Weinstein, C. E., and R. E. Mayer. "The Teaching of Learning Strategies." *Handbook of Research on Teaching.* Ed. M. C. Wittrock. 3rd ed. New York: Macmillian Publishing, 1986. 315-27.

Wentzel, K. R. "Adolescent Classroom Goals, Standards for Performance, and Academic Achievement: An Interactionist Perspective." *Journal of Educational Psychology* 81 (1989): 131-42.

White, R. T. "An Investigation of the Relationship Between Selected Instructional Methods and Selected Elements of Emotional Learning Style Upon Student Achievement in Seventh-Grade Social Studies." Diss. St John's Univeristy, 1980.

Whitleson, S. "The Brain Connection: the Corpus Callosum is Larger in Left-Handers." *Science* 229 (1985): 665-8.

---. "Sex Differences in the Neurology of Cognition: Social, Educational and Clinical Implications." *Le Fait Femenin.*

Wicker, F., et al. "Reframing Problems: A Bigger Boost to Insight than Visualization." *Journal of Educational Psychology* 70 (1978): 372-7.

Williams, Linda Verlee. *Teaching for the Two-Sided Mind.* New York: Simon & Schuster, 1983.

Wlodkowski, R. *Enhancing Adult Motivation to Learn.* San Francisco: Jossey-Bass Publishers, 1985.

Wolman, B., ed. *Handbook of General Psychology.* Englewood Cliffs: Prentice-Hall, 1973.

Wree, Andrea. "Sexes Differ in Brain Degeneration." *Anatomy and Embryology* 160 (1989): 105-19.

Wurtman, J. *Managing Your Mind & Mood Through Food.* New York: Harper/Collins, 1986.

---. *Dietary Phenyalanine and Brain Function.* Boston: Birkhauser, 1988. 374.

Wurtman, R. J. "Carbohydrate Craving" *Drugs* 39.3 [Suppl.] (1990): 49-52.

---, and E. Ritter-Walker. *Dietary Phenylanine and Brain Function.* Boston: Birkhauser, 1988.

---, and J. J. Wurtman. "Carbohydrates and Depression." *Scientific American* Jan. 1989: 68-75.

--- , et al. "Effect of Nutrient Intake on Premenstrual Depression." *American Journal of Obstretrics and Gynecology* 161.5 (1989): 1228-34.

Wynn, K. "Children's Understanding of Counting." *Cognition* 36.2 (1990): 155-93.

---. "Addition and Subtraction by Human Infants." *Nature* 27 Aug. 1992: 749-50.

Yeap, L. L. "Hemisphericity and Student Achievement." *International Journal of Neuroscience* 48 (1989): 225-32.

Zalewski, L. J., Sink, and D. J. Yachimowicz. "Using Cerebral Dominance for Education Programs." *Journal of General Psychology* 119.1 (1992): 45-57.

Subject Index

Networking Opportunities:

For a FREE catalog of over 100 Brain-Based Resources, trainings & products, you may want to contact:

Turning Point, Box 2551
Del Mar, CA 92014, USA
(619) 755-6670 or...Phone Toll-Free (800) 325-4769
(619) 792-2858 Fax 24 hours/day

Other organizations focused on "brain-compatible" learning:

1. The Brain-Based Learning Network (ASCD Network)
    CARE (Dr. Joan Caulfield)   Rockhurst College
    1100 Rockhurst Rd.   Kansas City, MO 64110-2561

2. International Alliance for Learning (formerly SALT)
    SuperCamp Program for Teens
    Learning Forum 1725 South Hill St.
    Oceanside, CA 92054   (619) 722-0072

3. The Accelerated Learning & Teaching Network (ASCD)
    Edge Enterprises
    1888 Montgomery   Cardiff, CA 92007, USA
    (619) 632-9195

4. Consortium for Whole Brain Learning
    Launa Ellison, teacher, author
    3348 47th Ave. South Minneapolis, MN 55406-2345

5. If you have an organization focused on the brain-based
    principles in this book and would like to be included
    in future editions, please write to the address above.

Brain-Based Resources

For a Speaker or Trainer Contact: For corporate trainings, conference speaking, district or school inservices and workshops, phone (619) 755-6670 or fax (619) 792-2858. Address: Box 2551, Del Mar, California 92014 USA.

For Certification Training as a brain-based trainer or teacher, the 6-day training is held each year. This book is just the beginning! See information elsewhere in this appendix for details and registration.

Distributor Inquiries Welcome: If you distribute a catalogue or do workshops, your audience may be interested in learning more about these practical brain-strategies. To provide a valuable service and earn additional income, contact our publishing office for distributor price list. Call (619) 755-6670 or fax inquiries to: (619) 792-2858.

Publisher Inquries Welcome: If you are a publisher in Europe, Asia, Africa, South America, Australia, England, New Zealand, Mexico or Canada, please contact our office for details on publishing rights.

Order The New, Amazing, Learn-to-Learn Study Skills program based on accelerated learning, amazing brain-based methodology and multiple intelligences. Includes 12 colorful posters, two booklets, a notebook, six audiotapes & pen. Call (800)325-4769 or (619)755-6670 fax 619-792-2858 or write: Turning Point, Box 2551, Del Mar, CA 92014 USA.

Feedback, Suggestions and Corrections: Please feel free to write, call or fax the author with any information that might be useful for upcoming editions (Volume II) or reprints: P.O. Box 2551, Del Mar, CA 92014 USA

For a FREE Catalogue of Brain-Based Learning Products for teaching, training and personal use, including:

* Books	* Videos
* Audiotapes	* Special Reports
* Bulletins	* Kits & Programs

Call (800) 325-4769 or (619) 755-6670 or mail your name and address to: Turning Point, P.O. Box 2551, Del Mar, CA 92014 USA

The Learning Brain Video

At your school, you can boost learning, motivation and recall. You can lower stress, make learning more fun and push achievement scores through the roof. Hundreds of schools have done it. Now, you can too! Order your own exciting and compelling two-part 76 min. video on this book for your school or business. Using state-of-the-art virtual reality, it highlights the key research in this book, making a persuasive and motivating case for the use of brain-based learning in education. Hear teacher interviews and see schools that really work. Use this video to better understand and utilize the brain's amazing potential. Use as a school-wide or district in-service. The video explores these key areas:

*	Physiology/Biology	*	Emotions in Learning
*	Timetables/Rhythms	*	Strategies & Styles
*	Memory & Recall	*	Different Learners
*	Intelligence	*	Mapping & Patterns
*	States/Attention	*	Music/Environments
*	Stress/Threats	*	Motivation & Rewards
*	How to apply all this knowledge to learning & education		

___**YES!** Send me the exciting *Brain-Based Learning Video* for $89
___**YES!** I'd also like the facilitator's guide for just $10 extra ($99 total)
___**YES!** Instead, I'd like the Deluxe Staff Development Kit (facilitator's guide, posters, 2 books, transparencies, discussion cards & consulting time ($375 total) I understand my satisfaction is guaranteed with a full 90 days satisfaction or money back guarantee.
___**ADD** $7.95 for shipping & handling. <u>Circle one of the following:</u>

check (U.S. Dollars)   purchase order   VISA   Mastercard

_____   _____
VISA or Mastercard   expiration date

Name printed as it appears on card: _____

Your name (print) _____

Occupation and title_____

Address _____ City _____

State_____ Postal/Zip Code _____

Country _____ Version: VHS   PAL Format

Phone (_____) _____Fax (_____) _____

To order, write, fax or call today. U.S. residents send check, purchase order or bankcard information to: Turning Point, Box 2551, Del Mar, CA 92014. Or, call toll-free 800-325-4769, 619-755-6670 or fax (619) 792-2858. Overseas orders: please use bankcard and call or fax first for shipping & handling charges.
Satisfaction guaranteed.

FREE Bulletins--Mail this today!

All three of the special bulletins listed below are yours,
absolutely FREE. Send your name, address & mail to
the address on the reverse side. Limit one order per person.

* How to Really Understand the Opposite Sex
* 21 Ways to Boost Personal Learning Skills
* The "Almost-Genius" High-energy Learning Diet

Name (print please) _____

Address _____ # _____

City _____ State _____ Zip _____ Country_____

--fold here--

YOUR COMMENTS, IDEAS, BOOK SUGGESTIONS

Please send your ideas for the sequel to this book, or your
comments and suggestions about how to improve this one.

_____

_____

_____

Your contributions are appreciated & will be acknowledged!

cut here & mail

Brain & Learning
Workshop-Seminar

* *Increase your market value and boost income*
* *Make a bigger difference & feel good about it*
* *Learn an "in-demand" cutting edge skill*
* *Network, make friends with "like-minded" people*
* *Discover how to use these strategies in your work*
* *Boost attention, learning, recall & implementation*

If you'd like to become a **Level 1 Certified Brain-based Learning Trainer**, it's easy and it's fun. Attend our exciting and innovative 6-day, 42 hour course that transforms the way you teach or train. Held each year (begins the second Monday in July in San Diego, California, USA), it's a perfect way to learn, embody and master the success learning, teaching and training strategies of the cutting edge in brain research. Your trainer will be Eric Jensen, the author of this book, a former teacher, staff development trainer, and corporate trainer with over 10 years of brain-based successful training experience with over 20,000 satisfied participants. You can expect to learn & experience:

___ What are the 12 essentials to know about the brain & learning
___ How to boost persuasiveness, congruency and impact
___ The 5 newest learning styles you don't know about---but should
___ How to deal with troublemakers and hecklers with ease and confidence
___ The newest "smart drugs" & "mind foods" for learning & thinking
___ 19 Rituals which boost learning and maintain optimal states
___ Which types of music are best for learning and when to use them
___ Simple ways to boost thinking, intelligence & self-esteem
___ How to make best use of the 7 multiple intelligences
___ The 5 secrets to permanently eliminating discipline problems
___ How to guarantee that your audience will recall & use what they learn
___ The 17 secrets to boost concentration and attention in learning
___ The amazing 6 types of memory & which one to not use
___ How to make the learning enjoyable and highly effective
___ 11 specific strategies to deal with the body's timetables
___ 15 ways to engage the emotions to insure long-term memory
___ How to create and maintain the optimal learning environment
___ Best ways to program your mind to do exactly what you want it to do

Workshop Registration

Name (print) _____

Occupation (& title) _____

Address _____

City _____/Postal Code _____

State_____ Country _____

Phone (_____) _____

Fax (_____) _____

YES! Register me for the workshop in the year: _____
      (Begins second Monday in July in San Diego, Calif. USA)

I'm sending my registration fee and deposit for $95
      (U.S.Dollars)   or   VISA Mastercard

_____   _____
    VISA or Mastercard number   expiration date

Print name as it appears on card: _____

Registration
Fax a copy of this page today

Space is limited, so you may want to enroll today. Six-day tuition is $675, registration fee and deposit is $95. Register early and get a FREE $50 resources credit good for books & videos. Course materials and certification included. Transportation, meals and lodging extra. For more details, call 800-325-4769, outside U.S., call 619-755-6670 or fax (619) 792-2858. Or, write: Turning Point, Box 2551, Del Mar, CA 92014, USA.

Note: There is a growing demand worldwide for more information about the brain in personal development, teaching, supervision, training, management and health care. Get in on the explosion of new information. Learn the latest on brain research, mind foods, better thinking, memory, smart drugs, attention, emotions, intelligence, toxins and more. It's a terrific career-boosting experience you'll long remember. Join us today!

About the Author

Eric Jensen is deeply committed to making a positive, significant, lasting difference in the way the world learns. He is a former classroom teacher who received his B.A. in English from San Diego State University and M.A. in Psychology from the University of California. He has taught at three universities and is a former Outstanding Young Man of America selection.

Jensen was the co-founder of SuperCamp, the nation's first and largest accelerated learning program for teens. He authored the bestselling *Student Success Secrets, The Little Book of Big Motivation, Thirty Days to Bs and As, Brain-Based Learning & Teaching* and *SuperTeaching*. He was a key part of the New Futures Program, The Education For The Future Project, The Global Youth Summit and Australia's MetWest Accelerated Learning Initiative, one of the largest brain-based teacher training programs in the world.

Trainers from AT & T, Disney, IBM, Digital, GTE, Hewlitt-Packard, ICA, Burroughs, SAS and three branches of the military have used his methods. Jensen provides successful trainings for conferences, schools, organizations, and Fortune 500 corporations, and is an international speaker, writer and consultant.

For a Speaker or Trainer Contact: For corporate trainings, conference speaking, district or school inservices and workshops, phone (619) 755-6670 or fax (619) 792-2858. Address: Box 2551, Del Mar, California 92014 USA.